Flames of Faith

An Introduction to Chasidic Thought

Adapted from the Torah Classes of
Rav Moshe Wolfson, *Shlit"a*

by
Rabbi Zev Reichman

KODESH PRESS

Distributed by
Kodesh Press L.L.C.
www.KodeshPress.com
kodeshpress@gmail.com
New York, NY

We feel that this volume makes available to a wide audience material that can have a deep impact on the Jewish consciousness.

We are blessed to be a part of Rabbi Zev and Chana Reichman's dedication to Torah and their ability to impact so many in the ways of Hashem. We pray to Hashem that they continue in their great work and inspire the Jewish people to Torah and Mitzvos.

With thanks to Hashem we
dedicate this volume to our children

ברוך ארי

שמעון יהושע

יהודה משה

and all generations that follow.

May this merit allow them to have in their heart the covenant of Avraham and to value Tzadikim and may they be granted lives of Torah and Mitzvos. May this book also serve as an eternal memorial and zechus in memory of our father, their grandfather,
Bernard Korman

Debra and Scott Korman

Dedicated to the eternal memory of

Ahron (Ari)
ben Mordechai Yehoshua
Frommer z"l

ARI FULLY EMBRACED THE JOYS OF JUDAISM.

HE CHOSE TO SEE THE HALACHIC LIFESTYLE AS
A PRIVILEGE RATHER THAN A BURDEN.

HOPEFULLY, THE JOY THIS BOOK WILL BRING
TO OTHERS WILL BE A MERIT FOR HIM.

הרב משה וואלפסאן
RABBI MOSHE WOLFSON
1619 - 43rd STREET
BROOKLYN, NEW YORK
11218

ב"ה

בה כ"ה אדר תשס"ג

לכבוד ידידי היקר הרב הגאון הנעלה מוהר"ר צבי רייכמן שליט"א

שמחתי על מה שראותי את הרעיונות של ספרך הנפלא האין סוף

של ספר תורה קדוש מאת רבנו האדמו"ר הזקן בעל התניא אקדמו ר'

שניאור זלמן זצוקללה"ה. הספר נכתב בטוב טעם ודעת, וסגנונו

כולו אומר כבוד וינעם כי כריך הס"ת אוזק כדלי סופר מהיר,

אשר יבאו, אף אני אוזה אמן, שהרי בתאר דברים

נאמרת אמן, וגם הוספת תוספת מרובה של ביאורים כהירים

ונתנים, ועשית אותו כרעיונות נשגבים שטאות אפי חתן

התכיר הרב הגאון והנאאו מוהר מרזכי משה גריצר שליט"א,

קח נא את דירכתי שתצכה לתפוץ ולהפרק את קהלתך הטאארה

של אמוץ התורה ויראת טמים, ויפלו מעינותיך חולה לנבות את

הררים ולהגרל כתלמושים, ונזכה שהספר יתקרל ראהרה ורצון

ויהנו רו ויהנו אמנן רדים וטלוים, ואחק ואמן ויקום וילאה.

בצע ידידות

משה וואלפסאן

TABLE OF CONTENTS

ACKNOWLEDGEMENTS

IT IS IMPOSSIBLE to adequately thank all those who helped me in the development of this work. However, I must attempt to at least partially recognize those who helped turn the dream of an English introduction to Chasidus into a reality.

No words can express my feelings of gratitude to Rav Moshe Wolfson, *shlit"a*. Rav Wolfson's Torah ideas have shaped my perspective on life, and despite a busy schedule the *Mashgiach* made time to review this book and encourage its publication. Rav Wolfson made many important corrections to the manuscript. I am deeply humbled that the *Mashgiach* invested so many hours in this project. All I can say is a prayer, "May Hashem bless him to see much *nachas*, Jewish joy, from his children and students for many years to come."

Through Rav Wolfson's synagogue, I met Rav Aharon Kovitz, Rav Leibish Lish, and Rav Efrayim Glassman, each of whom helped me with the content in this book.

I am most indebted to Yeshiva University and its leadership for all they have provided to me. Rabbi Dr. Norman Lamm and Rabbi Zevulun Charlop deserve special praise for their efforts on behalf of Yeshiva and its students. They, together with Ms. Susan Wexner and Mrs. Bella Wexner, created the Harry and Bella Wexner Kollel Elyon. The Wexner Kollel was an intellectual home for me where I learned Torah from sages such as Rabbi Michael Rosensweig, Rabbi Mordechai Willig, and my father, Rabbi H. Reichman. In addition to Torah learning, the Wexner program provided classes in practical rabbinic skills, such as psychology, business practices, public speaking, and writing. Of all the instructors in the program, I owe a special debt to Professor Leslie Newman, the English writing coach. Professor Newman donated many hours of her time to refining this work.

When the Wexners were honored for their generosity in creating the Kollel, Mrs. Bella Wexner, of blessed memory, charged the students to provide her with some *nachas*. Mrs. Wexner is no longer alive, but I pray that the inspiration Jewish hearts will garner from this work will provide much *nachas* and merit to her everlasting soul.

In addition to training, Yeshiva provided me with the opportunity to teach the ideas that are in this book. I am most grateful to Rabbi M. Schmidman and Rabbi D. Rapp who first hired me to teach in the James Striar School of General Jewish Studies at Yeshiva University. The students in my classes helped refine the concepts in these lessons and have served as a source of inspiration and intellectual challenge. I am also thankful to the other leaders of Yeshiva, especially our President, Richard Joel, and Rabbi Dr. Hillel Davis.

When I consider the great efforts the administrators of Yeshiva expend in developing this singular institution I am reminded of the traditional prayer for *oskim be-tzarchei ha-tzibbur be-emunah*, those who are faithfully involved in communal need, "May the Holy One provide them with their reward, and remove from them any illness, and heal their bodies, and forgive all their sins, and may He send blessing and success to all that they do."

Traditionally, a matchmaker was paid when a match he proposed was settled. If the matchmaker proposed a bride to a young man but the couple did not end up marrying each other he would not receive a fee. Chasidim relate that the *Divrei Chaim*, Rabbi Chaim of Tzanz, would pay every matchmaker, even those who suggested matches for his children that did not work out. The Rebbe explained that in Heaven, before a child's birth, God declares the identity of the individual the child will eventually marry as well as all the proposed mates for the child. To arrive at the correct spouse one must first pass through all the suggested partners. A matchmaker who suggests a coupling helps to bring the real match closer and therefore deserves remuneration.

In keeping with the tradition of the *Divrei Chaim* I thank the many individuals who helped develop this book at its various stages. I am most thankful to Rabbi Daniel Green, Rabbi Lavi Greenspan, Rabbi Rob Shur, Rabbi Feivel Smiles, Gavriel Bellino, David Sacks, Josh Marter, Yaakov Kaszemacher, Ezra Altman, and Emily Steinberg for their help.

I have the privilege to serve as the Rabbi of the East Hill Synagogue of Englewood, New Jersey. The people I have met at East Hill have changed my life and the life of my family for the better. I am especially thankful to all of the members of the shul for their encouragement, probing questions, and friendship. Many members of the shul helped with various aspects of producing this book. Specifically I must thank Mr. Daniel Straus, Dr. Ron Strobel, Mr. Brian Haim, Mr. Elliot Maza, Dr. Ron Krinik, Dr. Harvey Rice, Mr. Mordy Dicker, Dr. Henry Anhalt, Dr. Larry Shemen, Moshe Greif, Mrs. Jodi Scherl, Mrs. Carol Levy, Mrs. Pam Machefsky, and Mrs. Rochelle Weisberger. Finally, special thanks to Mrs. Ruth Frommer, East Hill's capable administrator who helped type drafts of this book.

I am most grateful to Mr. and Mrs. Nader Bolour, Mr. and Mrs. Josef Bolour, Mr. and Mrs. Dan Weingarten, Mr. and Mrs. Jerry Gontownik, and Mr. and Mrs. Drew Parker for their financial help during this book's initial phases. Last, Mr. and Mrs. Scott Korman provided the bulk of the funding for this book and as such are equal partners in the Torah that will be learned from it. May your acts of *chesed* and Torah support serve as a merit to your family and an example for all to emulate.

This book was first published in 5764/2004. Ten years later, Rabbi Alec Goldstein, Kodesh Press, and Rabbi Chaim Laufer carefully reviewed and improved the text. I am most grateful to them for their efforts.

No words of mine could ever begin to thank the Almighty for blessing me with a family and teachers who guide me to the path of Torah and Mitzvos. May it be His will that this book help us and the entire family of Israel reach higher levels of Torah learning, devotional prayer, acts of kindness, and love for fellow Jews.

Zev Reichman
New York, NY
May 2014

FOREWORD

THERE WAS ONCE a king whose only son was a source of enormous pride and joy. Then disaster struck. The young man contracted a mysterious illness, collapsed into a deathly coma, and none of the royal doctors could revive him.

In desperation, a professor of herbal medicine was summoned to the palace. The specialist examined the boy and prescribed an unconventional remedy.

"Grind a twenty-eight karat ruby gem-stone to a pulp, and then mix it with several common herbs and mineral water and feed it to the boy."

Many of the king's attendants heard the professor's words as quackery. The rare and precious stone he had requested was the centerpiece of the setting on the king's crown. These skeptics felt that the king's crown should not be destroyed on the directives of a charlatan. Other officials contended that their king certainly wanted his court to attempt every possible cure, regardless of cost or plausibility. The professor did not wait for the two groups to resolve their fight. He seized the crown, tore out the jewel that was its heart, and crushed the stone into granules. After feeding the potion to the prince, the boy immediately opened his eyes, and recovered fully.[1]

The King in the parable is God, the Ultimate Sovereign. The Jewish nation is the crown prince, as we are called in the Torah, "children of God." The Torah refers to our relationship with God in paternal terms (see Deut. 8:5). The wise professor who saved the prince was Rabbi

---

1. This parable was related by Rabbi Shneur Zalman of Liadi (1745-1813), one of the greatest thinkers of the Chasidic movement. His book, called the *Tanya* or *Likkutei Amarim*, is the essential handbook of Chasidic thought. He related the story to explain the timing of the appearance of the Chasidic movement.

Yisrael Baal Shem Tov,[2] known by the abbreviation "Besht," who started a movement of ecstatic Jewish observance, Chasidus.

In the mid-eighteenth century, the Jewish nation in Europe underwent a momentous change. After centuries of discrimination and suffering, sounds of civic, economic, and political emancipation began to resonate in small towns throughout Eastern Europe. Yet this emancipation engendered a debilitating spiritual infection, which struck the Jewish people and fully emerged once the Jews stepped beyond the strictures of the ghetto and took their place among the ranks of European citizenry. Jews began to forsake the traditions of their ancestors and assimilate into Gentile societies. To ingratiate themselves with newfound Gentile friends, millions of Jews forsook their identity and religious heritage. R. Yisrael Baal Shem Tov, the founder of the Chasidic movement, fashioned a unique remedy to this epidemic.

He seized the initiative. He took the Torah, God's crown, and extracted the wisdom of *Sod*, Jewish mysticism, the most precious jewel of the Torah. To enable the digestion of the stone, he ground it up; he translated mystical concepts into the realm of the common man; he explicated principles, popularized esoteric imagery, and encouraged spiritual practice for all. He organized the devotees of his lessons into a movement that is still vibrant in our times, Chasidus.

The secrets from the inner meaning of Torah form the soul of the Chasidic movement's thought. They inspire, revive, and inflame Jewish souls with a passion to constantly increase observance and devotion.[3]

---

2. He was born circa 1698 and passed away in 1760. The phrase *Baal Shem Tov* literally means "master of the good name." He had a good name for he always judged the deeds of others favorably, and his prayers for others brought about miracles.

3. Chasidic thought is an encounter with the depths of Jewish experience. Once your soul has been lit with the spark of Chasidus other sections of Jewish knowledge, such as Talmud study (in Hebrew called *Gemara*), will display similar flames. One usually considers Talmud study to be a cold, intellectual, endeavor. However, Rabbi Aharon Karliner (1736-1772), a contemporary of Rabbi Shneur Zalman of Liadi, would teach that the word "*Gemara*" means a "burning ember," *gumra de-isha*. "For when someone learns Torah for its own sake, his heart burns with a desire to dedicate his entire being to the Master of the Universe" (*Beis Aharon*, pg. 5a). Rabbi Shraga Feivel Mendelovitz, of blessed memory, the founder of Mesivta Torah Vodaath, taught Chasidic thought to his American born students in Torah Vodaath for he felt that once inspired with the profundity of Chasidus his boys would experience Talmud study and mitzvah observance in a warmer, more passionate, and joy-filled manner (Rav Wolfson).

This ecstatic Jewish practice and belief has stood the test of time. For more than two centuries it has inoculated millions against the ravages of secularism and preserved the spiritual life of the Jewish nation.

Chasidus emerged as a protection from the storm winds of modernity. Today's Jewish community might benefit from a new look at the Chasidic movement's beginnings and reflections. Intermarriage is rampant, and assimilation into American culture has become the norm. Even those Jews who fulfill their religious obligations frequently perform rituals in a lifeless and superficial way. Were we to discover the depth and soulful vitality that fill Chasidic literature, a renewed passion might flame our faltering Jewish experience with the warmth of Torah. Unfortunately, for many of my contemporary American Jews, access to the gem-stones of the Chasidim has been denied.

Chasidic works are overwhelmingly in Hebrew, and few good translations exist. For the American Jew whose Hebrew is not fluent, these books are welded shut. Even those who can read Rabbinic Hebrew find Chasidic literature challenging for the Chasidic masters assumed that their readers were knowledgeable in basic mystical concepts and terms. Absent an introductory course, many try to absorb the warmth of Chasidic Torah and then give up in frustration when the texts do not seem to explain their basic assumptions.[4] This book is an attempt to fill that void. It attempts to provide an introduction to the basic terms and ideas of Chasidic texts so that once it is mastered the reader will be able to comprehend the works of the Chasidic masters directly.

This book is written for the interested lay reader who may be new to Torah study. That is why I have endeavored to translate all terms into English.[5] It is also directed to the yeshiva student who is knowledgeable

---

4. See *Chasidic Masters*, Chapter 1.

5. At times this book draws upon the depths of insight that emerge from the Hebrew language. Chasidus discovers inspiration through the etymology of Hebrew words. Many ideas in this book are derived from the meaning of words in different contexts. Further, the letters of the Hebrew alphabet have assigned numeric values. This book draws on the wisdom of "*gematria,*" calculating the numerical value of a word and phrase and explicating its relationship to other words or phrases that equal the same sum.

about Biblical narratives and Talmudic law but may be new to the world of Chasidus. Hopefully, these introductory lessons will open the door to new dimensions of observance, piety, and study.

Another linguistic device is *roshei teivos*, different types of abbreviations, such as acronyms and acrostics. Lessons in this book might interpret a word as an acronym for a phrase with each letter representing an entire word that begins with that letter. For instance the Hebrew word *shevi* (שב"י), "captive," represents the phrase Shimon (ש) bar (ב) Yochai (י), Simon son of Yochai, one of the Talmudic teachers of Jewish mysticism. Since this book is designed to be understood by someone who is not fluent in Hebrew, I have attempted to explain, in plain English, all Hebrew word interpretations, so that everyone will be able to understand the ideas of this book.

Introductory Notes
on Style & Content

Chasidus and Kabbalah

THIS IS A book of Chasidus not Kabbalah (Jewish mysticism). Rabbi Aryeh Kaplan explained the difference: "The earlier Kabbalah tried to bring man into heaven. The main idea of Chasidus was to bring heaven into man."[6] Chasidic thought is predicated on Kabbalah, but Chasidic works differ greatly from Kabbalistic tracts. Chasidus emphasizes practical application, while Kabbalah describes Heavenly domains.

The following story accentuates this distinction. Rabbi Aryeh Leib Heller, the author of *Ketzos Ha-Choshen*,[7] once challenged Rabbi Zvi, the Chasidic Grand Rabbi of Zhiditchov[8]:

> "What is unique about the Baal Shem Tov? Why are thousands of simple Jews excitedly following him? He is merely a teacher of Lurianic Mysticism. Rabbi Luriah's[9] lectures did not excite such passion amongst the masses."

6. Rabbi Aryeh Kaplan, *Chasidic Masters* pg. 4.
7. Rabbi Aryeh Leib Heller (1745-1813) was one of the greatest Talmudic scholars of his era, and his work, *Ketzos Ha-Choshen* is a classic commentary about Jewish financial law.
8. Rabbi Zvi Hirsch Eichenstein (1763-1831) of Zhiditchov was a great Kabbalist, Torah giant, and Chasidic Rebbe in Galicia, Poland. He was a student of the Chozeh of Lublin. He was a great expert of the *Zohar*. His primary student was his nephew, Rabbi Yitzchak Eizik Safrin of Kamarna.
9. Rabbi Isaac Luriah was one of the foremost mystics in Jewish history. Born in Jerusalem in 1534, he led the Jewish mystics of Safed during their period of prolific scholarship, until he passed away in 1572. His work is the definitive guide for Kabbalah, and he is known as the *Ari Ha-Kadosh*, "the Godly Rabbi Isaac." The word "*Ari*," literally, "lion," is the acronym of the Hebrew phrase, "Eloki (Godly) Rabbeinu Yitzchak."

R. Zvi answered, "Picture a land whose king died abruptly. The populace plunged into self-pity, certain that no adequate replacement would be found. A search committee was formed, and its agents set out to find a regent. An investigator heard vague rumors about a man from the distant east, 'He is tall, handsome, and wise; blessed with royal ancestry, and a kind, gracious heart.' He seemingly possessed the desired qualifications for the throne. Unfortunately, due to the vast distance between the candidate and his prospective subjects, the reports lacked details and sounded vague and unsure. As a result, most of the kingdom's citizens felt that they were sheep bereft of hope for a shepherd.

"A short time later a traveler arrived from the Far East who was a close friend of the prospective leader. The traveler described the strengths of the candidate with great clarity. His presentation was convincing, and the leaders of the community announced that a king had been found. However, the simple-folk remained depressed. Preoccupied as they were with the daily struggle for subsistence they could not pay attention to the visitor with exciting news.

"One man thought to relieve the tension of the commoners. He brought the candidate himself to the people. Once the nation saw him and experienced his speeches, they were all impressed by his stature and wisdom. The masses joined the leaders, spontaneously all shouting, 'Behold our king! Long live our new king!'"

R. Zvi then explained, "This parable is the story of Jewish mystical thought. R. Shimon bar Yochai [the author of the Zohar][10] revealed a glimpse of the secret world. The Jews of that historical period needed an insight into the Heavenly worlds to inspire devotion, but his lessons were couched in esoteric language, and they were like the distant rumors about

---

10. The word *Zohar* literally means "glow" or "splendor." It is also the title for a work that collects mystical lessons from sages from the times of the Mishnah, which dates to the second century. The *Zohar* is the basic Jewish mystical text.

the king, only a small and elite class fully appreciated them. The Ari Ha-Kadosh's time needed more of this heavenly light. As a result, Providence blessed Rabbi Luriah with an intimate knowledge of the sacred dimension. He described the secret realms with great precision. His reach was broader than Rabbi Shimon bar Yochai's, yet his work too was only meaningful to righteous people and intellectual giants. In the current era, we need these lights on a scale for the layman. The Baal Shem Tov is the man who travels to the peasants and reveals to them, 'Behold here is your king!' He shows that God is everywhere. He takes the secret wisdom and explains how it can be actualized into daily living. His message is accessible to all since it is reached in an experiential and not merely intellectual way. As a result the masses join him and excitedly shout, 'We see our King (God)! Long live our King!'"[11]

---

11. I adapted this story from the Torah commentary *Divrei Tzaddikim* written by Rabbi Dov Berish of Ushpitzin.

Rabbi Moshe Chaim Luzzatto (1707-1746), one of the greatest mystical masters, revealed that Rabbi Shimon bar Yochai had a special soul which came to earth to help lead wayward Jews back to observance. His logic can be extended to include Rabbi Isaac Luria and the Baal Shem Tov:

> When Moses rose to the highest spiritual levels he took out of the light of *binah*, the force of return to God, a special soul. This soul became Rabbi Shimon bar Yochai. That is why it is written, *Alisa la-marom shavisa shevi*, "You rose to the heavens and took [*shevi*] a captive" (Ps. 68:19). This "captive" was the soul of Rabbi Shimon, which is why his name is hinted in the letters of the word *shevi*. The Hebrew letters *shin*, *bet*, and *yud* are the three-letter acronym of his name Shimon bar Yochai and they are the letters of the word *shevi*... (Rabbi Luzzatto's *Addir Ba-Marom*).

Rabbi Isaac Luriah was the son of Shlomo, his Hebrew name is Yitzchak ben Shlomo. The first letters of his name are *yud*, *bet*, and *shin*. The Baal Shem Tov's Hebrew name was Yisrael, and his mother's name was Sarah. The acronym for Yisrael ben Sarah is also *yud*, *bet*, and *shin*. An individual's essence is contained within the letters of his name. These three individuals shared the same leading letters, for these personalities were partners in a common mission, to reveal the innermost secrets of the Torah and thus encourage Jews to renew their ties with the Almighty (Rav Wolfson).

The Chasid seeks to answer the charge of application, "How does one translate the secrets of the universe into service of God?"[12] For example, Kabbalah discusses the different manifestations of the *Sephiros*, distinct gradations of God's light, in the varying spiritual universes. Chasidus uses the *Sephiros* to develop a psychological map of man's personality and then guide man as how best to approach Divinity.

The various customs designed to preserve mysticism for the scholars do not refer to Chasidic thought. Kabbalah with its other-worldly focus is traditionally studied by experts of Jewish thought. Chasidus, however, focuses Kabbalistic lessons toward man's behavior in this world. When Kabbalah is used to encourage practical actions, when its ideas are expressed in the human realm, then all should study it. Consider the lesson of Rabbi Chaim of Tzanz:[13]

It is written, "the honor of God [demands that one] conceal the matter; and the honor of Kings [requires the] study of the matter" (Prov. 25:2). This means that if a student seeks to study Kabbalah in order to know how many spiritual worlds there really are and how many *Sephiros* exist, namely the "honor of God," then conceal the matter and do not teach such a person. However if he wishes to study Kabbalah in order to know how to serve God with dedication, sanctify all of his two hundred and forty-eight limbs, and turn them into a *merkavah la-Shechinah*, channels filled with God's light,[14] namely the "honor of Kings" then study the matter

---

12. This question is referred to in Chasidic literature with the phrase *al derech ha-avodah*, "According to the way of service to God." Every Torah concept can be applied to *derech avodah*; it can be interpreted as advice about serving the Almighty.
13. Rabbi Chaim Halberstam of Tzanz was born in 1793 and passed away in 1876. He was a renowned Talmudist and Chasidic leader who fathered several great Chasidic dynasties.
14. According to Jewish thought the physical body can become a *merkavah*—chariot—to the *Shechinah*, the Divine presence. Our physical bodies can be sanctified to the point that the Divine is felt on them, and they become billboards that increase His Glory. Literally *merkavah* means "chariot." Travel

and reveal Kabbalah to such a seeker.[15]

CHASIDIC THOUGHT REVEALS ONENESS

A Chasidic term that befuddles many students is *bechinah*, and it is a hard term to translate. Some render it, "aspect." In Chasidic texts many items are described as a *bechinah* of something else, and multiple *bechinos* may be ascribed to a single item.

Bechinah denotes an analogy or a relative value. For example, male is to female as giver is to receiver, for to create life male gives seed that female receives. The sun gives light that the moon receives, thus the sun is *bechinas zachar*, a masculine aspect, while the moon is *bechinas nekeivah*, analogous to the feminine.

Personalities are thus a *bechinah* of certain times or places. Some Rabbis are a *bechinah* of Shabbos (Sabbath)[16] while others are a *bechinah*

usually causes a person to have less honor, for in the new location he is unknown (see further Rashi at the beginning of *Parashas Lech Lecha*). Travel in a chariot increases the honor of the passenger (because the chariot engenders respect, and through his journey more people learn that he is a nobleman). Similarly, physical life usually causes a decrease in God's honor, but for those who are a *merkavah*, their sojourn of life is like a chariot, and their deeds and life-story bring added glory to God (*Pachad Yitzchak, Pesach Ma'amar* 1). Each of our forefathers was a *merkavah*. They were exclusively dedicated to serving God, and God's attributes were discernible from their deeds. See further *Bereishis Rabbah* 47, *Michtav Me-Eliyahu* vol. 2, *Lech Lecha*, *Da'as Tefillah* pgs. 75-78.

Rabbi Jacob I. Schochet explained the idea of a *merkavah* in the following passage:

> *Tzaddikim* are a *merkavah* [chariot, vehicle] for Godliness. That is, just as a chariot has no will of its own but is in total submission to the will and directions of the charioteer, so is the *tzaddik* with total self-negation altogether submissive to the Divine Will even with his body and bodily functions.... To see and meet them [such *tzaddikim*] is tantamount to seeing and meeting the "Face of the *Shechinah*." Why are they called the "Face of the *Shechinah*"? Because the *Shechinah* is concealed within the manifest *tzaddik* (*Chasidic Dimensions* pg. 100).

15. Introduction to *Imrei Yosef* (Spinka). See further *Bereishis Rabbah* 9:1.
16. See further *Zohar* 3:144b.

of *Yom Tov* (holidays). Shabbos is the day of complete rest. Holidays are times of partial rest, when some forms of work, food preparation in particular, are allowed. Shabbos individuals are constantly at rest. Due to their faith and trust in God, they do not engage the material world at all. Their great faith is rewarded and miraculously their material needs are met. Other sages resemble Yom Tov; their faith is not as complete as the belief of the Shabbos scholars. As holidays on which some work is performed, they expend minimal effort in the material realm.[17]

Relativity allows for many different *bechinos* within an item, for an item can be contrasted by many disparate phenomena. If we look at the relationship between sun and moon, the sun is male while the moon is female. But if we look at the relationship between the Creator and His creations, God represents the male concept and the sun is female. This leads to items symbolizing different concepts, some of them contradictory, such as the sun being the symbol of both the masculine and the feminine.

One God created our world and, as a result, a powerful unity underlies all of creation. Chasidus seeks to reveal this unity. Chasidic thought delights in finding the common themes of different details within a particular lesson, even when a different principle is suggested for the same material in another lesson. Thus, Abraham in one lesson might be defined as the ultimate personification (*bechinah*) of Shabbos, while in another lesson Abraham is the personality of kindness, and Joseph is presented as the paragon of Shabbos-like living. In truth, both Abraham and Joseph had multiple elements to their personalities, one of which was a Shabbos-like quality.

In this work, I have attempted to remain faithful to the Chasidic mode of thought. In many of the lessons I tried to link together seemingly distinct entities through revealing the *bechinos* of an item. I have avoided the use of the term *bechinah* since it is so difficult to translate. Instead, I have tried to spell out the points of comparison to the extent that I understand them.

---

17. See further *Emunas Etecha* to *Parashas Naso* pg. 120.

THE ESSENCE OF CHASIDUS

In R. Zvi's parable, the Baal Shem Tov showed the king to the peasants. Chasidus encourages a perspective on life that sees God everywhere, guiding every personal experience and maintaining the existence of every physical item.[18] Rabbi Menachem Mendel of Kotzk[19] once said, "Where is God? Wherever you let Him in."[20] Over the centuries of the existence of Chasidus, thousands of devotees, from all walks of life, allowed God into every aspect of their lives. Their theology painted the world with dazzling new colors. Once you acquire their point of view, wherever you turn, you'll find infinite light.[21]

Seeing the King excited the peasants. Seeing is a physical sensation—an experience—not a logical argument. The essence of Chasidus lies in experience and passion. A verbal definition of Chasidus is inherently deficient. Words cannot do justice to the tearful eye of a teenager singing *"Tzamah Lecha Nafshi"* ("My soul is thirsting for You, God"). Nor can verbiage accurately convey the joy of the dancer leaping in honor of God.

---

18. "In truth every item in the physical world needs constant care from God. Without God constantly renewing an item's life it would disappear. Every item only seems to exist on its own; in truth, God is continually affirming its existence. If you seek the inner reality and reject externals, you will find God everywhere. Do not focus on the mirage; focus on the essence and then you will be able to point with your finger at God who inheres within every sphere of the physical world" (*Mishbetzos Zahav* pgs. 210-213, *Shabbos Ha-Gadol* 5753).

Rabbi Levi Yitzchak of Berditchev (1740-1810) encapsulated this view of the world with a song called "A Dudele." In Yiddish the word *du* means "you" in a very intimate manner. The lyrics are: "To the east, Du / To the west, Du / To the north, Du / To the south, Du / In front, Du / Behind Du / Du, Du, Du, Du." Rabbi Levi Yitzchak was teaching that he saw God everywhere.

19. Rabbi Menachem Mendel Morgenstern (1787-1859) of Kotzk was a passionate Chasidic leader. He is most remembered for his insistence on absolute truth and his critiques of any form of hypocrisy.

20. See *Chasidic Masters* page 4.

21. See Rabbi Tzadok Ha-Cohen of Lublin's *Dover Tzedek* pg. 12. Rabbi Tzadok Ha-Cohen Rabinovitch of Lublin was a great Talmudic scholar and an original Chasidic thinker. He was born in 1823 to a distinguished rabbinic family, and he passed away in 1900.

The highest emotion is love. Chasidus calls upon man to fall in love with Holiness. Its devotees enter into a state of rhapsodic ecstasy and revel in the personal bond they feel with their Maker.[22]

Genuine seekers of spirituality should not satisfy themselves with study of this or any other book. They should travel to Chasidic centers and sense the emotional power of Chasidic life.[23]

The key to understanding Chasidic thought lies in experiencing Chasidic teachings directly. This work is presented as a series of lessons filled with Chasidic insight. Hopefully, these will serve as an introduction to Chasidus in general and, once mastered, as a springboard to the comprehension of classic Chasidic texts.

SOURCES

The overwhelming majority of ideas contained herein has been gleaned from the lectures of my teacher, Rav Moshe Wolfson, *shlit"a*, the *Mashgiach Ruchani* (spiritual guidance counselor) of Yeshiva Torah Vodaath[24]

---

22. Rabbi Aryeh Kaplan points out that since Chasidus calls on man to love God, it demands of all, even the common man, to achieve sanctity. This ideal is a realistic one for the Chasidic community for, "Where love exists, nothing is difficult, and when love for God is absolute, even sainthood may not be an overwhelming goal" (*Chasidic Masters*, pg. 5).

23. Rabbi Kaplan expressed the essential role of feeling in Chasidus in the following way:

> In the teachings of the Hasidic Masters, one comes across a new way of approaching God and the spiritual. Neither Kabbalah nor philosophy, but experience is the proper way to approach God. "Serve God with gladness!" "Taste and see that God is good!" "For me the closeness of God is best." The words of the Psalmist became the watchwords of the Hasidic movement (ibid. pg. 3).

24. Torah Vodaath is one of New York's oldest and most prestigious Yeshivas. Rabbi Wolfson was a student at Torah Vodaath and was a close disciple of Rabbi Shraga Feivel Mendelovitz, of blessed memory, the institution's founder. Today Rav Wolfson provides inspiration and guidance to the students at Torah Vodaath.

and the Rabbi of Beis Medrash Emunas Yisrael. As an introduction to Chasidus, the *Mashgiach* taught an English language class on the *Tanya* for three years. This work is based upon my notes from those lectures.[25] In addition, I have listened to lectures on the *Tanya* by the Rebbe of Stitchin, Rav Mordechai Zilber, *shlit"a*, the *Mashgiach*'s son-in-law. The Rebbe's deep presentations have also helped me immeasurably in the preparation of this work. I have also added material from the writings of Rabbi Wolfson and other Chasidic masters.[26] There are works from the *Musar* schools of thought that seemed to deal with the same themes the *Mashgiach* advanced, and I have attempted to incorporate their insights as well. I have tried to note in the footnotes the sources for all the ideas that I did not hear directly from Rav Wolfson.

The *Mashgiach* is a selfless teacher. He has shared his wisdom and life with thousands, many of whom seek him out on a daily basis. He has been a major influence and source of inspiration in my life and in the lives of countless other students of Torah. I will never be able to sufficiently express my gratitude to the Almighty for bringing me to the *Mashgiach*. His outlook and personality have had an enormous impact upon me.

Some ideas in the book are from sources that I do not remember. Whatever sources I did recall I have tried to note, and I hope that I did not violate the Talmudic dictum demanding that lessons be taught in the name of its originator. Finally, I pray that if I misrepresented a concept its author will forgive me.

---

25. The *Tanya* is the basic text of Chasidic thought, and while there are different approaches than that of the *Baal Ha-Tanya*, his work is integral to understanding Chasidus.

26. In particular I have drawn upon Rav Wolfson's writings, *Emunas Etecha* and *Tzion Ve-Arehah*. I have also tried to incorporate insights from *Mishbetzos Zahav*, the writings of the Stitchiner Rebbe.

A Prayer

One of the few pieces of literature written by the Baal Shem Tov is a letter he sent to his brother-in-law. In it, the Besht related a dreamlike experience in which he ascended the heavenly ladder and met the soul of *Mashiach* (the Messiah):

> I spoke to *Mashiach* and asked him, "When is your majesty coming?"
>
> He replied, "This is your sign: It will be at a time when your teachings become widespread in the world, and 'your springs spread their waters afar.'"[27]

Hopefully this book will help spread the waters of the springs of Chasidus a little further.

---

27. *Chasidic Masters* pg.13.

LESSON ONE

THE COMMITMENT AT BIRTH

THE TALMUD[28] TEACHES that the most exquisite moments of life are spent in the womb. The embryo gains insight, as it sits together with its own personal angel and is taught the entirety of Torah. A glowing candle allows them to see from one end of the world to the other. As the soul leaves the womb, the angel guides it in a final and irrevocable oath:

> I will be a *tzaddik*, a righteous individual. I will never take pride for virtue even if the whole world calls me a saint. In my eyes I will [always] remain like a *rasha*, a wicked person [who must still grow and improve].[29]

Upon entering this world, the child is touched by his celestial mentor, and the illuminating candle, the doting angel, the Torah learning, and the solemn oath vanish from memory.

Three questions arise from this Talmudic account: First, since we have no memory of this pre-natal oath, why were we led to accept it? Next, according to Jewish law, only the oaths of adults can create legal and binding obligations; therefore, why is an unborn child taking an oath? Last, considering that an oath usually serves as a guarantor to the truth of one's words, why is the pure soul of the child not accepted as trustworthy without the oath?

The questions may be answered as follows: an oath is not merely a verbal guarantee; rather it is a process that imbues an individual with

28. *Niddah* 30b.
29. Ibid.

added strength. We glean this understanding of the oath-taking process from two sources, the usage of such verbal commitments in the Torah and the etymology of the Hebrew word *shevua*, "oath."

Oaths in the Torah

In the book of Genesis, after the death of Sarah, Abraham sends his trusted servant Eliezer to find a wife for Isaac, Abraham's son. Abraham saw the rampant corruption among the indigenous Canaanites, and he sought a suitable daughter-in-law from a different society. Not satisfied merely to request that Eliezer avoid choosing a Canaanite, Abraham led him in an oath:

> I will make you swear by God, the God of heaven and earth, that you will not take a wife for my son from among the daughters of the Canaanites in whose midst I dwell. But you should go into my country and to my relatives and take a wife for my son for Isaac (Gen. 24:3-4).

Abraham's insistence on this oath is disturbing. Would he not trust Eliezer's solemn commitment? Eliezer had been Abraham's most loyal student.[30] The two had fought together and depended on one another in battle.[31] Abraham had trusted Eliezer's loyalty to defend his life; why would he not trust Eliezer's word? One might posit that Eliezer's word was not trustworthy in the absence of an oath since he was not a member of Abraham's family. This solution would not apply to a different circumstance of oath-taking in the Torah.

According to Jewish mystics, Joseph was the paradigm of virtue and righteousness, the personification of *tzaddik yesod olam*, a man of such holiness that his merit sustains the entire world. Joseph was also Jacob's favorite son, and they shared a special relationship.[32] When Jacob

---

30. See Gen. 15:2 and the commentary of Rashi, s.v. *u-vein meshek beisi* and *Dammesek*.
31. See Gen.14:14 and Rashi's commentary on that verse.
32. See Gen. 30:25 and Rashi's comment on that verse; Gen. 37:2 and the respective Rashi; also Gen. 37:11, 37:35, 45:27-28.

lay dying he called Joseph and requested burial in the Land of Israel. Although Joseph promised that he would ensure his father's interment in Israel (Gen. 47:30), Jacob was not satisfied and demanded that an oath be sworn in God's name: "And he [Jacob] said 'Swear to me' and he [Joseph] swore to him, and Israel [another name for Jacob] bowed back toward the head of the bed" (Gen. 47:31).

Did Jacob really suspect that Joseph would not fulfill his final request? It is a Mitzvah to fulfill the last wishes of a dying man.[33] Did Jacob fear that the paradigmatic *tzaddik* would not fulfill a moral charge? Did he think that his most beloved son's word could not be trusted?

Evidently, oaths function in the Bible as more than mere guarantees of truth-telling. They give the oath-taker added strength to attain what might otherwise be too difficult to accomplish. Abraham trusted Eliezer, and Jacob trusted Joseph, yet the goals that Joseph and Eliezer were charged to achieve were seemingly unattainable. To find a suitable spouse for his master's son, Eliezer had to overcome his personal interests, having a daughter of marriageable age, and the opposition of both the boorish Bethuel (Besuel) and Laban (Lavan), relatives of Abraham who rejected Abraham's mission.[34] To bury Jacob in Israel, Joseph had to overcome the opposition of Pharaoh, a tyrant who believed that Jacob's physical presence in Egypt brought blessings to the land and prevented the recurrence of famine. Without their oaths, Eliezer and Joseph might have quit if their initial efforts proved unsuccessful. Perhaps they would have invoked the Talmud's rule that "the coerced are not liable." Their oaths called forth added strength from the core of their soul. The extra determination and fortitude enabled them to successfully complete their missions.[35]

---

33. *Gittin* 15a.

34. Furthermore, Eliezer had to leave Abraham's house. When Eliezer arrived to Bethuel's home, Eliezer had to convince Bethuel and Laban to allow Rebekah (Rivkah) to marry Isaac. Abraham's home was suffused with a spirit of sanctity, while the home of Besuel was a den of iniquity. Abraham feared that the atmosphere of Besuel's home would affect Eliezer. In Aram, Eliezer would not be able to overcome his own biases, and he would falter and leave the task unfulfilled (Rav Wolfson).

35. See *Or Gedalyahu* on *Parashas Vayetze*, contrasted with the *Sfas Emes* at the beginning of *Vayetze*. See also the *Sfas Emes* on *Parashas Mattos* (5634),

THE WORDS *SHEVUA* AND *SHEVA*

Hebrew words are derivations and variations of three-letter roots. The root of the word *shevua*, "oath," is also the root of the word *sheva*, "seven." The verbal confluence reflects a connection between an oath and the symbolic message of the number seven.

The number seven recalls the days of the week and also God's creation of the world. On each of the seven days of creation, He formed a different elemental spiritual force. These spiritual forces devolved into the material world.[36] The number seven symbolizes these forces and the totality of the natural world's origins.[37]

How is an oath related to seven? Oath-taking invokes all of the natural forces within man. In critical situations a person may discover the enormous potential strength latent within him. A mother might manage to dash through flames to rescue her child who was trapped in an inferno. Caring relatives might spend weeks with inadequate nourishment and sleep to take care of a sick family member. During moments of trial, the adrenaline in our bloodstream increases to give us added vigor and enables us to perform at seemingly superhuman levels. Usually, in normal daily living, we utilize only a fraction of our physical strength, mental concentration, and spiritual capacity—that is, unless we enter into an oath.

---

who writes, "My teacher and master, my grandfather, explained the concept of *shevua*. When man accepts upon himself a commitment with his entire heart, [he swears and] this is the *shevua*, the gathering together of all the seven *middos* [character parts] within man. Once fully devoted, the name of God rests upon him." In later lessons there will be a further explication of the seven character parts of man.

36. See further later lessons where the further depths to the creation narrative are revealed.

37. See the *Collected Writings of Rabbi Samson Raphael Hirsch* (1808-1888), vol. 3, pgs. 96-111. Rabbi Hirsch develops the theory that the number seven represents completeness, as in the verse, "Wisdom has hewed out its seven pillars" (Prov. 9:1). The seven pillars of wisdom represent all the knowledge in the world. Rabbi Hirsch then symbolically interprets details of many laws such as the seven sprinklings of blood of animals offered as offerings, and the seven branches of the menorah as representing a totality.

Oath-taking calls forth and dedicates every ounce of willpower and strength. If one swears in God's name that a statement is true, that person is committing his or her entire being to the fulfillment of these words. An oath is a guarantor of truth because it arouses the most passionate of commitments.

According to the Sages, when God declared in the Ten Commandments, "Do not take my name in vain [through swearing]," the entire universe shook.[38] Why did this command frighten the entirety of creation? Perhaps because a *shevua* summons all *sheva*, all the seven spiritual roots of creation, and invests them in the cause.[39] A human is a miniature universe. Since I parallel the world, whatever I do with my soul causes a corresponding effect on the soul of the world.[40] When I swear I arouse all the parts of my heart; the physical world then finds all the sources of its existence aroused as well. A false oath weakens every root of mine, and that causes all the channels through which God pours life down to the world to shake with instability.

Hebrew has a variety of letter sounds that are similar and therefore interchangeable. Commentators sometimes replace letters in a word with similar sounding letters in order to obtain an additional layer of meaning.[41] One such interchangeable pair is the letters *bet* and *peh*.[42] Through their interchange *sheva* acquires a relationship to the word *shefa*, an overflow of energy. Every *shevua* is really an awakening of a Divine emanation of spiritual energy and the source for renewed strength and commitment.

---

38. *Shevuos* 38b.

39. Nachmanides writes, "The secret is that the word *shevua* is from the word *sheva*" (commentary to Num. 30:3). See further *Emunas Etecha, Parashas Chayei Sarah*, pg. 70 s.v. *ve-chein matzinu*.

40. See further Lessons Five and Six, where this concept is explained in greater detail.

41. The name for this concept is *Osiyos Mischalfos*, letters which interchange. An example is the letters, *ayin, ches, heh*, and *aleph*, all of which are interchangeable with each other. *Osiyos Mischalfos* is the guiding principle of Rabbi Samson Raphael Hirsch's analysis of the Hebrew language; see the Introduction to the *Etymological Dictionary of Biblical Hebrew* by Matityahu Clark. See also Rashi on Lev. 19:16, who explains that the letters *bet* and *peh* interchange, as well as the letters *gimmel, kaf*, and *kuf*; *nun, lamed*, and *resh*; *zayin* and *tzadi*.

42. In the *ktav ashuri* (Assyrian script) of Hebrew, within the black ink of the letter *peh* (פ), is a white letter *bet* (ב).

THE MEANING OF THE UNBORN CHILD'S OATH

The oath of the yet to be born child is a charge of strength that gives each human added energies and determination to succeed in this life's journey. This world can be a house of horrors that is filled with trials and doubts that undermine faith. The wicked often seem to prosper and the righteous to suffer. Maintaining the inner faith that is harbored within our souls and following the faint voice of conscience despite the deafening protestations of lust and self-interest are most difficult feats. To resist the seductions of the profane and fully devote our energies to God's work, we must commit all the spiritual forces within us. Before birth, we did not lift our hands onto a Torah scroll and swear, but every fiber of our being was charged with passion for our mission. We may have forgotten the encounter with the angel, but the invigoration from that parting persists. We have an enormous latent force, an overflowing river of spiritual energy, committed to the task to be a *tzaddik*.

The oath of birth is continually renewed through the celebration of Shabbos. Lesson Two will detail the role of Shabbos and how it resembles the pre-natal oath.

Lesson Two

The Role of Shabbos

In Jewish practice, we continually renew the seven-fold commitment of birth through commemorating Shabbos, the seventh day. Shabbos resembles a *shevua*, an "oath." On Shabbos, the silent devotional prayers contain seven blessings. These prayers are like an oath; they invigorate the seven parts of the heart and personality. In Chasidic literature, Shabbos is called Beer Sheva, a seven-fold well. Shabbos is similar to a well, a source of life-renewing water for the seven parts of the personality. Shabbos energizes every spiritual part of the soul so that we might redouble our efforts to serve God in this world.

In the writings of Slonimer Chasidim the role of Shabbos is explained by means of the following parable:

In pre-modern Eastern Europe there was an itinerant peddler who would trudge from town to town selling meager wares. One time, while making his way through the forest between hamlets, the sky darkened and a winter storm erupted. The overcast sky soon disappeared in the black darkness of night and a thick layer of snow covered the forest paths. He lost his way and found himself alone with snowflakes and biting winds. As the hours progressed and he marched on helplessly, he lost all feeling in his fingers and toes, while his cheeks turned crimson red due to the frost. Suddenly, in the distance he saw a shimmering light. Realizing that the light must be a sign of human settlement he marshaled his final reserves of strength and made his way toward the beacon. He arrived at the light source and found that it was a travelers' inn. He entered the motel and sat down next to the roaring fire. He then ate the dinner that was served and quickly fell asleep. The next morning, after a hearty breakfast, he received directions from the innkeeper to the next town. He then stepped out into the snow-covered forest confident that he would find his way.[43]

Shabbos is the inn, the fire and the food, the respite from the storm. Life is the journey through the forest and the inclement weather. Each soul is sent down from a Heavenly perch to this lowly earth to fulfill its mission of increasing the glory of God. Our experiences during the week, when we engage the material world, are akin to the storm in the forest; it is dangerous for the soul, and we easily lose our way. That danger, though, is also the reason for eventual reward.

Another parable might help elucidate this concept:

A king once sought to display the broad reaches of his empire. He issued an edict that called on his subjects to provide him with precious stones from the different parts of his kingdom, for he desired to fashion a crown that would demonstrate to all the breadth of his rule. The loyal subjects scaled mountains and dug deep mines to find the many different types of gems in the king's territories. A simple peasant decided that he would provide evidence that the king's rule reached the depths of the ocean. He set out in a small boat to the middle of the sea. Then he dove into the frothing waters, to try and procure a pearl from the ocean floor. It was a dangerous dive, undercurrents swept him away from his goal, sharks lurked beneath the waves, and his lungs quickly felt as if they would burst from exhaustion. He had to rise to the surface and gulp air many times, yet he persevered and kept diving below. Eventually, he found a tiny pearl. Exhausted, he brought the pearl to the king. The king, touched by the peasant's dedication, took the small and simple stone and made it the centerpiece of his crown.[44]

---

43. *Divrei Shmuel*, Shabbos Note 22.
44. *Sidduro shel Shabbos*, Part 5, 1:15.

Each of us can be the simple peasant in the story. We were sent to this sphere of existence to display the breadth of God's rule.[45] When we obey His commands, while in a lustful, physical body and in a tempting material environment, we demonstrate that God is King even in the depths of the physical realm.

The mission is a dangerous endeavor. Many fail. They drown in the ocean of natural urges[46] and ignore their higher calling. The danger is ultimately for the good. The fact that our souls take risks, the fact that we are struggling to sanctify God's name despite material desires, is what gives the Almighty great joy and earns the soul infinite reward in the World-to-Come. Were there to be no risks of sin, such as if we would live in an exclusively spiritual state, our observance of Mitzvos would not be a display of dedication. Now that we are in a physical realm and blessed with difficult temptations, our observance of God's Mitzvos and avoidance of misdeeds solely because He commanded, shows our love for the King.[47]

---

45. King Solomon taught, "All that God made He made for His sake, even the evildoer for the day of retribution" (Prov. 16:4). The Gaon of Vilna explains that the verse is revealing the purpose of life, to reveal God as Ultimate Sovereign. Righteous individuals fulfill this purpose through observance of God's commandments. Obeying His directives demonstrates that He is King. Wicked individuals ignore God's ethical mandates. They reveal God as King when they are punished for their misdeeds. Thus, since all were created for the sake of increasing God's glory, the wicked will suffer punishment for their misdeeds if they do not repent.

46. The Hebrew word for "nature" is *teva*. The same letters in a different context mean drowning. The connection between the two meanings of the word is that, "The natural world of desires and animal instincts drowns an individual" (*Chiddushei Ha-Rim*, the first Gerrer Rebbe).

47. Rabbi Levi Yitzchak of Berditchev once sought to demonstrate the dedication of the Jewish people. On the morning of the third day of Passover he turned to his followers and asked them to find for him some contraband, "I would like to save two rubles and avoid the government's tax," he explained. The word quickly spread, "The Rebbe desires some illegal material." Within thirty minutes a Chasid came forward and brought the Rebbe a spool of yarn that had been smuggled illegally across the border. Then the Rebbe said, "Find me some leavened bread in the house of a Jew! I will pay two thousand rubles for a single slice." His followers protested, "That is impossible, Rebbe. The Torah prohibits the possession of *chametz* during these days; there is not a single piece of bread in any Jewish home in Berditchev!" At this point, the Rebbe turned to God and said aloud, "God, see the love of your people! The Czar has thousands of soldiers and police. He prohibited possession of this yarn with a penalty of

The peddler's journey through the forest stands for the same life-long mission that the peasant's dive into the sea represented. The dangers of the sea and the winter storm of the forest are representations of the material pitfalls that can drive us off task and cause us to lose our way. The peddler who is lost is the person who has forgotten the goal of increasing God's glory. (The peddler lost in the wilderness began to suffer from the cold and deprivation.) When we forget our goal in life and ignore our Divine obligations, the soul suffers spiritual frostbite and hunger. Shabbos is the light in the distance that guides and provides a glimmer of hope from the midst of the tempest.

When Shabbos comes, we retreat from the world to warm our bodies and nourish our souls, so that we might redirect our lives and renew our faith in God. Then we are ready to re-engage and sanctify existence as commanded by our Creator. Shabbos is a moment of *sheva* and *shefa*, when the seven forces of creation, represented by the seven days of creation, coalesce and recharge. It is the day in which our souls re-enact the oath-taking of our births and recommit to be *tzaddikim*, righteous individuals.[48]

---

death. His soldiers are looking for these infractions and eagerly punish those they catch; people are afraid of his men, Nevertheless, with a meager sum of two rubles I could display disobedience of this human king. You have neither policemen nor soldiers. You wrote in your Torah that Jews should not have *chametz* on Passover; and see, no Jew in Berditchev has a drop of *chametz*! I offered thousands of rubles and the people thought I was mad, they had no desire for such funds; they observe your commands with disregard of monetary loss and gain. Why is this so? Because they are committed to You!" (ZR)

48. The connection between Shabbos and the pre-natal oath can be found in a lesson of the *Sfas Emes*:

"Our Sages teach that the angel makes him swear 'I will be a *tzaddik*....'" Can a soul undergo an oath?! Can it hold a Torah scroll?! Rather, the meaning of that passage is that at the point before birth it is clear to the soul that life comes exclusively from the Almighty and should be utilized to fulfill a mission; the realization of God's willed commands. Similarly, the Shabbos is called a *shevua*; this is why the Torah was given to Israel on a Shabbos. We refer to the experience at Sinai as being an occasion when we all entered into an oath, since at Sinai as well, it became clear that life comes from Him and all our energies were charged and directed, which is the meaning of *shevua* (*Parashas Mattos* 5634-1874).

In mystical literature,[49] the Biblical personality of Noah is identified as a paradigm of Shabbos-like living. Perhaps the reason for this is that Noah represents renewal. His world was destroyed in the deluge that swept away a sinful creation, and he merited to see mankind begin anew.[50] Shabbos is a day of renewal; after Shabbos we are reborn. At birth, the baby is dedicated with full passion, as Shabbos departs and we start afresh, we are charged with renewed vigor to march firmly along the path of holiness.

Oaths and Shabbos are examples of a *davar kelali,* entities that encapsulate in microcosmic form the entire physical world. Shabbos touches all seven forces through the dimension of time whereas an oath-taking localizes them in the construct of personality.[51] This *davar kelali* appears in another manifestation as well.

SHABBOS IN THREE DIMENSIONS

The mystical aspect of Torah teaches that a profound unity underlies mundane reality. Phenomena and objects that commonly appear to be different and distinct may be identical in their abstract essence. The *Book of Creation*[52] teaches that each spiritual concept in the world necessarily appears in three dimensions: space, time, and soul.[53]

The holidays, called *Mo'adim* (Lev. 4-8), display this principle. The room in the Temple in which God spoke to Moses was also called *Ohel Mo'ed*—the Tent of Meeting. Here then, in a word, is a connection between the holidays (part of time) and the Tent of Meeting (a part of

49. *Tikkunei Zohar* 21.
50. See further *Bereishis Rabbah, Noach* 30:8.
51. See *Shem Mi-Shmuel* (Commentary to Genesis, pg. 5) who explains, "Shabbos unites all and encompasses all, that is why it is described with the word *kol* [all], as in the verse, *va-yechullu ha-shamayim ve-ha-aretz ve-chol tzevaam, va-yechal Elokim ba-yom ha-shevi'i....* On Shabbos, heaven and earth became part of *kol,* since the microcosm that integrated all appeared."
52. In Hebrew it is called *Sefer Yetzirah.* Many sources attribute it to Abraham; others say it bears the handiwork of Rabbi Akiva. See further *Innerspace* pg.4 and notes 22 and 23.
53. The acronym for this idea is *Asha"n,* indicating the common denominator of *olam* (places in the world) *shanah* (time of the year), and *nefesh* (individuals within society and parts of the human being).

space). The selfsame holiness of the Divine Presence that filled the Tent of Meeting infuses the holidays.[54] During the holidays, God is so close that He can be seen.[55] The Tent of Meeting was the place where His presence was so palpable that it was as if He were seen there.

The Midrash reinterprets a verse in Leviticus in a manner consistent with the principle of unity in different dimensions. The Torah states, *eleh mo'adei Hashem asher tikrau osam*, "These are the meeting times of God that you shall proclaim...." The Midrash suggests that the closing, *asher tikrau osam*, literally, "that you should call them," should be interpreted to refer to people, and read as, *asher tikrau attem*, "that you will call yourselves." The Midrash is applying the concept of *Mo'ed* to the realm of person. Some individuals are similar to *Mo'adim*; they see God, and when you see them you might be inspired to seek and discover the Divine.[56]

---

54. Rabbi Samson Raphael Hirsch also points out that the *Mo'ed* in time corresponds to the *Mo'ed* in place, although he explains their relationship in a way that is different from the metaphysical explanation provided in the text.

> *Mo'adim*, appointed seasons, summon us entirely to the contemplation and inner realization of those ideas which lie at their foundation. *Just as the Mo'ed in the spatial sense refers to the locality which men have as their appointed place of assembly for an appointed purpose, so Mo'ed in Time is a point in Time which summons us communally to an appointed activity* [emphasis added]—in this case an inner activity. Thus *Mo'adim* are the days which stand out from the other days of the year. They summon us from our everyday life to halt and to dedicate all our spiritual activities to them (*Horeb* 161).

55. See also *Hagigah* 2a, and Rashi s.v. *yireh yeira'eh*.
56. See further *Likkutei Moharan*, Lesson 4, who teaches that seeing the face of a righteous individual can cause a person to fully devote themselves to God. Rabbi Dr. Akiva Tatz described how a righteous face leads one to Divinity in the following passage:

> There is a mystical idea that the highest level of the personality is crystal-clear and transparent, but the lower self, the ego clouds it. (Spiritual beauty is expressed as being transparent, Hashem's [God's] light shines through. When one sees a *tzaddik*, one perceives something of God; the limited human dimension has been clarified and a higher reality becomes visible. In fact the opposite of beauty, ugliness, is *caur*, the same root as *acur*, "opaque.") (*Living Inspired*, pg. 104.)

In Lesson One, we discovered that Shabbos is an all-encompassing force of holiness in the realm of time. Because all forces appear in triplicate form, Shabbos-like holiness must also manifest simultaneously in the realms of place and soul.

SHABBOS IS JERUSALEM

The liturgy for Shabbos, in a seemingly incongruous diversion, prays for Jerusalem. The highlight of the prayers to inaugurate Shabbos is the song of *Lechah Dodi*. The second stanza refers to the teaching of Shabbos at Sinai in the Ten Commandments. In the third stanza we sing,

> To welcome the Shabbos come let us go,
> For it is the source of blessing;
> From the beginning, from antiquity she was honored,
> Last in deed but first in thought.[57]

Then, there is an abrupt change of subject. Instead of Shabbos, the song speaks of Jerusalem. We call on this royal city to leave the destruction and its vale of tears (the fourth stanza), and to awaken and reveal its Godly

---

Another application of this principle of the *Sefer Yetzirah* pertains to Yom Kippur, the holiest day of the year. The Torah calls this day *Shabbos Shabboson*, "the Sabbath of Sabbaths," the source of all holiness. Just as there is a day, so too, there is a place that is the foundation of all holiness—the *Kodesh Ha-Kodoshim*, "the holiest of holies," the innermost sanctum in the Temple of Jerusalem. Similarly there is a person who is filled with this type of spiritual energy: Aaron the High Priest, who is described in the verse as *kodesh kodoshim hu*, "he is holy of holies" (1 Chron. 23:13). On Yom Kippur a great unification occurs when the holiest of souls, enters the holiest place, at the holiest time. This union of themes arouses divine blessings for the coming year (*Arvei Nachal, Parashas Emor*).

Rav Wolfson points out that the connection between Aaron and the Holy of Holies may explain why Aaron passed away on *Rosh Chodesh Av*, the first of the month of *Av*. The first day of a month is called *rosh*, "head of the month," for its function is like that of the human head. It expresses the essence of the month and contains in microcosmic form all of that month's events and energy. Because *Av* is the month in which the Temples in Jerusalem were destroyed, Aaron (the personification of those places), passed away on its first day (*Emunas Etecha, Parashas Mattos*).

57. *ArtScroll Siddur*, pg. 317.

light (the sixth stanza). Finally, we declare that, with the Redemption, the city will expand to the right and left, and all of Jewry will rejoice in her success (the ninth stanza). Only in the final stanza does the song return to the topic of Shabbos, welcoming her as a bride into Jewish hearts and homes.

Why do we sing of Jerusalem in the prayers of Shabbos? The answer is that Jerusalem is Shabbos. What Shabbos is in the dimension of time, Jerusalem is in the dimension of place; they share the same type of Godly revelation.[58]

According to the Talmud, when God began the creation of the universe, He first created a middle point and that center then expanded until the entire universe was formed. According to the deeper wisdom of Torah, that starting point contained within itself the entire world in a form of latent potential. Mystics add that the creation process is constantly occurring anew. King David wrote that the Divine words that formed the Heavens still hover in the ether, since God renews the entire creative process every moment (see Ps. 119:89). Thus, even today, thousands of years after the happenings in the Book of Genesis, the central starting place contains within it a microcosm of the entire universe that emerged and will re-emerge from it. That point is Jerusalem.

Shabbos contains within it the entirety of time; it encapsulates the other days and itself, while Jerusalem is a microcosm of the realm of place. Shabbos is the portal through which the Divine blessings for the coming six days shower down to earth. Similarly, Jerusalem was described by Jacob as "the Gate of Heaven" (Gen. 28:17). All of the earth's blessings for the dimension of space flow to Jerusalem and from there emanate to the rest of the universe. Jerusalem is an international city. All nations desire a foothold within her walls, because spiritually all sources of life for all countries inhere within her streets.

---

58. Shabbos displays that man is not the master of his fate and livelihood; God is the master of the universe. During the times of the Temple there was no private ownership of homes in Jerusalem, For instance, during the holidays any Jew could stay in any home in Jerusalem without paying rent, for in Jerusalem the homes belong to God. Jerusalem teaches the lesson of Shabbos that God is the only master of the world. See further *Tzion Ve-Arehah*, pgs. 100-107.

Just as Shabbos sanctifies every fiber of our feelings, so does Jerusalem. The holy city provides added strength and inspiration to every part of one's being.[59] Through observance of the Shabbos in the

---

59. In truth, the entire Land of Israel parallels Shabbos. That is why in *Pirkei de-Rabbi Eliezer* it is written that just as God created six days of work with a seventh as Shabbos, He also created six important bodies of land, the six continents, and a seventh important land, the Land of Israel. Based on this Midrash, a question of liturgical accuracy can be resolved. In the prayers for Shabbos, it is written *chemdas yamim oso karasa*, "You called it the most beloved of days." Yet nowhere in the Holy Scriptures is Shabbos called "the most beloved of days." In light of the above, Shabbos has the holiness and quality of the Land of Israel; adjectives about Israel are therefore true about Shabbos. The Land of Israel was called by God "most beloved" in the verse *Va-yimasu be-eretz chemdah*, "And they [the generation of the desert] rejected the most beloved land" (Ps. 106:24, *Tzion Ve-Arehah* pg. 23; see further the final lesson of the book).

On Shabbos each Jew receives an added soul. The Land of Israel has the holiness of Shabbos; thus, one who lives in Israel also possesses a dual complement of soul. Outside of Israel, Jewish law insists that each holy day (other than Shabbos), such as the beginning of Sukkos, be observed for two days while in Israel the holy day's duration is only one day. Since residents of Israel have a double soul they can internalize the holiness of the festival in a single day, Those outside of Israel only posses half such spiritual capabilities, this is why they must observe the holy day twice to internalize its blessings (Rabbi Isaac Luriah).

Since the entire Land of Israel is like Shabbos, the *shefa chaim*, the "Godly life-flow for the entire world," flows through the Land of Israel. Israel is to the rest of the universe what the heart is to the human body. The heart distributes nutrients to the limbs, and Israel distributes Godly nutrition to the rest of the world. On the level of soul, all countries are related to Israel, and that is why the nations of the world seek to stake out a claim in the holy land and refuse to accept that it belongs exclusively to the Jewish nation (*Emunas Etecha, Bereishis*, pg, 3, s.v. *u-va-zeh muvenes*).

The Talmud states that Israel is the highest land and that the Temple Mount in Jerusalem is the highest point within Israel. What is the meaning of this statement? From a geological perspective there are many mountain ranges that are taller than Israel. How can Israel and the Temple Mount be considered higher than the Himalayas? Rabbi Moshe Sofer (1762-1838) answered that Israel and Jerusalem as the starting points for creation are the keys to unlocking the meaning of the Talmud's claim. Our earth and the universe as a whole are circles. The beginning of the circle can be called its highest part. Since the Temple Mount was the first place God created, it is the highest point along the circle of earth. Since Israel was created right after Jerusalem, when one compares Israel to the rest of the world's lands it is the first and thus called the highest (heard from Rav Wolfson).

dimension of time, we will be worthy of reclaiming the Shabbos of place, the rebuilt city of Jerusalem.[60]

Shabbos in Man

There are individuals who are Shabbos, and they have an all-encompassing holiness. These individuals have within their souls a little bit of every other soul that exists. They touch all and provide added strength to the totality of the natural world. All the blessings for the coming six days, the realm of time, flow through Shabbos, and the Divine blessings for all lands, the realm of space, flow through Jerusalem. Similarly, there is an individual through which all souls are blessed.[61] The *tzaddik* is this

---

Both Jerusalem and the Land of Israel can be Shabbos. First, Jerusalem as the capital of the Land of Israel has within it a concentrated version of the entire Land of Israel. Furthermore, our sages teach that Jerusalem in the future will extend and fill the entire Land of Israel (*Shir Ha-Shirim Rabbah* 7:10). It may be that the latent Jerusalem quality in the Land of Israel makes the Land of Israel Shabbos in place. Finally, Chasidus and Kabbalah are not attempting to draw fine distinctions. These disciplines seek to display underlying unity. They therefore highlight those aspects of institutions that bear a similarity, Thus, Jerusalem is the place of Shabbos when one compares Jerusalem to the rest of the Land of Israel, and if one compares the Land of Israel to the rest of the world, the Land of Israel is Shabbos and the other lands are the days of the week.

60. The *Midrash Yalkut* on *Parashas Behaaloscha* links Shabbos with the renewal of Jerusalem stating, "If you will observe [the obligation of] the lighting of Shabbos candles, I will show you the candle of Zion [the rebuilding of Jerusalem]." The blessing for lighting Shabbos candles, through which Jewish women enter into Shabbos, contains the phrase *ve-tzivvanu le-hadlik ner shel Shabbos*, "And has commanded us to light the candle of Shabbos." The numeric value of the phrase is the same as the numeric value of the phrase *Li-Yirushalayim mevasser ettein*, "I will appoint a harbinger of redemption for Jerusalem." Due to their innate congruence, observance of Shabbos will cause God to restore the glory of Jerusalem.

61. "The Land of Israel in general, and Jerusalem in particular, are the very heart and center of the world as a whole. The life-force for the world, all blessings and emanations from Above, therefore, issue to all countries through Jerusalem and the Land of Israel.... It is the very same with the people of Israel. It is the very heart of all mankind. Thus Israel is the channel for the sustenance and all blessings of the world.... In analogous terms, the *tzaddik*, the leader and shepherd of Israel, is the very heart of the people of Israel. Thus he is the very specific channel connecting Above and below" (*Chasidic Dimensions*, pgs, 114-115).

person, the personification of Shabbos.[62]

The Baal Shem Tov taught that God only shows a person the sights that he deserves to see. If you see the performance of a sin, it is because you have that misdeed within you in some form. God might reveal to you an exaggerated form of your flaw so that you will examine yourself and improve your character.[63]

The Baal Shem Tov once witnessed a Jew violating Shabbos. He realized that his witnessing Shabbos desecration meant that, in some way, he too was a violator of the holy day. The Baal Shem examined his deeds on past Shabboses and concluded that his observance of Shabbos had been perfect. But after extensive analysis, the Baal Shem realized that he had committed a sin of "Shabbos desecration." He had seen an individual insult a Torah scholar, and did not attempt to defend the scholar's honor. Torah scholars (since they are *tzaddikim*) are individuals who possess the holiness of Shabbos. The desecration of their honor, which the Besht was complicit in, was in a certain sense the desecration of Shabbos.[64]

To understand why a *tzaddik* merits to reach all human souls it is necessary to refine the definition of who is indeed a *tzaddik*.

---

62. Since the *tzaddik* is the person of Shabbos and Israel is the land of Shabbos there is a special relationship between the Holy Land and the *tzaddik*. An example of this is the Biblical figure Noah. Noah is called a *tzaddik* (Gen. 6:9), and he was saved from the deluge that destroyed the earth. According to Rabbinic tradition, the Land of Israel was never touched by the flood. Noah embodied Israel, which was why he experienced the Land of Israel wherever he went (*Tzion Ve-Arehah* pg. 15, *Emunas Etecha, Bereishis*, pg, 3 s.v. *ve-yadua*).

63. Torah law obligates the witnesses who testify to the court about a crime that carries the penalty of stoning to cast the first stones. This is due to the principle of the Baal Shem Tov (quoted in *Heichal Ha-Berachah, Devarim*, pg, 208b) that if one sees a misdeed performed by someone else it is a sign that the one who sees has it the same flaw in, at least, a minute measure. Witnesses who saw idol-worship have within them the flaw of paganism. This is why the witnesses must participate in administering the punishment. Through casting the first stones they are to learn to rectify their flaws in the realm of that sin (*Emunas Etecha, Parashas Shoftim*, pg. 232 s.v. *yad*). See further *Emunas Etecha, Parashas Naso*, s. v. *ve-chipper*.

64. *Not Just Stories*, pg. 58. Rav Wolfson added that to rectify the flaw of not honoring Torah scholars sufficiently, the Baal Shem Tov immediately traveled to the author of the work *Pnei Yehoshua* and helped light the pipe of the great Rabbi to fulfill the Mitzvah of serving Torah scholars.

Lesson Three

The *Tzaddik*

The *tzaddik* is the foundation of the world (Prov. 10:25).

For the *tzaddik* will fall seven times and rise
while the wicked will stumble within Evil (Prov. 24:16).

Rava taught: Job wanted to absolve all from accountability. He said to the Almighty, "Master of the Universe, You created the ox with split hooves and the donkey with webbed feet. You created Eden and you created *Gehinnom*. You created *tzaddikim* and you created wicked individuals. Who forces You to do anything? (*Bava Basra* 16a). How could Job ascribe sainthood to birth? The Talmud seems to teach that only man determines whether or not he will be righteous.[65]

WE FREQUENTLY ASSUME that man's spiritual status hinges upon the measure of his deeds. God places man's actions on the Divine scale: Mitzvos on one side and *aveiros* (violations of God's commands) on the other. Those who are weightier with Mitzvos are *tzaddikim* while an excess of *aveiros* characterizes *resha'im*, "sinners." The few with perfectly split behaviors belong to a third category, *beinonim*, "intermediate individuals." Chasidus argues that this simplistic definition is not wholly accurate.

Rabbi Shneur Zalman of Liadi, the founder of Lubavitch Chasidus, dedicated the first part of his book *Likkutei Amarim* (*Tanya*) to the premise that a *tzaddik* is not merely a person whose deeds are usually Mitzvos. The Talmud records a dispute between two sages, Abaye and Rabbah, as to whether the latter was a *beinoni* or a *tzaddik*. Rabbah insisted that he was a *beinoni*, while Abaye argued that if Rabbah was

---

65. *Tanya*, Chapter One, pg. 5.

a *beinoni*, it would be impossible for anyone to be a *tzaddik*.[66] Rabbah definitely performed more good than evil[67] yet felt undeserving of being called a *tzaddik*. The *Tanya* deduced that a *tzaddik* is not just a practitioner of good deeds. His inner life is virtuous. Sin repulses him, and he is attracted only to virtue.

A handful of individuals are born *tzaddikim*. Job referred to the natural *tzaddik* when he said, "God, You created *tzaddikim*."[68] While the Talmud states that the angel of predestination[69] does not declare the spiritual level the child will attain because each individual must attain holiness through his own efforts, that is merely the norm. Every rule has exceptions. The natural *tzaddik* that Job referred to is such an exception. From birth, this *tzaddik* is predisposed to a life of holiness, and internally he hardly feels that sin is a viable option for him. King David was a different type of *tzaddik*; he was born with powerful and sinful urges.

---

66. *Berachos* 61b.

67. According to *Bava Metzia* 86a, Rabbah constantly studied Torah and never had time to sin.

68. *Bava Basra* 16a. This is a partial reason for the existence of Chasidic dynasties. It is felt in certain groups that owing to the merit of great ancestors their Rebbes are born *tzaddikim*. Purportedly, when the *Sfas Emes* was offered the leadership of Gerrer Chasidim he protested that he was too young and inexperienced to lead such an important group of Jews. One of the elder Chasidim answered with a story:

> A group of professional mountain-climbers decided to climb Mt. Everest. After several difficult days of climbing many hardened climbers tired of the challenge and left the group and only a small set of the most expert climbers continued with the climb. Eventually they reached the peak, where they discovered a young child sitting alone atop the mountain. They were astounded, "How did such a young boy climb a mountain that experienced rock-climbers could not scale?" The boy answered, "I was born here."

The Chasid explained to the *Sfas Emes*, "Despite your youth, you can be our leader since you were born at the top of a mountain that your forefathers scaled."

69. This is the view of Rav Chanina, who taught that the angel *Lailah* (night) is the authority for conception. *Lailah* takes the seed and brings it before the Heavenly throne and queries the Almighty, "Master of the World, what will this one be, strong or weak? Wealthy or poor? Wise or foolish?" But he does not ask whether it will be a *tzaddik* or a *rasha*, for Rav Chanina taught, "All is in the hands of Heaven bar the fear of heaven, that is in the hands of man" (*Niddah* 16b).

Through mortification of his material body and rigorous Torah study, he killed his evil urge and reached the spiritual level of a *tzaddik*.[70] A *tzaddik*, whether by birth or through spiritual achievements, is not afflicted by the struggle between lust and conscience. The only desire of the *tzaddik* is attachment to the Divine.

EXAMPLES OF *TZADDIKIM*

Most souls presently on earth are not on their first trip to this planet. We were here in previous lives, did not accomplish our Divine task, and as a result are sent down to earth again[71] for another *gilgul*—transmigration of the soul—in order to relive the trials of life and this time reach *tikkun*, rectification of the spirit. Most of mankind cannot remember their earlier lives. A select few righteous individuals recall their prior identities.

Rabbi Moshe Teitelbaum[72] remembered the time when he was a leaving Egypt. When his grandson[73] asked whether he supported Moses after Korah rebelled, he replied that he stayed neutral.

The Apter Rav,[74] during the *Avodah* prayers of Yom Kippur, which detail the High Priest's service on that day, would not recite the traditional *ve-kach hayah omer*, "and this is what he [the High Priest] said." Rather, he would say, *ve-kach hayiti omer*, "and so I would say." He also recalled a life as a King of Israel.

Rabbi Yisrael of Rizhin[75] remembered when his soul was a sheep of our forefather Jacob, and he revealed to his Chasidim the song that Jacob would sing to his sheep.

---

70. Perhaps this class of *tzaddik* was referred to in Proverbs 24 as the *tzaddik* who falls seven times yet rises.

71. See Rabbi Yisrael Yaakov Klapholtz's compendium *Nishmas Yisrael*, where he collects all the Rabbinic sources for the concept of *gilgulim*, "transmigrations of souls."

72. He was born in 1759 and passed away in 1841. He served as rabbi of Ujhely. He authored the work *Yismach Mosheh*.

73. Rabbi Yekutiel Yehudah Teitelbaum of Sighet (1808-1883). He was a student of Rabbi Chaim of Tzanz and the author of the work *Yitav Lev*.

74. Rabbi Avraham Yehoshua Heschel (1755-1825) was the author of *Ohaiv Yisrael*, and was renowned for his piety and love for all Jews.

75. He was born in 1797, and he passed away in 1850. He was a grandson of Rav Avraham the Angel, the son of the Maggid of Mezeritch. The Maggid was the student of the Besht who led the entire Chasidic movement after the passing of the Besht. Rabbi Yisrael was renowned for his religious devotion and regal manner.

These great men remembered what most of us have forgotten because they did not need full freedom of choice. For most of us, fixing our soul (*tikkun ha-neshamah*) demands engaging in the internal struggle of good versus evil and ensuring that holiness triumphs. As we learned in Lesson Two, "The king rewarded the peasant diver because he tried and succeeded in displaying the king's rule in the dangerous depths of the sea." The fact that our life is dangerous for the soul, the fact that strong forces seek to shove our behavior into the realm of misdeed, and yet we persevere and seek to serve God is why God loves our service and rewards us in the World-to-Come. If we would remember the migrations of our souls, then we would sense the urgency of life's purpose, deviance would lose its appeal, and we would not battle. Our life's journey would then be like a stroll along a well marked path instead of a dive into a raging ocean, and life would not be as meaningful to the Almighty.

Those who do not need the challenge of choice can afford to have the good within them weighted with the memory of their earlier lives. *Tzaddikim* like the Rabbi of Rizhin already succeeded in their mission during prior lives. Before their souls were sent again to this earth, they justly argued, "Why must we risk the eternal accomplishments that we earned?" God agreed and gave them an existence devoid of spiritual danger.

Such *tzaddikim* differ from all other humans. Most of us came to this world to perfect our own souls. Souls like Rabbi Moshe Teitelbaum were sent to help the world. They serve humanity as role models and sources of merit.[76] Since the holiness of the *tzaddik* reaches even the innermost human realm, inclinations and desires, he is the most appropriate vessel for God to use to transmit blessings to mankind.

THE COSMIC ROLE OF THE *TZADDIK*

Tzaddik yesod olam (Prov. 10:25) is the verse that teaches that the *tzaddik* is the foundation of the world. The physical world that we see is sustained by the spiritual gifts and flows of blessing that God continually

---

76. The Talmud in *Yoma* 38b is referring to *tzaddikim* like the Rizhiner when Rav Chiya bar Abba taught in the name of Rav Yochanan, "The Holy One, blessed be He, saw that there were few *tzaddikim*, so he planted several in each and every generation."

pours into it. This *shefa eloki*—divine abundance of good—comes through the purest human soul, the *tzaddik*. The *tzaddik* loves every Jew and all of God's creatures with thoroughly dedicated affection.[77] His love of existence connects all of creation to the *tzaddik*, and they receive their

---

77. The Maharal (Rabbi Yehudah Loew of Prague, 1512-1609, a great Kabbalist, philosopher, and educator) in his commentary to the *Aggadah* explains that a Jewish leader such as the High Priest is the heart of the nation. All limbs are connected to the heart and receive their life from it, and all Jews are attached to the *tzaddik* and are nourished through him (*Makkos* 11a). "The *tzaddik*, the leader and shepherd of Israel, is the very heart of the people of Israel" (*Chasidic Dimensions*, pg. 115, quoting *Tikkunei Zohar* 21:50b).

> The *tzaddikim* of all times share the common denominator of absolute attachment, commitment, and devotion to God, Torah and Israel. As such they follow and share in the qualities of the first and greatest leader and shepherd of Israel: Moses. In fact, they are regarded as extensions and reflections of Moses. Thus it is said that there is not a generation without a leader like Moses. This is not simply in terms of an analogy, but in a quite real sense: an extension and emanation of Moses exists in every generation, in every *tzaddik*....
> This Moses-aspect goes further: Moses had a *neshamah kelalit*, a comprehensive soul. His soul was a root-soul which compounded all the souls of his generation: they were all rooted in his soul. Thus it is also with the *tzaddikim*-leaders of every generation: they, too, are comprehensive root-souls compounding the souls of their respective generations. In this sense they are the leaders and the shepherds of their generations in every respect that Moses was in his. For the head of the generation is the whole of that generation (*Chasidic Dimensions*, pgs. 101-102).

The *tzaddik*'s overwhelming love for creation leads him to be gentle to all. As a result, even when rebuking sinners he will express his displeasure in muted terms:

> I remember that they once related to my father, of blessed memory, that when our great master, Rabbi Ahron Rokeach of Belz, may his merit protect us, was in Munkatch policemen came to arrest him. These evildoers beat him, pushed him, and treated him so roughly that he could not stand their evil, and he said, "They are slightly strange, these *Goyim*." This was already a very harsh critique for his standards. I remember when they related this to my father he smiled slightly. This is the way of *tzaddikim*, they are good to all (Rabbi Yekutiel Yehudah Halberstam [1905-1994], the Rebbe of Tzanz-Klausenberg, in his book *Imros Tzaddikim*, pg. 22, Story 5).

life through him.[78]

78. See *Tanya*, Chapter 2. Even the sinners are connected to the *tzaddik*, and they benefit from him. The Almighty will periodically cause the *tzaddik* to sin, so that he can fall to the realm of sinners, connect with them, and then mystically elevate their souls with his subsequent return and elevation.

The Rebbe of Klausenberg explained that the *tzaddik* loves his nation; that is why his personal penances for his own misdeeds are performed for the sake of all the sinners in the nation, and thousands of souls are uplifted in a hidden and mystical manner through his personal improvement.

> The true path of the Baal Shem Tov and his disciples was that they would perfect themselves first before they would pass judgment on others. When the Baal Shem isolated himself in the Carpathian Mountains, he rolled in the snow to atone for his misdeeds, and he broke the frozen ice atop the river in order to immerse himself in the waters beneath the ice. During those moments tens of thousands of Jews felt the removal of the foreskins covering their hearts and remembered their Maker. This is the meaning of the verse, "There is no speech and there are no words; their sound is unheard" (Ps. 19:4) and despite that, "Their line goes forth throughout the earth, and their word reaches the farthest ends of the land" (v. 5). In this manner the Baal Shem's students made thousands of returnees to the faith. The masters R. Elimelech of Lizhensk (1717-1786) and Rabbi Aharon of Karlin (1736-1772) brought eighty thousand Jews back to observance. They accomplished this through the maxim of Hillel, "Love the creations and bring them closer to Torah." They loved all. They knew to defend and find merit in the behavior of Jews, and they accepted all guilt upon themselves. As Rabbi Yishmael stated in the Mishnah, "Children of Israel, I am your atonement." Through fixing their own internal minute flaws, they caused the entire world to be filled with a spirit of *teshuvah*, return to God (*Imros Tzaddikim*, pg. 23-24).

Our forefather Abraham brought people to observance through meeting them and impressing upon them the truth of monotheism. Our forefather Isaac was very restricted; he did not venture forth into human society, yet he too brought thousands of strangers under the rubric of observance. Isaac's influence was affected in the *tzaddik* mode. When he learned Torah, or improved himself, these acts caused thousands of others to move closer to monotheistic belief and practice (Rav Wolfson).

> Even as the *tzaddik* is the channel for the Divine effluences to the world in general, so he is also an intermediary for the people of his generation to ascend to Divinity.
>
> A common denominator establishes a relationship. On the spiritual level, any commonality, even if limited to a single aspect, already estab-

The Talmud relates that Rabbi Chanina ben Dosa was a *tzaddik*.[79] It then teaches:

> Rabbi Yehudah taught in the name of Rav: Every day a Heavenly voice emerges from Mt. Sinai and proclaims, "The entire world is sustained *bishvil* [through or because of] Chanina my son. And as for Chanina my son, he is satisfied with a small measure of carobs as his weekly total of food.

---

lishes an inherent oneness. When joining different parts of water they become one for every species attaches itself to its own kind. So, too, the *tzaddik* is unified with those who became sanctified through his holiness and is able to raise them along with him. Moreover, as he is the comprehensive soul of his generation, he can elevate all and everything that is rooted in his soul. By means of his own good deeds and service of G-d he can elevate even the souls of the wicked.

In this context, the *tzaddik* will sometimes appear involved with mundane affairs. He is seen engaging in mundane speech or the telling of seemingly inconsequential stories, or otherwise dealing with the masses on their own level. This behavior would seem incompatible with his sublime status. Externally he appears to have lowered and degraded himself, to have stepped aside from his attachment to G-d. In truth, however, he is and remains in a constant state of *deveikus* [attachment to God] in all he does. His anomalous behavior is but for the establishing of a relationship with the simple and the lowly. Thus he is able to raise them to higher levels (*Chasidic Dimensions*, pgs. 109-110).

R. Aryeh Leib, the author of *Aryeh de-Bei Ila'ah*, once said,

> When I was a young man I thought that I would lead the entire world to a path of holiness. As the years went by I realized, I cannot change the entire world, but I thought that at least I will change my entire hometown. Eventually I saw that this too was unattainable so I decided that I will correct my entire family. Now in my old age I say, "I wish and hope that I will be able to fix myself." I believe that the meaning of this saying was that in his older years he recognized that when he learns Torah in holiness and purity he does not need to seek out sinners and impress upon them to return to observance, the holiness that shines in the world from his Torah will accomplish that job for him (*Imros Tzaddikim*, pg. 32).

79. See further *Berachos* 17b, and Rashi s. v. *ve-heim*.

In Hebrew, *bishvil* can mean "because of" or "along the path." The Baal Shem Tov taught that when the Talmud said, "*bishvil* Rabbi Chanina," it also intended the meaning of path. The *tzaddik* like Rabbi Chanina is the path through which all blessings flow.[80]

WHY CHASIDIM HAVE REBBES

Chasidim seek attachment with their Rebbe to strengthen their bond with the *tzaddik*. The Rebbe is considered a possible foundational *tzaddik*, the source of life-affirming good. Therefore, the stronger one is connected to him the more life one derives directly through the *tzaddik*.[81]

To receive vitality in the holiest manner[82] there is a need for a direct

---

80. It is taught:

> The *tzaddik* is like a path or a channel through which liquids flow. Through his righteous deeds he pulls down Divine flows of blessing from Heaven. Just like a pipe does not benefit from the water that flows through it, so too the *tzaddik* has no desire for his own benefit, he only desires that others, the members of the world, receive plenty. This is the meaning of the voice from Heaven, *kol ha-olam nizon bishvil Chanana beni*, "The entire world is sustained through the channel of Chanina my son." Why does he resemble a channel? He does not seek his own benefit. He is satisfied with a small measure of carobs as his weekly total... (*Avodas Yisrael, Likkutim* pg. 275, quoting the Baal Shem Tov).

81. Rabbi Jacob Immanuel Schochet expressed this idea in the following passage:

> In view of the special and ideal nature of the *tzaddik*, it is of great significance to seek his presence, to be associated with him as much as possible. For "He who walks with the wise, shall be wise" (Prov. 13:20). This is analogous to entering a perfumery: though one will not sell or buy anything there, nonetheless, when leaving the shop he and his garments will have absorbed the pleasant scent, and this good scent will not depart from him all day long. Likewise, he who associates with *tzaddikim* is influenced by their ways and good deeds (*Chasidic Dimensions*, pg. 94, quoting *Pirkei de-R. Eliezer*, Chapter 25).

82. The Stitchiner Rebbe explained that life received directly through the *tzaddik* has a unique quality. The essence of the *tzaddik* is his abnegation of self,

channel to the *tzaddik*. One can get life in other ways. Evil gets life from God even though it is not connected to the *tzaddik* in a direct way. However, evil receives flawed vitality.

The world of evil is superficial. Sin is a product of externalism. For instance, lusts tantalize with promises of pleasure yet they are rarely a path to satisfaction. Once they are realized, man is left with an aching emptiness, for evil is hollow within. A holy person is an inner person who rises above an extrinsic perspective.

There is a superficial connection to the *tzaddik* and an internal attachment to the *tzaddik*. Physically being a Chasid, a follower, while in practice not emulating his ways is a superficial attachment. The attendant who hovers around the *tzaddik*, setting the holy man's schedule or serving him lunch, is only externally close to the *tzaddik*. True connection requires a relationship on an inner level, where one learns and grows from the example of the *tzaddik*.[83] The quiet student who is inspired by the presence of the *tzaddik* or works to serve God with added devotion and to emulate the *tzaddik* has the inner bond even if he never introduces himself to the *tzaddik*. The student who resembles

his *mesiras nefesh*. The *tzaddik* does not perform Mitzvos for material benefit nor for spiritual rewards. He has nullified any sense of self and is exclusively dedicated to servicing the Almighty for Divine reasons. (See *Imros Tzaddikim* pg. 23, story 2, where the Klausenberger Rebbe related an example of the dedication of *tzaddikim*. The son of the *Divrei Chaim* would wholeheartedly express and manifest a willingness to suffer enormous pain and hardship of the sake of God at every moment of his life. See also *Chagigah* 12b. The Talmud teaches that *tzaddikim* are constantly offering all that they possess, including their lives, to God. This sacrifice continues even after their earthly passing. In the next world, every day they offer their souls to God again.) As a result, the *tzaddik* is willing to sacrifice all, from physical pleasure to spiritual delight, for the sake of God's commands. A businessman attached to the *tzaddik* will receive a divine *shefa* of wealth that first went through the *tzaddik* (while belonging to the *tzaddik*, the *shefa*-gift was in a sensitive form and not necessarily wealth). Since the *tzaddik* is always giving to Heaven, the businessman's wealth is charged with the character of the *tzaddik*. It has a spiritual quality, and possessing it ennobles and sensitizes the businessman, and he will find that it is easy to give this wealth to the poor and other Divine causes. The businessman who does not emulate the *tzaddik* at all and is disconnected from him might receive Divine blessings of wealth but they will not have a holy charge. His wealth will lead him to arrogance and only after great effort will he succeed in using it for holy causes.

83. Heard from the Stitchiner Rebbe.

the *tzaddik* is the true Chasid. The attendant is a Chasid only in name. He and the *tzaddik* reside in different worlds, and he does not receive life directly through the *tzaddik*.

Personally becoming a *tzaddik yesod olam* might seem to be an unrealistic goal for many of us. The *Tanya* teaches that many souls do not have the potential of reaching such a pristine level. However, all souls can attain great spiritual levels. An awareness of the different types of souls within mankind can help each of us actualize our unique, latent, proclivities for holy behavior. Lesson Four will elucidate the different types of human individuals.

Lesson Four

Humanity's Five Categories

THERE ARE FIVE types of individuals within mankind, three holy and two sinful: a *tzaddik gamur* (complete *tzaddik*), a *tzaddik she-eino gamur* (incomplete *tzaddik*), a *beinoni* (who is drawn equally to God and sin), a *rasha she-eino gamur* (someone who is mostly wicked), and a *rasha gamur* (completely wicked).

The *tzaddik gamur*, "complete *tzaddik*," lacks an evil inclination. The part of the personality that is usually expressed as a drive for physical urges and evil behaviors has been transformed,[84] and it now only seeks virtue.

Tzaddikim called *malachim*, "angels," belong to this group because the *tzaddik gamur* is as dedicated as an angel. Celestial beings do not have an urge to violate God's commands. A *tzaddik gamur* also has no urge for sin. In the final prophetic work, Malachi wrote, *sifsei cohen yishmeru da'as ve-Torah yevakshu mi-pihu ki malach Hashem Tzevakos hu*, "The lips of the priest preserve wisdom, and Torah is sought from his mouth, for he is an angel [*malach*] of God, the Lord of Hosts" (Mal. 2:7). Literally, *malach* means "messenger." We are all God's messengers, sent to accomplish the mission of living a life with God, observing His commandments, learning His Torah, and thus sanctifying His world.[85] Unfortunately, we too often ignore our calling. A true *tzaddik* lives with a constant awareness of mission, and as a result, Malachi named him a *malach*, a constant Messenger.[86]

---

84. As King David said, *libbi chalal be-kirbi*, "My Heart is empty within me" (Ps. 109:22). David was saying that he had successfully emptied the stone part of his heart. The desire for sin, that is unfeeling of the spiritual, is referred to in the Talmud as the stone heart.

85. See further *Sfas Emes* to *Parashas Shelach* (5631).

86. R. Tzadok Ha-Cohen of Lublin, *Sichas Malachei Ha-Shareis*, pg. 5.

The second individual is a *tzaddik she-eino gamur*, an "incomplete *tzaddik*," who is primarily attracted to morality. He also possesses a weak drive for evil and sin. His desire for the holy is supreme and he consistently chooses virtue. Within his heart the advocate for holiness is loudest so it is said to rule over the evil inclination. Such an individual is also called *tzaddik ve-ra lo*, a *tzaddik* who suffers, literally "a *tzaddik* whom evil is his."[87] He has some *ra*, "evil," but *lo*, it is "his," since he controls it.

The third individual is a *beinoni*, a middle of the road type, who is drawn equally to the ungodly and the Heavenly yet never follows the call of evil. Externally, he is perfect for all his deeds are Mitzvos. Internally, this man's body is a battleground with two forces, one angelic the other demonic, wrestling for supremacy. With the help of God and his own efforts, he always acts with virtue.[88] While he may succeed in overcoming lowliness, he is constantly aware that the physical within is a sleeping giant, primed to arise with virulent intensity. The task of the *beinoni* is to remain vigilant and avoid complacency. He is called *oveid Hashem*, "The one who works for God," and not *eved Hashem*, "The Servant of God," since he is in the throes of a struggle and has not fully achieved spiritual heights in a permanent manner.[89]

---

87. A *tzaddik* might suffer if his essence is not fully pure; there is still some evil that he harbors within.

88. According to the *Tanya*, the *beinoni* never allows the evil urge to fully conquer his actions, speech, or thought. Man possesses a core deeper than conscious thought. In this subconscious realm, the *beinoni* possesses a seething volcano of material desires. This volcanic urge is equal to the inner advocate of holiness (*Tanya*, Chapter 12). According to the *Tanya*, the primary way to succeed in this struggle is by means of love for God. In his system, true love of God can only emerge from intellectual inquiry in the mind. Think about the greatness of God, consider how relative to God nothing exists, realize that God is the source for your life. These meditations will give birth to love of God (*Tanya*, Chapter 13). The *Tanya* also describes other methods by which one can become a *beinoni*. R. Tzadok Ha-Cohen explains that virtue can succeed to gain the upper hand, by means of shame in the presence of God. Internalize an awareness of constantly standing before the Infinite (*Sichas Malachei Ha-Shareis*, pg. 7-8). This attitude causes one to be ashamed of sin and a devotee of the internal voice for Mitzvah.

89. *Tanya*, Chapter 15.

Then there are two types of *resha'im*, "evil-doers." The first is a *rasha ve-tov lo*, a sinner who has enhanced his lust for physical pleasures due to sins he has committed. Materialism is more enticing for him than the moral, but he maintains a residual advocate for holiness. As with the *beinoni*, his inner life is a combat area with two armies battling over the small city (his body). Most of his deeds and desires are sinful, yet the good advocate inevitably resurfaces for a moment and causes regret for the misdeed, and his life is filled with guilt. This class contains most of mankind.[90]

The final individual is the *rasha ve-ra lo*, also called a *rasha gamur*, "complete *rasha*." This is the polar opposite of a *tzaddik gamur*; he is all bad with no desire to perform good deeds.[91] Hitler, may his name be obliterated, was part of this class. He had no regrets or contrition for his misdeeds. Apparently, he obliterated his inner advocate for good. The ancient Pharaoh of Egypt was also such a villain; as a result of his many decisions to adopt evil behaviors, God punished him with forfeiture of his innate advocate for the holy; essentially he lost the ability for good.[92]

Now it may be understood why Rabbah called himself a *beinoni*. Rabbah constantly performed Mitzvos yet he claimed that his essential core, his desires, still needed refinement. Abaye argued that Rabbah's remarkable achievements indicated a magnificent internal state and Rabbah had little or no desire for evil, making him either a *tzaddik gamur* or a *tzaddik she-eino gamur*.

RAMIFICATIONS OF THE DIFFERENT LEVELS OF VIRTUE

Every Jew can reach the level of *beinoni*, since God has given man free choice. While our physical nature pulls us to laziness, haughtiness, anger, and desire we can overcome these vices. We personally may not reach a point where we emotionally abhor evil, but we can reach a level of perfection in speech, thought, and deed.[93]

---

90. *Tanya*, Chapter 11.
91. *Tanya*, end of Chapter 11.
92. Maimonides, "Laws of Return," 6:3.
93. *Tanya*, Chapter 14.

Consideration of the meaning of the *beinoni* concept can serve as a source of succor and support. We should never feel guilty about harboring desires for evil or lusts after temptation. We may have been created with the potential of a *beinoni* and do not have an innate ability to reach the level of a *tzaddik*, who is not even attracted to misdeed. Man's purpose is to provide pleasure to the Divine through living a life of Torah. God may not want of us to be a *tzaddik*. He might desire that we serve Him as a *beinoni* in the context of battle. This service may be even more beloved to Him than the service of a *tzaddik* for it entails effort.

It is important for all to study the characteristics and nature of a *tzaddik* since there are moments when a *beinoni* can temporarily become a *tzaddik*, such as when overcome with love towards God. If we think about the awesome size of the universe, when we focus and repeatedly meditate about the wisdom of the microscopic creations and how they were all created for our enjoyment, a passionate love of the Creator will fill our heart. At the height of passion, we may reach the level of *tzaddik*. The material is repulsive, God's infinite love and generosity fill us with a burning passion to come close to Him, to cleave to Him and feel Him in every fiber of our being.

Tzaddik-hood is also relevant due to *ibbur neshamah*, "soul impregnation," which happened to Pinchas. According to the *Zohar*, Pinchas was impregnated with the souls of Nadav and Avihu[94] as a reward for his bravery that saved the Jewish nation. The Torah, therefore, describes him as "Pinchas son of Elazar, son of the priest Aaron." The seemingly misplaced comma after the word Elazar indicates that Pinchas was the son of Elazar by virtue of his own soul and also the son of Aaron the High Priest due to the souls of Nadav and Avihu (Aaron's sons who had died earlier) that had entered his body.[95]

---

94. *Zohar, Parashas Pinchas*, pg. 213b. See also the writings of the Ari, *Sha'ar Ha-Gilgulim, Hakdamah* 32, that Pinchas really had four different souls within him: he was born with one soul, then he received the soul of Nadav and Avihu, later on he received the soul of Eliyahu Ha-Tishbi, and the soul of Elijah from Benjamin.

95. Another example of *ibbur neshamah* is found in the writings of the *Me'or Enayim* (Rabbi Menachem Nachum Twersky of Chernobyl, 1730-1797). The *Me'or Enayim* explained that the reason why there is a powerful urge to share good news is *ibbur neshamah*. At the moment when one brings good tidings,

The Talmud's lesson[96] about the pre-natal oath is understandable in light of the different spiritual levels of the *tzaddik, beinoni,* and *rasha.* The commitment of the young soul to be a *tzaddik* is to strive towards the internal wholeness of the *tzaddik gamur.* "Even if the entire world calls you a *tzaddik,* view yourself as a *rasha*" means that one should never assume that they have reached the level of *tzaddik.* Even when every act, feeling, and thought, is pure, see yourself as a *beinoni,* with lusts and desires as virulent as those of a *rasha,* and this way you see yourself as if you were evil but not actually a *rasha.* This perspective will ensure that you do not grow complacent or arrogant, while allowing you to maintain a healthy self-esteem. To discover the route to fulfillment of the pre-natal oath we must study the Godly and physical souls within man.

---

the soul of Elijah the prophet, the *Mevasser Tov,* the person who will bring the news of the ultimate redemption, enters into one's soul.

Using this principle one can understand why Serach bas Asher was counted as two individuals in the count of the members of Jacob's family that went down to Egypt (see *Bereishis Rabbah, Parashas Vayigash* 94:9). Since she brought the good news of Joseph's survival to Jacob, she had two souls, her own and the soul of Elijah, so she was counted twice. Perhaps it was this soul of Elijah within her that caused her to enter Heaven alive, as Elijah did. (The *Targum Yonasan, Parashas Vayigash,* writes that Serach entered Heaven while still alive.)

Serach's added soul teaches an important lesson about exile. Exile is not a permanent state. At the onset of Jewish subjugation a member of the community harbored the soul of Elijah, the harbinger of redemption. Thus the light of redemption started to glow with the beginning of exile to comfort the Jews and inform them that their salvation was already set in place, and it only had to be revealed. The full spelling of the letters of Serach's name is *sin, yud, nun,* then *resh, yud, shin,* then *ches, yud, tav,* which has the *gematria* 1288, same as the phrase, *Yittaka be-shofar gadol u-vau ha-ovdim,* "[On that day the ultimate redemption] will be heralded through a great shofar and the lost ones will come [to God's home in Jerusalem]" (Isa. 27:13). This correlation further indicates that Serach had the soul of Elijah who, like the great shofar, sounds the call of the ultimate return to Israel (*Emunas Etecha, Parashas Vayigash,* 5756).
96. *Niddah* 30b.

Lesson Five

Body Versus Soul

God formed man out of dust of the earth, and blew into his
nostrils a soul of life, and man became a living creature
(Gen. 2:7).

For you are dust and to dust you shall return (Gen. 3:19).

MAN IS COMPOSED of two opposing components. He has a body that was
initially formed from dust and is coarse like the physical world. Man is
also the guardian of a soul, a fragment of Divinity, which God "blew"
into Adam.[97] Since God is not human who has a respiratory system,

---

97. The Midrash (*Bereishis Rabbah* 12:8, Rashi's version) describes the composite nature of man in the following text.

> Great is peace, for when God created His world He made peace between the higher [spiritual] creations and the lower [physical] creations. On the first day He created in both realms, as is written, "In the beginning God created Heaven and Earth." On the second day He created in the spiritual realm, as is written, "And God said: Let there be a firmament." On the third day He created in the lowly realm, as is written, "And God said: Let the earth sprout grasses." On the fourth day He created in the Heavenly realm, as is written, "And God said: Let the Heavenly lights appear." On the fifth day He created in the lower realm, as is written, "And God said: Let the waters swarm." On the sixth day He wished to create man. God then said, "If I create Him from the Heavenly, then the spiritual will exceed the physical by one creation and there will be no peace in the world. If I create him from the lowly then the physical will be one more than the spiritual and there will be no peace in the world. Therefore, I will create him from the higher and lower realms for the sake of peace." This is what is meant by the verse, "And God formed man dust from the earth"—[man is] from the lowly, and, "He blew in his nostril a soul of life"—[man is also] from the Heavenly.

what does the Torah verse mean when it speaks of God's breath?

God's breath symbolizes His essence and vitality. In Jewish thought, breath equals life. Time of death is determined in Jewish law as the point when respiration ceases,[98] and the Hebrew word for "soul," *neshamah*, shares a root with the word for "breath," *neshimah*. Life is essence. Thus, human breath represents man's existence, and God's breath is symbolic language for His essential vitality.

To blow means to push out breath from the depths of one's being. "G-d blew into man" means He reached to the essence of Himself, cut off a piece, and endowed it to man as the human soul. Body (earthiness) and soul (pure Godliness) are opposite entities joined together.

A parable helps explain their relationship: There was once a cripple who was blessed with vigorous eyesight and a keen intellect. One day he learned that his daughter, who lived in the next town, was organizing a party in her home celebrating the birth of her first child. The invalid sorely wanted to attend the party. The next town was only a few miles away, but he could not walk, and he could not afford to pay for a horse and buggy to transport him.

In the same town as the invalid lived a blind man who was healthy and strong. He had heard that a medical professor, expert in vision restoration, was in the next town for a short visit. The blind man desperately desired to visit the doctor. However, he knew that he could not attempt the trip on his own. Were he to try and grope along the roads he would quickly lose his way at the various turns and would be easy prey for the bandits who ambush passersby.

Hebrew names manifest the essential nature of an item. The essence of man can be found in his name *Adam*. The letter *aleph* is a composite of three letters, two letters *yud* (one on the right and the other to the left) and a *vav*. The *gematria* equals 26, which is the numerical value of God's name of being (*yud* then *heh* then *vav* and *heh*). The *aleph* of *Adam* recalls *Alufo shel olam*, "The Master of the world," for man has a part of Divinity within him. The remaining two letters spell the word *dam*, "blood." Blood is the home for the animal soul of man. Thus man is a union of Divine Soul with animal flesh (Rav Wolfson). See further *Da'as Tefillah*, pg. 270, *Innerspace*, pg. 128, *Kometz Ha-Minchah*, pg. 34, *The Light Beyond*, pgs. 110-111.

98. Heard from the Stitchiner Rebbe.

The invalid asked a friend to bring him to the town's central square to find a ride to the next town. The blind man also came to the square for the same purpose. They ended up sitting next to each other. They both waited for hours but no ride materialized. Eventually, they started talking to each other, and the invalid realized that he and the blind man both sought the same destination.

He recommended that the blind man carry him. He would look out and guide the blind man along treacherous turns and watch from his elevated perch for ambushers who may be lying in wait, while the blind man's vigorous strength would easily carry them both to their goal. Together they arrived in the next town.[99]

The blind man is the body while the invalid is the soul.[100]

The body does not see well. The body accepts pleasure as the purpose of life. The body desires to sleep and waste time. It is quick to anger, and it revels in foolish speech and thought. The body is often depressed, and it seeks pride and power. The soul however has perfect vision. The soul knows that we are on earth in order to display the Divine's rule and thus mend His world. The soul sees ultimate reality, what truly matters and what real pleasure is. Alone, the soul is an impotent invalid. For its *tikkun*, to accomplish its mission of performing Mitzvos and learning Torah in this sphere of existence, it needs a body.

It was most important for the blind man to walk and the invalid to ride. Imagine if the order had been inversed, would they have achieved their goal? If the blind man had ridden atop the invalid, he would not have been able to see afar in order to protect the invalid from robbers who lay in ambush, nor would the invalid with his atrophied legs have been able to carry the blind man's weight. The soul must control the body and have the body serve it. People in whom the soul serves the body lack the correct perspective on life, they enslave their moral thinking to legitimize base behaviors, and they torment their soul with the lowest desires.[101]

---

99. Adapted from *Vayikra Rabbah* 4.

100. The next town is the World-to-Come where celebration and Divine pleasure reign supreme.

101. The highest point of the soul is concentrated in the mind, that is why the prayer recited before placing *tefillin* (phylacteries) on the arm and head declares,

THE DIFFERING ATTRACTIONS
OF THE BODY AND THE SOUL

Everything in nature seeks to return to its root. So as well is a child always attracted to his parental home. Home as the source of one's life has the quality of a root, and branches are attracted to their roots. Consider the strength of the bond between father and child. The father is the source of the son, he is a root, and the son is an offshoot. Since the attraction to source is so powerful the son seeks to emulate his father and earn his father's approval.[102] Similarly every man is attracted to his wife, and when single he feels forlorn and incomplete. This too stems from the need to reconnect to one's roots. Before birth each soul is a duality, with a male half and a female half. When we are born, only half of a soul enters the world at a time. There is another half, of the opposite gender, that is born into another family. The urge for marriage is a desire to return to the perfect state, the most natural form in which we were originally created. Marriage is not a union of disparate individuals; it is a reunion of the halves that were initially one soul.[103]

"[the *tefillah* box] on the head stands opposite the brain so that the *neshamah she-be-mochi*, the soul, whose location is in the head, together with my other proclivities and abilities will be fully committed to the service of God." Thus, thought is associated with the soul, while impulses are expressions of the body.

Rabbi Samson Raphael Hirsch explains that many of the commandments are in fact measures to insure that man's soul (his logical thoughts) rule his lower animal self (his impulses and desires). See his commentary to Lev. 19:27, and *Horeb* Chapters 65, 68, and 69; see also his *Jewish Symbolism* (vol. 3 of his Collected Writings), pgs. 175-178 (where he interprets the commandment of *shaatnez*).

102. *Tzion Ve-Arehah*, pg. 31.

103. See further *Made in Heaven*, pg. 1, note 1. The primordial unity of souls is hinted at in the verse *hemmah me-hevel yachad*, "They are together from mist." Since the point of mere soul mist, male was together with female. Perhaps this concept can explain a difficulty that is found in Rabbinic sources about marriage. Legal authorities stress that marriage should be performed with symbolic omens of blessing. For instance, ideally one should marry at the beginning of the lunar month when the moon, the symbol of the Jewish nation, is growing in luster. Second, there is a widespread custom to place the wedding canopy under the stars, the artifact of God's blessing to Abraham that Jews will be as plentiful as the celestial lights. Yet the Rabbis derived the laws of marriage from the

The body and soul have different roots. The body is from the earth. It is organic and chemical like the earth. Since the body is attracted to its root, it is drawn to an animalistic life, one of passions, laziness, emptiness, and false pride. The soul however is also attracted to its root.

purchase of the *machpelah* cave, the Tomb of the Patriarchs, where Adam and Eve, Abraham and Sarah, Isaac and Rebekah, and Jacob and Leah are interred. Can a cemetery and death be a good omen? The answer is yes, the *machpelah* cave indicates the heights of union married individuals can reach. Marriage is not merely a partnership of bodies and lives, it is a reunion of souls. As a result it does not have to end. The body stops living at the point of death but the soul lives on and a marriage where husband and wife are fully connected to each other, continues after death. Even in the next world the two souls are fused. That is why our patriarchs and matriarchs were buried as couples in the same cave, to indicate that during their lifetimes they had fully fused their personalities, and therefore the bond fully continued on a soulful level after death. Perhaps the name *Chevron* (where the *machpelah* cave is located) reflects this concept, since *Chevron* stems from the word *chibbur*, "connection." Deriving the laws of marriage from the purchase of the *machpelah* cave is a wonderful omen, showing that in marriage an absolute unity can be achieved during the lifetime of the couple and that union can continue after physical death (*Emunas Etecha, Parashas Vayetze*, pg. 86).

Every nation's root is their homeland; that is why Englishmen are loyal to England and Americans are loyal to America. The root of the Jewish nation is the Land of Israel. That is why Jews are innately attracted to the Land of Israel. In the realm of person, the roots of the Jewish people are our forefathers Abraham, Isaac, and Jacob. God introduced Himself to each with commandments about the Land of Israel. God's first words to Abraham were *Lech lecha*, "Leave your land, birthplace, and family and go to the Land that I will show you [Israel]" (Gen. 12:1). To Isaac, He said, "Do not go down to Egypt; reside in the land that I will command you to stay there. Stay in this land [Israel]" (Gen. 25:2-3). And Jacob's first message was, "I am the God of Abraham.... The land that you are lying on will be given to you and your descendants" (Gen. 28:13). Since the land of Israel is the root of the nation in the dimension of space, in the dimension of people our roots first began their relationships with God through hearing of the bond to the land (*Emunas Etecha, Parashas Lech Lecha* 5759).

The ultimate redemption will return Jewry to their land and thus will return us to our root. Since marriage is also a return to the root, marriage is the symbol of the redemption. That is why in the blessings celebrating marriage the seventh blessing requests the ultimate redemption. At a time of return to a root it is fitting to pray for the ultimate return to the Source. Thus, the prophet Jeremiah promised, "Once again it will be heard in the cities of Judea and in the outskirts of Jerusalem the sounds of joy and gladness, the sounds of groom and bride, the sounds of people declaring, let us thank God" (Jer. 33:10-11).

The soul stems directly from God's breath. The soul pulls us up to God Himself. The soul attracts man to the highest ideals. It inspires morality, and it demands behavior that connects man to God.[104] The concentrated life force of the body is called *nefesh ha-bahamis*, "the animal soul," since animals also have organic "spirits" that provide their life and attract them to lowly desires.

The soul is the *nefesh Elokis*, "the Godly soul," since it is a piece that was hewed off of the Divine. The *nefesh ha-bahamis* is concentrated in the blood, which is why loss of much blood causes death to the body. The Torah severely prohibits[105] ingestion of animal blood because what you eat influences your character.[106] Since the blood contains an intense form of the animal's vitality and nature, eating it would cause the human *nefesh ha-bahamis* to become too strong.[107] The organ with the most blood in the body is the liver. The *nefesh ha-bahamis* is therefore said to be located in the liver, or the left half of the heart, a section of the heart that has excessive amounts of blood. The home of the *nefesh Elokis* is the mind, and it is concentrated in the right half of the brain. The *nefesh ha-bahamis* is sometimes called *yetzer hara*, "evil inclination," for it draws the person to evil, the selfish behaviors of the animal world. The *nefesh Elokis* pulls man to attachment with the Divine and is called *yetzer tov*, "the inclination for good."

"The candle of God is the human soul" (Prov. 20:27). Just as in a candle the flame seeks to leap ever higher, the *nefesh Elokis* seeks to leap out of the body into the embrace of the Heavens. The wick tethers the flame, and the body tethers the soul, keeping it grounded and constrained.[108]

These conflicting urges may be the source for the custom to *shuckle*—sway back and forth—while praying and studying Torah. To remove an

---

104. See *Horeb*, Chapter 61, which explains the obligation of burial as a requirement to return the body to its root, just as the soul has returned to its root in Heaven through death.

105. Ingesting blood carries the punishment of *kares*; the soul is disconnected from the Divine, and the individual dies at an early age.

106. See further Nachmanides' commentary to Lev. 11:1 3; *Mesillas Yesharim*, Chapter 11; *Sha'ar Ha-Kedushah*, 1:2, *Degel Machaneh Ephraim, Parashas Eikev* s. v. *u-maltem*.

107. See further *Or Ha-Chaim* on Lev. 17:10.

108. *Tanya*, Chapter 16. See further *Chasidic Masters*, pg. 33.

embedded tooth, a dentist must pull it. Resisting dislocation, it shakes back and forth. When praying or learning, the soul seeks to leap out of the body; it wants to rejoin its root and feel God without the limitation of flesh.[109] Yet the body keeps the soul in this world. The two drives face off against each other, and as a result, there is a swaying back and forth.

The greatest miracle is the human specimen. According to Rav Moshe Isserles,[110] the blessing recited after using the lavatory expresses thanks for the wonder of human life. The blessing concludes with praise to God: *Baruch attah Hashem, rofeh chol basar u-mafli la-asos,* "Blessed are You, God, who heals all flesh and created a wondrous creation." The final few words seem incongruous. The ability to use the privy preserves health, but what is so wondrous about them? Seeing the intricacies of the microscopic realm or the magnificence of a waterfall does not elicit a blessing with the term "wondrous creation" in it, why does excretion? Rabbi Moshe Isserles answered that the paradoxical nature of man makes his existence wondrous. On the one hand, man is a physical being who eats, procreates, and excretes as the lowest animals do. On the other hand, man is a soul with the ability to praise God, thank the Almighty, and experience transcendent Divinity. Joining these two forces is a supernatural feat. Thus, after the most physical of activities, when we are reminded of the coarse nature of man it is the time to thank God for maintaining the union of body and soul.[111]

Body and soul seem to be opposite forces destined to eternal conflict for supremacy. A deeper look, however, reveals that the body can help you learn about the soul, and that the body is neither exclusively nor permanently an opponent to the soul.

---

109. Rav Moshe Chaim Luzzatto writes in his work *Da'as Tevunos,* "The soul is a fragment of Divinity. Its only desire is to return to and cleave to its Source, to reach Him; [this is because the soul is] like all effects that seek their cause, and the soul will only rest and feel inner peace once it accomplishes this goal."
110. Rabbi Moshe Isserles was born in 1530, and he passed away in 1572. He was regarded as the "Maimonides of Polish Jewry." He was one of the greatest *halachic* authorities of all time and he served as the Rabbi of Cracow, Poland. He is often known by the acronym *Rema.*
111. *Rema, Orach Chaim* 6:1.

An Introduction to Chasidic Thought

The Story of the Turkey Prince

Rebbe Nachman of Breslov[112] related the following story:

> Once the king's son went mad and thought he was a turkey. He felt compelled to sit under the table without any clothes on, pulling at bits of bread and bones like a turkey. None of the doctors could do anything to heal him or cure him, and they gave up in despair. The king was very sad.
>
> Then a wise man came and said, "I can cure him."
>
> What did the wise man do? He took off all his clothes, and sat down naked under the table next to the prince and also pecked at crumbs and bones.
>
> The prince asked him, "Who are you and what are you doing here?"
>
> "And what are you doing here?" he replied.
>
> "I am a turkey," said the prince.
>
> "I am also a turkey," said the wise man.
>
> The two of them sat together like this for some time, until they were used to one another.
>
> Then the wise man gave a sign, and the king's men threw them shirts. The wise man-turkey said to the prince, "Do you think a turkey can't wear a shirt? You can wear a shirt and still be a turkey." The two of them put on shirts.
>
> After a while he gave another sign, and guards threw them trousers. Again the wise man said, "Do you think if you wear trousers you can't be a turkey?" They put on trousers.
>
> One by one they put on the rest of their clothes in the same way.
>
> Afterwards, the wise man gave a sign and they put down human food from the table. The wise man said to the prince, "Do you think if you eat good food you can't be a turkey any more? You can eat this food and still be a turkey." They ate.

112. Rav Wolfson's teacher, Rabbi Shraga Feivel Mendelovitz would refer to Rebbe Nachman as "The poet of Chasidus." Rebbe Nachman was the great-grandson of the Besht. He was born in Mezhibozh in 1772, and he passed away in Uman in 1811.

Then he said to him, "Do you think a turkey has to sit under the table? You can be a turkey and sit up at the table."

This was how the wise man dealt with the prince, until in the end he cured him completely.

Rabbi Nachman's parable can be understood as a display of the ideas in this lesson. Every human has a body that is his animal or turkey part, and a soul, that is a prince as the son of God.[113] We should stress our soul and the fact that we are the children of the King of Kings. Yet the prince thinks he is a turkey. We so often immerse ourselves in bodily concerns that we view them as the sum of our essence. Physical desires become our needs and the body's urges our obligatory behavior. We are the prince who is certain that he is a turkey.[114]

The wise man used the turkey misconception to heal the prince and free him from his delusions. As a turkey, the prince had to act like the other turkey (the wise man), since turkeys cannot be different from each other. Guided correctly, the body itself, its physical urges, can further the cause of holiness and eventually become saintly.

---

113. On the verse, *Ve-gam ha-nefesh lo timmalei*, "And the soul as well will not be satisfied" (Eccl. 6:7), the Midrash compares the relationship of body and soul to a marriage of unequals:

> It is like a village peasant who marries the king's daughter. Even if he were to bring her many luxurious items they would be worthless in her eyes since she is the daughter of the regent. He can never provide for her according to what she expects. So too the soul is the daughter of the King; even if the body brings her all the physical pleasures of the world she will not be satisfied, for she is Heavenly.

114. In the Song of Songs (1:9-10), King Solomon compared the beloved to the chained horse of Pharaoh's chariot. The work *Afikei Yehudah* explains the verse to refer to the themes of Rebbe Nachman. The horse is the body, and the charioteer is the soul. When the chariot leaves the stable, the horse is in the lead and it imagines that it is the master. The body, since man is aware of it first, thinks it is the master and the essence of life. A few minutes after the stable doors open, the viewer will see the charioteer and the ropes that control the horse. An individual who controls his body displays his soul as his truest self (quoted in *Limmudei Nisan*, Part 1, pg, 322).

Rebbe Nachman's lesson can serve as a source of comfort. Even if I feel that I am lost in a morass of physical urges and I am naked of my spiritual dignity, there is still hope. I can be rescued by a wise man, a *tzaddik*, who will descend to my level and attach himself to me. The *tzaddik* will then show me how to channel my physicality and turn a turkey into a prince of God's kingdom.[115]

Study of the body is one of the ways in which the material aspect of man might help further the cause of his soul. Why can the body help further the soul's agenda? Why should these opposites complement each other? Lesson Six will attempt to answer these questions.

---

115. Rabbi Wolfson did not quote this story of Rabbi Nachman in this lesson. I inserted it and adapted its explanation from Avraham Greenbaum's *Under the Table and How to Get Up: Jewish Pathways of Spiritual Growth*.

Lesson Six

The Body Can Complement the Soul

A SUPERFICIAL VIEW of body and soul and their relationship to each other would lead one to view them as eternal opponents. Yet, once one delves deeper one can see how the body can help the cause of the soul.

THE BODY CLOTHES THE DIVINE SOUL[116]

The inner wisdom of Torah teaches that the relationship between the physical body and the Divine soul is like that of a garment; the body clothes the soul. In mystical terminology, *oros*, "lights," is the term for soul-like forces,[117] while *keilim*, "clothes" or "vessels," is the term for body-like entities.

116. I heard most of this segment from the Stitchiner Rebbe. See further *Mishbetzos Zahav, Shavuos* 5751, pg. 194.
117. Mystics use the term "light" to describe the soul and other spiritual entities. Light is one of the least physical of items in our material world. It cannot be grasped and held, thus it represents the spiritual, non-tangible, entities. Light also provides a clear field of vision and is a universal symbol of purity. Furthermore, it spreads out quickly just as spirituality causes a person to spread himself out and do acts that bring honor to God. Additionally, light was the first creation and thus it represents the source of existence. Rabbi Yechiel Bar Lev suggested that light represents an extremely strong degree of connection to root. If you cut a branch off a tree, the branch will no longer grow but it will not disappear; it continues to exist. However, if you sunder a ray of light from its root, for example by closing a window, thus separating the rays from the sun, the room will become dark because light detached from its root ceases to exist. Light represents the spiritual dimension since we must be totally connected to the root and if we are not connected to the Divine we cannot exist. See further *Yedid Nefesh* pgs. 35-36.

Consider a lamp in your living room as an example of *oros* and *keilim*. Light in the elemental form is soul-like. It is the *or*, "light." Essential light is clothed in the *keli*, "vessel," of the light bulb. Light itself—pure, absolute, and unlimited in any way—would be so bright that no one would benefit from it. In a light bulb, light is restrained so that it can be appreciated. This is the function of all *keilim*. They limit the *oros* to enable benefit.

The light bulb is an *or*, a soul-like light, relative to the lamp shade, its *keli*—vessel. The light bulb on its own would be too bright for anyone to benefit, the shade around it reduces the glare so that its rays are soft and helpful. Body is light to clothes as its vessel. The clothes conceal the body so that it is not seen in its naturalness.

The soul is light to the body as vessel. The soul on its own is like pure unlimited light. It is overwhelming. Just as a light fixture limits absolute radiance and cloaks it in a manageable form, the body obscures the light of the soul.[118] Body as vessel to soul as light seems to mean that the two are opposing forces since concealing is the opposite of revealing.

The soul is the source of life; it is what gives life. The body receives life from the soul. The body is a receiver to soul as a giver. Here again, body and soul are opposites for taking is the opposite of giving, just as dimming is the opposite of illuminating. A deeper look will reveal that the definition of body and soul as light and vessel is the reason why study of the body can teach about the soul.

We can delve deeper. A vessel need not always dim the light. Sometimes the vessel becomes pure and radiant. Then the vessel itself becomes light-like. For instance, a lampshade can become translucent so that the light bulb shines through it without being dimmed at all. In such cases the lampshade is indistinguishable from the bulb, and one might say that the lampshade produces light, for it loses its identity to the light bulb. The body is the vessel of the soul, yet once the body is purified it will not oppose the soul nor will it hide the soul.[119]

---

118. Another pair of terms that describe this relationship is *chomer* and *tzurah*. *Chomer* literally means "matter," and it is body-like or vessel-like. *Tzurah* literally means "form," and it is the soul or light to matter. Within man the soul is the *tzurah*, and the body is the *chomer*. See further *Yedid Nefesh* 1:5.

119. "The body should reflect the *neshamah* perfectly; [it] should serve the soul

Even prior to the absolute purification of the body, the body can help you grow spiritually.[120] Every *keli* can become an *or*, and the ability to become a light is constantly latent within it. Thus a study of the vessel that discovers its latent abilities will teach about the light's characteristics.

LESSONS OF THE BODY

Lust is the body's strongest impulse. At the same time, lust is a mask of a Heavenly and soulful force, *chesed*, the desire to spread out and connect with others.[121] Lust is when I seek to connect with them for my own selfish pleasure. *Chesed* is the elevated form of this urge; the desire to connect with others in order to give and to help them and an urge to attach oneself to God. Lust as the most virulent bodily desire teaches that generous giving is the most powerful urge of the soul. The body's lust drive is enormously powerful; that should teach us how deeply the soul desires *chesed*.

---

in perfect loyalty. Never should the body stray after its own desires. It should be a vessel, a tool which obeys its control dimension totally selflessly. It should be like a vehicle driven only from within, its very existence justified only as a loyal servant. At the Creation, the body of Adam was just that. It was an ethereal, luminescent structure which revealed the spiritual content" (*Living Inspired*, pg. 118).

"The garments of the world, the covering of Adam before he sinned were of *or*, 'light.' After the sin, the covering became skin. The root *or* has the silent *aleph*—it is light, spiritual, all revelation. The root [for the Hebrew word for skin] spells not only "skin" but "blind" too—the covering which revealed has become a covering which obstructs" (*Living Inspired*, pg. 120). When one purifies his body he is, in some measure, returning to the state of Adam before the sin.
120. The body clothes the soul. "Clothes hide but also reveal—although the wearer is hidden by his clothes, his dignity is revealed by his clothes. Royal robes cover the king, but they reveal his royalty. [*Oteh or ke-salma*, "God wears light like a garment"—nature hides God, but accurately reveals His presence!]" (*Living Inspired*, pg. 120). Thus the body obscures the soul and reveals the soul.
121. In Lev. 20:17, the Torah states, *Ve-ish asher yikkach es achoso bas aviv o vas immo... chesed hu ve-nichresu le-einei benei ammam*, "A man who marries his sister, daughter of his father, or daughter of his mother... it is *chesed*, and they will be cut off before their nation...." The Baal Shem Tov explained that the verse included the word *chesed* to teach that lowly lustful desires are a misapplication of the Heavenly drive for *chesed*. The verse is bemoaning the disgrace saying, "Lust? How could you do that, to misapply *chesed*, the most radiant and important of character traits?"

Perhaps the following thought might help one overcome improper drives: The animal soul is ascendant when lust is actualized. If one acts according to the dictates of selfish desires one is little better than the beasts of the wild. On the other hand, the Heavenly soul shines through the body when one displays selfless giving. When experiencing lust temptation, the body is reflecting a fallen urge of the soul. It is a moment to engage in *chesed*—selfless giving to other humans and to the cause of holiness.[122]

The reason for the centrality of lust and generosity is that *chesed*, the Divine and elevated form of this drive, was the foundation of the world; as scripture states, *olam chesed yibbaneh*, "The world was built on *chesed*" (Ps. 89:3). God's creation was an act of total love, and he placed *chesed* as the foundation of a Heavenly personality.[123]

Even the physical form of the body can teach lessons about the *nefesh Elokis*, the Godly soul. Look at the body; from the form of the body, and the various functions its parts fulfill, you may learn about the nature of the soul. For instance, the tongue is the vessel for speech. The tongue has unique characteristics. It does not have a bone. It can easily be burnt and damaged. This is a lesson about the soul. Soulful speech is soft and delicate. Soulful rebuke is delivered to others through a context of love

---

122. Raising lust is a very high level of service of the Almighty. When overcome with such feelings contemplation that at its root it is a desire for divinity and turning those passions towards feeling love towards Him or His children is a difficult task. Chasidim demanded it of themselves.

The Baal Shem Tov taught that God created human emotions to teach man how to serve his Master. The Besht explicitly said, "Man must believe that when an evil lust falls into his heart it was sent to him from God, for the time has come for him to serve God with love of Holiness. Heaven is hinting to him, 'Turn love to the love of God.' Once the heart is already in a state of desire it is easier to reach love of Divinity. Similarly, when a great fright falls upon man, he should know with certitude that this fear was sent from Heaven to tell him, 'Now is the time to arouse your own innate fear of God.' So it is with all the emotions" (*Divrei Shalom, Purim*, pg. 38; see also *Degel Machaneh Ephraim, Parashas Eikev*).

123. See *Pachad Yitzchak* on Rosh Hashanah for his discussions of *chesed*, and see the *Kuntres Ha-Chesed* in *Michtav Me-Eliyahu*.

and in an oblique manner that does not offend.[124]

Another lesson about the soul can be found in the sum of components that comprise the human body. The body has 248 primary limbs and 365 sinews.[125] The limbs are the major bones of the body; the sinews are what hold muscles to bone and contain blood within their channels. Bones are white while sinews (that are filled with blood) are red. Thus there are 248 white parts of the body and 365 red parts of the body. The soul has matching segments.

There are 248 "white lights" and 365 "red lights" in the soul. Each soul "light" (part of the soul) is Godly holiness clothed in one of the physical parts of the body. The soul-part is what gives life to that portion of the body. The white lights are clothed in the limbs, in the white bones, and the red lights are sheathed within the sinews.[126]

Jewish observance is divided into two parts: *mitzvos aseh*, commandments that require a particular act from the Jew, and *mitzvos lo ta'aseh*, enjoinders prohibiting behaviors. The Torah contains 248 *mitzvos aseh* and 365 *mitzvos lo ta'aseh*. Performance of the *mitzvos aseh* draws life to the limbs from the "white" of the soul, while observing the prohibitions of *mitzvos lo ta'aseh* brings added strength and purity from the "red" of the soul. Thus each Mitzvah parallels a soul and a body part. The more Mitzvos one performs, the purer the body becomes, and that much

124. See further *Mishbetzos Zahav, Parashas Noach*. The tongue has two uses: it enjoys taste that no one else will enjoy, and it reveals to others insights through oral communication. This teaches that some ideas, such as lessons of the revealed Torah should be shared, while other concepts, such as the secrets of how God created the universe are to be hidden and each individual should enjoy them by himself (see further *Pachad Yitzchak* on Rosh Hashanah, *Ma'amar* 1).

The Maharal explains that the reason why the human body is naturally straight and we do not walk on all fours with our head to the earth is that God wanted to send a message to man through the human form. "Because God's presence is not visible in this world, it is easy for people to come to sin. God compensated for this physical blind-spot with the spiritual ability to perceive and fear God. Our erect human posture directs our gaze upwards to the Heavens. There we observe God's presence... and we are less inclined to sin" (Maharal of Prague on *Pirkei Avos*, pg. 81; see further *Derech Chaim*, end of the commentary to Mishnah 2:1).

125. The Mishnah in *Ohalos* 1:8 delineates the limbs and sinews.

126. *Shefa Tal*, pg. 2. See further *Chasidic Masters*, pg. 22 s.v. "One must."

more spiritual vigor may flow into it.[127]

In mysticism, the different colors along the spectrum symbolize different Divine attributes.[128] The color white symbolizes *chesed*, unbridled generosity and love. The color red represents *din*, "harsh justice." *Mitzvos aseh* require us to take actions; we must extend ourselves to express our love for God. What we do is the basis of who we are; thus our deeds provide added life to the white bones, the body part that frames a person's form and shape. *Mitzvos lo ta'aseh* are injunctions, forbidding acts that are injurious to our spiritual well-being. Observance of these laws entails constriction, pulling oneself in, and refraining from what our sensory urges seek. Scrupulous adherence to the commands of *Mitzvos lo ta'aseh* is thus an exhibition of *din*—fear and justice—setting boundaries and rigorously maintaining them.[129] The goal of *Mitzvos lo ta'aseh* is to preserve the spiritual well-being of the person; thus they parallel sinews that tie the muscles to the bones and maintain the person.[130]

---

127. Rabbi Tzadok Ha-Cohen of Lublin explains that for every physical illness of a Jew there is a spiritual cause. Return to God, *teshuvah*, erases the spiritual sin and effects physical healing (*Takkanas Ha-Shavin*, Note 1). Perhaps the idea in the text is the explanation of his lesson. Since each Mitzvah parallels a part of the body, lack of observance of a Mitzvah causes physical weakness and illness to the part of the body that corresponds to that Mitzvah. Return to God rectifies the spiritual soul-light and therefore brings about physical healing.

128. See further *Meditation and Kabbalah*, pgs. 179-183.

129. Our forefather Abraham was the ultimate paradigm of *chesed*, Heavenly giving and love. Abraham even sought to perform kindness with idolators and the sinners of Sodom (see *Parashas Vayeira*). Since *mitzvos aseh* are expression of giving, extending oneself for God's sake, Abraham is the personification of *mitzvos aseh*. The *gematria* of *Avraham* (1+2+200+5+40) is 248, which is the number of *mitzvos aseh*.

Isaac was the paradigm of *din* (sometimes called *gevurah*), setting limits and constriction. Isaac's greatest moment was when he allowed himself to be bound on the altar, an act of remarkable discipline and withdrawal. Isaac is the personification of *mitzvos lo ta'aseh*. As a result, when God first appeared to him and gave Isaac a Mitzvah to live in the Land of Israel, it was phrased as a prohibition, "Do not go down to Egypt, stay in this land..." (Gen. 25:2). (*Emunas Etecha*, *Lech Lecha*, 5759.)

130. The *nefesh* part of the soul is the part that has 613 "pieces" that correspond to the various body parts. See also Maharal in *Tiferes Yisrael*, Chapter Four. Rabbi Chaim Vital in *Sha'arei Kedushah*, *Sha'ar* 1. *Da'as Tefillah*, pgs. 97-98, *Razei Ha-Bosem*, pg. 154.

Death divides the soul from its physical body, and the soul then enters another dimension, the World-to-Come. A soul always needs some sort of vessel to contain it. Since death rids us of a body, what will clothe our soul in the next dimension? The answer is the Mitzvos that we performed. Since each Mitzvah parallels a soul part, if we fulfill all of the Mitzvos in the next world they will clothe us fully in a Heavenly body-like cloak.[131]

THE HEAVENLY BODY OF A *TZADDIK*

A *tzaddik* utilizes his body for the sake of his soul. He internalizes many of the lessons of holiness that the body teaches. He fulfills all the Mitzvos. As a result of his many good deeds he brings a new spirit to his person. While in this world, he already has some qualities of the next world. His body is constantly being purified through the Mitzvos that he performs and it becomes a vessel like the translucent lampshade. It does not oppose the soul; rather it reflects God's glory to all. When seeing such an individual, you immediately sense his soul and its message, for it shines right through the body.

We have a fundamental nature to see what is essential and not what is secondary. If you shake the gloved hand of a friend, you would not characterize it as "touching Jake's glove." Rather you would describe the event as, "I shook Jake's hand." Since the glove pales in importance to the hand it covers. Similarly, the body is merely the clothing of the soul. It should pale in importance to the soul. Where there is a conflict between the will of the body (the *nefesh ha-bahamis*) and that of the soul (the *nefesh Elokis*), the needs of the soul should come first, and in truth when we think of ourselves we should immediately think of our

---

131. Every Jew can fulfill all the Mitzvos, even though some commands only apply to priests and others were limited to the Land of Israel. A simple Israelite outside the Holy Land can study the Torah's discussion of the Mitzvos of priesthood or of the Land of Israel. Intellectual thought of these commandments and discussing their laws are partial fulfillments of these Mitzvos. Another way for each individual to fulfill all 613 obligations is through love. If a Jew binds himself with great attachment to all the Jews within the nation, the Mitzvos that the priests perform will accrue merit for him as well.

essence, our soul and not the clothes, the body.[132] The *tzaddik* reaches

132. The *gematria* of the word *ahavah*, "love," is 13, the same as for the word *echad*, "one." Total love demands singular devotion. One can only truly fully love one spouse or ideal. If so, how did the Torah demand love for fellow Jews once we were already commanded to love God our Lord? If the heart is filled with love for God where will there be room for love of fellow men? The answer is that the Torah demands love to one subject, God. If one sees souls and not bodies, then one sees the Divine in others and that Divinity is what is beloved. If one loves someone he loves that person's children who are extensions of the beloved. "You are children to God," according to the Torah, therefore, love of God demands love for the Jewish soul that emerges from Him (*Yismach Mosheh*).

The *gematria* of the Biblical verse for love of fellow Jews, *Ve-ahavta le-re'acha ka-mocha ani Hashem*, equals the verse, *Ve-ahavta es Hashem Elokecha*, "Love the Lord your God," for it is all one devotion. The *Zohar* teaches that God, Torah, and Israel are one. In truth, God clothed himself in the thoughts and words of Torah, and Jewish souls are pieces of the Divine as well; thus Torah, Israel and God are linked in an intrinsic manner, Rabbi Levi Yitzchak of Berditchev (1740-1810) explained a Scriptural ambiguity with this principle:

"As God commanded Moses, He counted them [the Jews] in the Sinai desert" (Num. 1:19): One can ask, it should have written, "He counted them in the Sinai desert as God commanded Moses"? Behold, God gave the Torah to the Jewish people, and the souls of Jews are the essence of the Torah, for there are 600,000 Jewish souls and 600,000 letters in the Torah scroll. In fact, the name *Yisrael* is an acronym for *yesh shishim ribbo osiyos la-torah*, "there are 600,000 letters to the Torah." Therefore, Jews are the Torah, for each Jew is a different letter in the Torah. When Moses counted the Jews he was learning Torah. This is why the verse changed its usual formulation to hint, "As God commanded Moses He counted the people," like the Torah that God commanded Moses was the [experience of] counting of the nation (*Kedushas Levi, Parashas Bemidbar,* s.v. *ka-asher*).

A classic Chasidic tale tells of Rabbi Moshe Leib Sassov's devotional midnight prayers. (The *Tikkun Chatzos* prayers were instituted by the Kabbalists to be recited at midnight in mourning for the loss of the Temple in Jerusalem.) One wintry day Rabbi Zvi Hirsch Zhiditchover decided that he had to witness his teacher's devotions, so he hid himself under R. Moshe Leib's bed to observe how R. Moshe Leib recited *Tikkun Chatzos.*

Shortly before midnight R. Moshe Leib awoke and dressed in the clothes of a Ukrainian peasant and left his house; Rabbi Zvi Hirsch surreptitiously followed. He walked out into the forest and chopped down a tree, he then carried this tree to a small shack at the edge of the town. He entered the shack, and turning to the poor Jewish widow who was shivering in the cold, he offered to sell her the extra log that he had on his back. The widow related how cold she

this level; he only sees souls; all he sees is the *nefesh Elokis*—the Divine within others.[133]

Lesson Seven will draw a rough sketch of the process the *tzaddik* engages in to transform his body.

---

was but she could not afford to pay for timber. Rabbi Moshe Leib responded that she could pay him at some other time, "Just go to the village square and ask for Ivan the Ukrainian. They will get me, and you will then be able to pay." While chopping the wood and warming the widow's home, Rabbi Moshe Leib recited *Tikkun Chatzos*.

Rabbi Moshe Leib was a transcendent *tzaddik*. He saw Divinity everywhere. His act of connecting to a fellow Jew through charity was an act of connecting to a soul, to a piece of God. Prayer is also a process of attachment to the Divine. Rabbi Moshe Leib linked his attachment to God through words of Psalms with attachment to Divinity of helping souls, for in truth souls are a piece of the Divine as well.

133. See further *Mishbetzos Zahav, Shabbos Ha-Gadol* 5753. The Stitchiner Rebbe explains there that Moses saw right through the external body, and always saw the spiritual, Heavenly soul when he interacted with others.

Lesson Seven

The Soul and Body of a *Tzaddik*

THE *TZADDIK* FIRST subdues and then entirely redirects his *nefesh ha-bahamis*, and only at the highest spiritual levels turns his body into a shining light, thus uniting body and soul.

The physical soul primarily seeks selfish pleasure. The *tzaddik* struggles with those desires, and develops a hatred for the hedonistic attitude. The *nefesh ha-bahamis* is said to receive its nourishment from the *sitra achra*, literally the "other side." The material, mundane, and sinful are all part of the non-saintly domain. This area is called *sitra achra* because like two sides of a sharp divide, one can only stand in one section. It is impossible to straddle the fence and place one's feet in both areas. Holiness is one world; material pleasure is a different one. To achieve sanctity, materialism must be eschewed. The *tzaddik* is on the side of the saintly; he therefore totally rejects materialism and finds it revolting.[134] *Tzaddikim* completely rid themselves of the external, physical perspective.

---

134. The lack of selfishness and desire for physical pleasure allows the *tzaddik* to engage in seemingly questionable behavior. The Talmud in *Kesubos* (17a) relates that Rav Acha would carry the bride on his shoulders when dancing at weddings. When the propriety of such behavior was questioned, Rav Acha replied that it is permissible for a man to carry an adult woman who is not his wife on his shoulders, if in his mind she is like a log of wood. Rav Acha was teaching that he had a *tzaddik*-like quality. He had risen above lust; to him a woman on his shoulders was like carrying inorganic matter. See further Rabbi Tzadok Ha-Cohen of Lublin, *Yisrael Kedoshim*, pg. 12.

Rabbi Isaak of Kamarna[135] related that his entire life, starting from age nine, when he would see a woman he would immediately see the name of God of *aleph, dalet, nun, yud*, which is the Godly manifestation that gives life to the feminine.

Evidently, he had suppressed his *nefesh ha-bahamis*, abhorred its lusts and dictates, and eventually rid himself of lustful desires and therefore constantly found Heavenly displays in all physical sights.[136]

After the *tzaddik* truly abhors physical pleasure, his *nefesh ha-bahamis* transforms and he finds Torah and Mitzvos appealing, exciting, and delightful in a physical manner. He feels the infinite pleasure that can be accessed within the performance of Mitzvos, experience of genuine *tefillah*, "prayer," and the joy of comprehending the Divine through Torah thought.[137]

In Berditchev, the Grand Rabbi, Rabbi Levi Yitzchak's[138] lighting of the menorah was a public event. Students of Rabbi Levi Yitzchak, other great sages, and simple townsfolk would all gather to witness

---

135. Rabbi Yitzchak Isaak Yehudah Yechiel of Kamarna was born in 1806 and passed away in 1874. He was blessed with remarkable spiritual abilities from birth. As a child he had the ability to reveal hidden mysteries and to predict future events. His uncle, Rabbi Zvi Hirsch of Zhiditchov, was afraid that his spiritual gifts might lead him to weakness in the realm of fear of Heaven, and as a result, at age six he lost his ability to see "from one end of the world to the other." He authored many important Chasidic works such as *Heichel Ha-Berachah, Derech Emunah, Otzar Mitzvosecha, Zohar Chai*, and *Megillas Setarim*.

136. Perhaps the goal of seeing divinity in all is the theme of Psalm 29. Rabbi Hirsch explains the very first verse of that psalm in the following manner: *Havu la-Hashem kavod va-oz*, "The verse may also be read in the accusative form; i.e., 'Bring unto the Lord, attribute and ascribe to Him everything that you admire as being endowed with strength.'" See further Rabbi Hirsch's *Commentary to the Psalms*, pgs, 204 -210.

137. The Chasam Sofer explained that the eating of an apple dipped in honey on Rosh Hashanah is a prayer that our good deeds, symbolized by an apple, should be sweet and enjoyable. We are praying to find their performance pleasurable, the way a *tzaddik* experiences Mitzvos.

138. Rabbi Levi Yitzchak of Berditchev was one of the most beloved personalities of Jewish history. He was a student of the Maggid of Mezerich, and after the passing of the Maggid (19 Kislev 5533; December 15, 1772) he served as the leader of Ukrainian Chasidus. He was a man of great love of God and love of Israel who would argue with Heaven, during his prayers, advocating blessings for all members of Israel. His work *Kedushas Levi* is one of the classics of Chasidic literature.

his devotions when he would kindle the Chanukah flames. One year, right when Rabbi Levi Yitzchak was to begin, the Rebbe (Grand Rabbi) seemed to needlessly delay. Eventually, Chatzkel the unsophisticated attendant of the Poritz (the Russian landowner) entered the room.

"Chatzkel, where are you coming from?" R. Levi Yitzchak called out.

"I just arrived from the home of the Poritz."

"How is the Poritz doing?" asked the Rebbe.

"Oh, life is good for him. He has expert chefs from Germany, Italy, and France who prepare for him the finest delicacies. And his table, what a table! The cutlery glitters and shines, and his plates are the finest china," Chatzkel enthused.

"How does the Poritz sleep?" continued the Rebbe, "Wow! The Poritz sleeps well. He has it good," gushed Chatzkel. "Rebbe, you sleep on a pile of straw. The Poritz has a mattress like the czar and a beautiful bed, with beautiful sheets, warm blankets, and soft pillows. And what a room! The floor is covered with antique Persian rugs, the walls are adorned with antique art and tapestries, and the ceiling supports the most exquisite chandeliers, Rebbe, the Poritz has it good!"

Finally, Rabbi Levi Yitzchak asked, "Does the Poritz light Chanukah candles?"

"Of course not," replied Chatzkel with a laugh.

Rabbi Levi Yitzchak grew animated and shouted with fervor, "The Poritz stuffs himself with food, and sleeps with feathers instead of hay? That is the good life? Without Chanukah candles!? We have it good! We have the joy of God's menorah!"

With that, Rabbi Levi Yitzchak began to shout with delight the words of the blessings for lighting the menorah.

Reb Levi Yitzchak's *nefesh ha-bahamis* was transformed. For him, pleasure from Mitzvah observance dwarfed the physical comforts of the Poritz.

Rav Aharon Karliner's Poritz loved sleigh-riding. One summer he brought thousands of bags of sugar (a rare commodity) to simulate snow and he rode in his sled on the mounds of the confection. A Chasid once wistfully told the Rebbe about the pleasure the Poritz must experience when riding a sled in the heat of August. The Rebbe responded, "That pleasure is not nearly as powerful as the enjoyment I feel when I recite on Shabbos the prayer, *Nishmas kol chai tivarech es shimcha Hashem Elokeinu*, 'The souls of every living creature will bless your name God our Lord.'"

According to the Talmud, holidays are times when half of one's day should be spent for oneself, engaged in physical pleasure, *chetzyo lachem*. The other half of the day should be dedicated to God and His service, *chetzyo la-Hashem*.

When Reb Uri of Strelisk[139] would complete his holiday prayers he would tell his community, "We have just completed *chetzyo lachem* [the physical half of the day]. Now that we are going to eat our holiday meal, we will fulfill the *chetzyo la-Hashem* [the half of the day that must be given to God]."[140]

R. Uri's body had been transformed. After all the years of battling his urges, he experienced prayer as a sensory pleasure. To him, eating was difficult and was an obligation performed solely because Jewish law demands food ingestion on the holiday. That is why in his holiday experience the prayers were the physical enjoyment while eating was the spiritual duty.[141]

Some *tzaddikim* reach an exalted state. They are personifications of an *atzilus*-type existence. *Atzilus* is a Heavenly universe whose name is

---

139. Reb Uri was born in 1757 and passed away in 1826. He was a student of Rabbi Shlomo of Karlin. He was a renowned *tzaddik* who would pray with such passion and displays of fervent feeling that he was called the *saraph*, "fiery angel." He had a great impact upon Rabbi Shalom of Belz.
140. *Imros Tzaddikim*, Klausenberg, pg. 24 story 1.
141. Rav Wolfson added that R. Moshe Leib of Sassov was also a *tzaddik* who experienced the spiritual as physically pleasing.

R. Moshe Leib was renowned for his dedication to redeeming Jewish prisoners. He would also frequently fast and pray for success in his dangerous exploits. One day, after a long and exhausting fast, he went to a Russian nobleman who was holding a Jew captive. When he entered the room the nobleman's lunch was brought in as well. Weakened with hunger, Rabbi Moshe Leib swooned at the aroma of the nobleman's food. He felt an overwhelming desire to request a taste of the dish. Intellectually, however, he knew that the food was not kosher. To overcome his hunger he thought of Shabbos. His spiritual feelings were so potent that considering Shabbos and the recital of *Nishmas* brought him so much pleasure that his body no longer hungered for the Gentile's meal (Rav Wolfson).

derived from the word *eitzel*, "next to." In this world light and vessel are one. In this universe body and soul are a total unity,[142] with oneness that transcends verbal description. A *tzaddik* who is on the level of an *atzilus*-type manifestation is like a head to the body, and leads his generation. *Atzilus* is integral for life of the spiritual worlds that are lower than it. Just as the head provides life to the body, and if its attachment is severed the body dies, this type of *tzaddik* is the life for the rest of the universe, and is *atzilus*-like.

To better understand the nature of the universe of *atzilus*, we must study all five of the spiritual universes. Understanding the parts of the Godly soul within man will facilitate comprehension of the heavenly universes that are the soul of the physical world. Lesson Eight will explain the nature of the human soul's components.

---

142. "In the book *Orach La-Tzaddik*, R. Elazar the son of R. Elimelech of Lizhensk related, 'My father said several times, "I wish people would have souls as pure as my body.'" This is something remarkable, consider how high a human can reach! We have no sense of how holy the body of R. Elimelech was" (*Imros Tzaddikim*, Klausenberg, pgs. 26-27).

Lesson Eight

The Five Parts of the Soul

THE HUMAN SOUL was created in a unique manner. All other creations were formed through command; God declared and the item appeared. For example, of the sky, Scripture states, *Bi-dvar Hashem shamayim na'asu*, "With the word[s] of God, Heavens were created" (Ps. 33:6).[143] The soul was not commanded to emerge rather God blew man's soul into him.[144]

---

143. The Hebrew language and the letters of the alphabet have a unique holiness since the world was created through God's speaking Hebrew. For instance, God said *shamayim*, and out of the letters *shin*, *mem*, *yud*, *mem*, the heavens eventually emerged. The Hebrew letters are the spiritual root of the world. A great *tzaddik* only sees these letters. (See page 82, where a story from the Kamarna Rebbe illustrating this concept is recorded.) When he sees the skies he sees the Hebrew word *shamayim* since it is the spiritual source of the physical heavens. Perhaps King David referred to this perception when he said in Psalm 29, *Kol Hashem ba-koach, kol Hashem be-hadar*, "The sound of the Almighty is within strength, the sound of the Divine is within glory." David was a *tzaddik*, and he was describing his perception of reality. All strength comes from the Almighty. God gives energy to the powerful. In truth they are impotent, and only God's force is significant. David also wrote, *Shivisi Hashem le-negdi tamid*, "I have placed the Almighty before me always." David only saw the Divine essence. This Divine essence is letter combinations of the holy language. The combinations spell out Divine names; that is why he proclaimed that he constantly had the Divine before his eyes, for he constantly perceived the Divine source. See further the Commentary of Rabbi S.R. Hirsch to Chapter 29 of the Psalms, *Bereishis Rabbah* 18:4, and R. Tzadok Ha-Cohen in *Sichas Malachei Ha-Shareis* pg. 44.

144. From Scripture's account it is clear that man's body was formed from the earth in a way that resembled the rest of creation; apparently it was formed through a command.

God does not recite words. What is meant by the image of God declaring the existence of a physical dimension? As we learned in Lesson Five, breath is the life of a person. Human speech limits breath, modulating it with the mouth and limiting it to particular sounds. Speech is a process in which the essence of man is clothed and limited. God's creation resembles human speech, the created world is a cover for God, His Essence was limited many myriad of times until He was clothed within the world. The image for the creation of the soul is one of direct breath, for the soul contrasted to the created world is like blowing versus speaking. The human soul, when compared to the rest of the created world, is "pure," essential, and unclothed Divinity.[145] An even deeper truth reveals that the image of a soul emerging out of blowing is a lesson about the parts of the soul—they resemble the different stages of breath a glassblower employs when blowing glass.[146] With glass, once the vessel is shaped the other steps in the process are lost, but in the Heavenly realm every stage of the formation leaves eternal results.[147]

First, the glassblower wishes to create a vessel. Then he decides what the vessel will look like and prepares for the process by filling his lungs with sufficient air. The glassblower then pushes the air through his lungs to his mouth and releases the breath out of his lips. The breath turns into a mini-wind. It enters the heated glass and changes its form. As the wind settles, the glass's shape is solidified.

God is the glassblower, my soul is His breath, and my body and personality comprise the glass vessel.

There are five parts to the soul, and they resemble the five stages of glass production.

The first part, or the lowest level, is *nefesh*, corresponding to the craftsman's breath that settled within and fully shaped the vessel. *Nefesh* is a derivative of the term *nafash* meaning "to rest."[148] *Nefesh* is the "resting soul." This is God's "breath" once it has reached its destination within man.

---

145. Heard from the Stitchiner Rebbe on tape 1 of his classes on *Tanya*. This principle should lead us to an enormous respect for every soul, for the soul is pure Godliness. Furthermore, it should teach us that our souls seek absolute and total attachment to the Divine, for each soul is a piece of absolute infinity.
146. *Innerspace* pgs. 17-20.
147. Rabbi Tzadok Ha-Cohen of Lublin, Chapter Three of *Sichas Malachei Ha-Shareis*.
148. *Innerspace* pg. 16.

Nefesh can be felt when a person is fully an empty vessel. It can be felt through the quietistic experience. Silence the external static that we are constantly processing; relax, and humble yourself. Open your heart as an empty vessel to be animated with God's light, and you might feel a bit of *nefesh*. *Nefesh* is the part of the soul that is most directly connected with the body and physical existence.[149] One merits receiving the holy form of *nefesh* soon after birth. A Jewish boy will receive his *nefesh* with his circumcision and a girl when her father names her in the synagogue.

The next stage of the soul, *ruach*, is received with adulthood. When a boy or girl, if they are righteous, celebrate their bar or bat mitzvah, they receive their *ruach*.

The Hebrew word *ruach* conjures a picture of a forceful wind. In the glass-making analogy, before the breath settled in the vessel, it was a powerful force that gave form to molten glass. Forceful and emotionally stirring spirituality is God's "wind," the *ruach* part of the soul.

Imagine a room filled with dancing Chasidim. They are singing, and when they reach the climax of the song, all are screaming, *Ki attah hu melech malchei ha-melachim malchuso netzach*, "That you God are the King above all kings; His rule is eternal." Their eyes are closed, and their bodies bob up and down throbbing with devotion. They pull you into their circle and you join their dance. You lose yourself in a passionate swirl. You feel that God is everything, and your deepest desire is to be loyal and close to Him. Those feelings are an expression of *ruach*.

A level higher than the wind is the breath at the lips of the glassblower. God's breath at His lips is the *neshamah*. This level of soul is felt in the experience of pure thought. Most of our thoughts are tainted; they are the result of physical biases and emotional inclinations. Pure, abstract, moral thought is an experience of Godly intimacy. The pleasure of comprehending and fully grasping the pure truth of Torah is a bit of *neshamah*. *Neshamah* is the highest part of the soul most of us will ever fully internalize. As a result, the soul as a whole is called *neshamah*.[150]

149. *Innerspace* pg.18; *Da'as Tefillah* pg. 271, *Nefesh Ha-Chaim* 1:14. The Vilna Gaon in his commentary on Prov. 22:5 writes that the *nefesh* is the lowest level of Godliness within man and is the "partner of the body."

150. In Lesson Five, the soul as a whole was called the *nefesh Elokis*. It is due to the *neshamah*-part of the soul that I wrote that the Godly soul is primarily located in the mind. This lesson provides a more detailed and precise picture of the soul and its components.

It enters a righteous, scholarly, married person at age twenty. If one is not righteous enough to internalize the holiness of the *neshamah*, it will hover above man, serving as a *makkif*, an "encompassing light," not a *penimi*, an "inner light."

Above *neshamah* are two levels of soul that are rarely fully internalized by humans: *chayah* and *yechidah*. *Chayah* is the breath of the glassblower before it reaches the mouth—it is the stage when he has first determined the mental picture of the vessel he will create and has filled his lungs with sufficient breath for the creation of the vessel. *Yechidah* is the first possible stage of glass-making, the will and desire to produce a vessel. It is the level of soul that parallels God's decision to create a being. *Yechidah* is God's will before He has even conceived of the form of man. It represents God's desire.

The different parts of the soul are concentrated in distinct body organs. *Nefesh* is in the blood. The Torah characterizes blood as *nefesh* when it prohibits the ingestion of blood, *Ki ha-dam hu ha-nefesh*, "for the blood is the *nefesh*" (Deut. 12:23). The blood of a person is his source of organic life. If blood stops flowing to a limb in the body, the limb will atrophy and waste away. The body part that has the most blood is the liver, and *nefesh* is primarily concentrated in the liver[151] and the left ventricle of the heart. The limbs of the body are the tools for all human action, thus bodily action, *ma'aseh*, of Mitzvos, such as stretching your hand to give charity, or walking to hear a Torah lecture, is an expression of the holy form of *nefesh*. *Nefesh* is attached to the body, and we learned in Lesson Five that the body seeks evil behavior. Hence it is said that *nefesh* has much evil potential.

According to the Midrash,[152] *ruach* is the part of the soul that "rises and descends." This soul part rises to the mind and then descends to the body, connecting our thought with our deeds. What is the intermediary

---

151. *Da'as Tefillah* pg, 271 in the name of the *Nefesh Ha-Chaim*.
152. *Bereishis Rabbah* 14:9 states, "She [the soul] has five names: *nefesh*, *ruach*, *neshamah*, *chayah*, and *yechidah*. *Nefesh* is the blood, as is written, "For the blood is the *nefesh*." *Ruach* rises and descends, as is written, "Who knows the *ruach* of men that rises on high" (Ecclesiastes 3). *Neshamah* is the intellect, and in the Baraisa it is taught the intellect is good. *Chayah* for all the limbs die and she lives on in the body. *Yechidah* for all the limbs have doubles while she is uniquely singular."

between the mind and the limbs? Feelings. All emotions stem from *ruach*. It is also related to *dibbur*, "speech,"[153] a wind that connects the mind's thoughts to the physical mouth.[154] Speech also connects people to each other.[155]

Speech primarily strengthens the emotions that you are feeling. Why do words have such an impact on the heart? Because emotions and speech are expressions of *ruach*, while an act is a manifestation of *nefesh*.[156] Our emotions usually dictate how we act. Thus *ruach* is usually the deciding part of the human personality. It is concentrated in the heart—the source of all emotions.[157] Feelings of purity, such as fear of violating Divine mandates, or love for fellow Jews, are expressions of a holy form of *ruach*.

---

153. Targum Onkelos, one of the oldest commentaries to the Torah, translates *nefesh chayah*, "living soul," as *ruach mimalalah*, a *ruach* that speaks, for *ruach* is manifest in speech.

154. *Daas Tefillah* 273-278, *Nefesh Ha-Chaim* 1:15. Rabbi Dr. Akiva Tatz expressed this thought in the following paragraph:

> Speech is the world of connection. Understood simply, speech connects the speaker and the listener. A relationship can develop, can flourish, because deep communication is possible by means of speech. In the Torah "speaking" is a euphemism for intimacy ("They saw her speaking with one...") this is not usage borrowed from a distance; the parallel is intrinsic.
>
> At a deeper level, speech represents the connection between higher and lower worlds. Speech is the mechanism by which an abstract idea which exists only in the higher dimension of thought can be brought down into the material world: when I speak, I transform ideas into the physical medium of sound, which is tangible enough for you to hear with the physical tools of hearing (*Worldmask*, pgs. 128-129).

155. See further *Derech Ha-Melech* on *Parashas Vayetze* 5690. The Piasetzne Rebbe (1889-1943, authored *Derech Ha-Melech*, *Chovas Ha-Talmidim*, *Aish Kodesh* and other classics, and led his Chasidim valiantly through the difficult years of World War II in the Warsaw Ghetto) points out that the Talmudic term for a form of marriage, the ultimate connection between two individuals, is *maamar*. *Maamar* also means a statement. The Rabbis chose this term for marriage to teach that heartfelt talking connects people.

156. Heard from the Stitchiner Rebbe.

157. *Daas Tefillah* pg. 273.

Neshamah is located primarily in the mind.[158] The *neshamah* is the most Godly of the soul parts. It is pure intellect. One feels God's "breath," with *machshavah*, "pure thoughts," such as when one fully understands an abstract, correct, and moral principle.

Chayah and *yechidah* are called *makkifim*, "enveloping lights." These are levels of holiness that are hardly attainable for most mortals. That is why they surround man and do not enter man. They form a protecting shield and occasionally send to the individual flashes of inspiration. Since these levels of soul are outside man's essential personality, they are not internalized within a physical body part.[159]

A Lesson from the Body

The most perfect hierarchy within man is one in which the *neshamah* rules the *ruach* and *nefesh*. Think clear and abstract thought, then allow untainted logic to inspire emotions and finally let those pure feelings control the body and guide its lusts. In symbolic terms the ideal arrangement is mind then heart and then liver. God teaches this lesson by the very makeup of a human being. God placed mind (which holds the *neshamah*) in the skull, the highest point of the body, the heart (the place of *ruach*) and liver (the seat of the *nefesh*) are beneath the head, thus indicating that the head should rule the others.

The Hebrew terms for mind, heart, and liver are *moach* (mind), *lev* (heart) and *kaved* (liver). An acronym of the terms is *melech*, literally, "king."[160] When man lives a life of mind first and then heart and liver,

---

158. *Da'as Tefillah* pg. 272.

159. They are symbolized by body parts and not internalized within body parts. The skull, which stands above the mind, symbolizes these soul parts, for these soul parts are above logic and rational intelligence.

160. Words in the Hebrew language have many layers of meaning. In addition to the literal meaning of the words, the letters of a word might refer to a complete sentence. This occurs when each letter in the word represents the opening letter of a word in a phrase. Thus a three-letter word is in truth an acronym for a three-word phrase. This process is called *roshei teivos*, "beginning of words."

he is king over his lower self.[161] Frequently, we reverse the order. Our lusts lead. For example, we desire someone else's money, or we are lazy and seek to avoid performing a moral duty. We then arouse our heart to love that path and we employ our mind to rationalize and justify misbehavior, saying, "He did not need that money anyway. I will use it for better purposes than he," or, "The duty will be performed by someone else, I can safely ignore it." In these instances our livers were really first, followed by the heart, and then the mind. The first letters of *kaved, lev, moach* (the reversed order) spell *kalem*, which means, "embarrassment, shame, and death." A life in which lusts rule inevitably ends with this unholy trinity.[162]

Man does not deserve a life of embarrassment. Man deserves great honor. Man carries the image of God and as a result deserves regard. Lesson Nine demonstrates how the five parts of the soul are the image of God that man contains.

---

161. A king can rule others if he first asserts total dominion over his lower self. This unity between king over others and self-control was clearly expressed by Rabbi Yehudah Ha-Levi in his *Kuzari*, which is a record of a discussion between a Gentile king and a Jewish scholar.

> AL KHAZARI: Give me a description of the doings of one of your pious men at the present time.
> THE RABBI: A pious man is, so to speak, the ruler of his country, who gives to its inhabitants provisions and all they need. He is so just that he wrongs no one, nor does he grant anyone more than his due. Then, when he requires them, he finds them obedient to His call. He orders, they execute. He forbids, they abstain.
> AI KHAZARI: I asked you about a pious man, not a prince.
> THE RABBI: The pious man is nothing but a prince who is obeyed by his senses, and by his mental as well as his physical faculties, which he governs corporeally, as it is written, "He that ruleth his spirit is better than he that taketh a city" (*Kuzari*, Part 3, quoting Prov. 16: 32).

162. *Da'as Tefillah* pg. 273.

Lesson Nine

The Image of God

MAN IS THE highlight of creation and deserves honor and respect for he carries the image of God.[163] What is the meaning of *tzelem Elokim*, "the image of God"? If I look at my reflection in a mirror, am I to think for a moment that I have seen God?! Judaism abhors any attempt to ascribe to God any physical characteristics, as Maimonides defined it, and it is one of the articles of faith that Jews recite on a daily basis, "I believe with complete faith that the Creator, Blessed is His Name, is not physical and is not affected by physical phenomena, and that there is no comparison whatsoever to Him."

God is totally incorporeal, so in what way is man in His image?

The mystics explain that each Hebrew name of God denotes a different way in which man perceives the Omnipotent. Sometimes, I feel the Almighty's boundless love, at other times I witness His awesome force and power, at still other points I might see His hand in nature. Each of the different attributes of God that man acknowledges is characterized with a unique name. The name Y-H-V-H[164] reflects our feeling His love, A-do-n-ai is the name for the fact that He is the master of all, and Shaddai reflects His power and dominion, His setting limits for the world.

---

163. The honor due man as the representative of God who carries His image is a basic theme in Chasidic thought. Supposedly, this was the last teaching of the Baal Shem Tov. On his deathbed, his final statement was, "An artist invests himself and expresses his deepest self in his work. Want to understand an artist? Look at his handiwork." The point of the lesson was that to appreciate God and to love God it is necessary to appreciate and love man. Man is God's greatest masterpiece—study the sculpture and appreciate it in order to appreciate the Divine. See further *Ma'asei Hashem*, vol. 1 pg. 55.

164. In deference to the saintliness of the names I have not spelled them out fully.

Man was formed in the image of *Elokim*. This name represents the awareness that God is *Baal ha-kochos kullam u-vaal ha-yecholes*, "Master of all powers and He has total authority."[165] Man in the image of *Elokim* means that man, too, in a certain sense, is the master over all the forces of creation and is endowed with unbridled power. *Tzelem Elokim* teaches the cosmic effect of human behavior. Our deeds affect the entire world and the entirety of creation follows man's lead.

An example of this principle is the story of the great flood. In *Parashas Noach*, the Torah tells of a time when all creatures were corrupted. Even animals and the inanimate earth violated nature's law. Lions copulated with bears, and a man would plant peach seeds only to reap apples. As a result of the pervasive corruption, God sent a deluge of water that destroyed almost all of humanity, the animals, plants, and several feet of topsoil. Only man has freedom of choice. Animals, plants, and the earth do not have the ability to decide between good and evil, so how did all of creation become corrupt? The answer is that man controls the rest of creation.[166] When man performs evil, the spirit of misconduct is increased throughout the world. Animals and the earth become infected too, and they start to perform in ways that are at variance with their law.

Mankind at the time of the flood was thoroughly rotten. They consistently chose evil. All the humans were sinners who polluted themselves, and they caused the rest of creation to be polluted as well. Noah was righteous, and his influence allowed for a minute sample of animal and plant life that maintained fidelity to its laws.

Currently, we confront a physical world that suffers from pollution, ozone depletion, and global warming. The earth's illnesses do not result merely from industrialization and its excesses. Spiritually there is an obvious cause for our planet's troubles; human society is an increasingly corrupt group. Presidents lie, corporate titans shamelessly deceive, and the various forms of media pull readers and viewers to the lowest of lowly urges. Innocent faith, old-fashioned honesty, decency, and morality have become rare commodities. The rest of creation reflects our misdeeds.

How does this cosmic power work? Why do the actions of man have such effects? The answer is that man is a miniaturization of the entire

---

165. *Tur, Orach Chaim*, Chapter 5. See also *Nefesh Ha-Chaim* 1:2.
166. See further *Beis Ha-Levi* on *Parashas Noach*.

spiritual realm. Man's soul parallels God's spiritual universes that form the foundation for this physical world.[167]

Imagine two harps tuned to the same pitch placed right next to each other. Play note A on one harp, its string will vibrate and produce a loud sound. Even though you have not touched the second harp, note A in the other harp will also vibrate softly. Man and the universe are parallel harps; when we cause our strings to vibrate, parallel strings in the supernal realms vibrate ever so softly, broadcasting the same notes throughout the world.[168]

THE SPIRITUAL DIMENSION AS SUPERNAL UNIVERSES

A great Rabbi once walked with his student along a grassy path. While they were talking, the student carelessly picked a flower from the ground and started to scatter its petals. The Rabbi stopped walking and said to his student, "In the Midrash[169] it is taught that every blade of grass has an angel that stands behind it hitting the grass saying, 'Grow.' When you

---

167. The technical term for this concept is *olam katan*, man is a miniature of the entire world. See further *Sichas Malachei Ha-Shareis* Chapter 2, and the Overview of ArtScroll's *Tehillim* by Rabbi A.C. Feuer. When God created man, He said, "Let us make man." Nachmanides explains the plural of "Let us" to mean that God invited all of creation to contribute to the creation of man; man has within him microcosmic traces of each created being. When a man displays strength and power that is the aspect of the lion within man, sometimes man is timid and fearful, that is when the nature of the lamb expresses itself in man. When people idle, doing nothing, it is a display of the plant element within man.

168. The imagery of two parallel harps is utilized by Rav Wolfson to explain a Talmudic story. The Talmud in *Berachos* 3b relates, "There was a harp hanging above the bed of David. When midnight would hit, a northern wind would blow. The harp would then play. David would awake and rise to study Torah until the morning."

This story sounds too fantastic to be true. Can a wind play tunes on a harp? The story is not to be understood in a literal manner; rather the Talmud is utilizing allegorical imagery. The harp above the bed is really David's heart, and the northern wind is the song of the souls of *tzaddikim* who reside in the northern part of the Garden of Eden. The righteous begin to sing at midnight. David's heart was perfectly attuned to the souls in the Garden of Eden. When they started to sing, like a parallel harp, his heart started to vibrate in harmony, and he then awoke and studied Torah.

169. *Bereishis Rabbah* 10.

picked the flower from the earth, you caused this flower's angel to die. Do you have a good reason for destroying the life of a celestial light?"

Our physical world is controlled by a spiritual world. Each blade of grass, for instance, has a spiritual channel, an angel that provides for its life. Jewish mysticism details the makeup of this spiritual dimension. In a broad sweep, this spiritual dimension is comprised of five spiritual universes.

Why is there a need for a spiritual dimension? Can't God direct us personally without any intermediates? The answer is that man's feeble physical and spiritual nature would be overwhelmed by the presence of God.[170]

God's essence is so overpowering that it does not allow for anything to exist independently before It. The spiritual universes are the steps in which God has limited His essence so that an independent existence can emerge. The key terms in understanding these steps are *tzimtzum*, "constriction," and *Or Ain Sof*, "Light without End."

Consider light. Light usually enables sight, yet too much light can blind.[171] Similarly, God is called Infinite Light (*Or Ain Sof*), with no end and no beginning. He is the ultimate Reality. His life and vitality is so powerful, it overwhelms all other existing items that face Him directly. To allow for creation God acted with *tzimtzum*—He pulled in His light. He then emanated from Himself a light that was less bright than His essence. Even this light was too much for existence, so out of this light He caused another further limited light to emerge, and then another and another. At the last stage of limited light a physical universe emerged out of the spiritual lights. *Olam* is a universe, and the words *he'elam* and *ne'elam*, "unknown" and "hidden," share the same Hebrew root. A universe is a "hiding of the Infinite," a diminution of Divine light. The process of limiting the light and turning the spiritual into a progressively more physical creation is called *seder hishtalshlus*, the "order of development."

170. When the Torah was given at Mt. Sinai, the Jews experienced a direct revelation of Godliness. The experience was so overwhelming that their souls left their bodies, and all of Jewry had to undergo a revival of the dead. Finite man cannot directly experience the breath of the Infinite.
171. The same is true with noise. A whisper can hardly be heard. Only if one raises the volume of speech is it audible. However, if one shouts at the top of his lungs, the heightened noise renders the words inaccessible.

Hishtalshlus shares a root with the word *shalsheles*, "chain." Creation is a chain for two reasons. First, in a chain each ring leads to another, and creation is a process of cause and effect, greater lights producing lesser lights, out of which are formed even smaller forces.[172] Second, in a chain, the rings interlock, the end of the first ring's airspace has within it the beginning of the second ring, and in the spiritual dimension each level is interwoven with the next level. For instance, the lowest level of the universe of *atzilus* (the first universe), is also the highest level in the universe of *beriah* (the second universe).

The different stages of the *seder hishtalshlus* are the universes that are the soul parts of the physical universe. The first supernal universe is so high that it too is a light that is almost infinite. This universe is hardly spoken about in Chasidic literature[173] and is called *Adam Kadmon*, "Initial Man," in Kabbalah; it parallels the human soul part of *yechidah*.

The second universe is *atzilus*. *Atzilus* means "next to," "noble," and "emanated or given off." This world is "next to" God; it is the first light that God gave off. An *atzil* is a nobleman;[174] he has power and importance because of his proximity to the king. Similarly, this universe is next to the King of Kings and that is where its importance stems from.

Prayer is a soulful sojourn through the universes. *Atzilus* is represented by the extremely righteous in their *Shemoneh Esreh* (Silent Devotional) part of prayers. For the silent devotion, one takes three steps forward to enter into a new dimension in which the prayers are recited silently. At this point of the service the petitioner is standing next to God, and that is why all can talk with Him in the hushed tones of an intimate whisper. Furthermore, according to *halachah* ideally this

---

172. "The *Nefesh Ha-Chaim* and many other sources tell us that there are many interlocking levels to the Creation. In an infinitely stretching chain beginning at the very Source of existence, many worlds are connected in sequence. Each of these higher worlds infuses the level below it with existence and energy; each is 'male' with regard to the world below it which is relatively speaking, 'female,' and together they 'bring out' yet another level below them. This process continues with myriad complexity until finally our finite world results" (*Living Inspired* pg. 71). This process is called the *seder hishtalshlus*.

173. The Ari Ha-Kadosh wrote that humans should not try to meditate and think about this world (*Sichas Malachei Ha-Shareis*, Chapter 3).

174. See further Exod. 24:11, *Ve-el atzilei bnei Yisrael*, "And to the noblemen of the Children of Israel...."

prayer should lead to leaving the physical self and getting lost in rapture of the Divine. During the silent prayer the *tzaddik* achieves *deveikus*, "absolute cleaving." *Deveikus* means becoming one with God. Oneness cannot be described nor defined; it can only be understood through the experience of a sensitive heart. Loss of all bodily sensation and absolute union with the Infinite is a human sensation that is *atzilus*-like; it is a sense of a wholly new dimension. The sense of absolute oneness with the Divine is an out-of-body experience that emerges from *atzilus*, the universe that is above our world and serves as a *makkif*, an enveloping light, to our physical dimension.

Atzilus is all good and it produces the *chayah* part of the human soul. *Chayah* is the source of *deveikus*, devotional oneness, and what *chayah* is in the human is what *atzilus* is to the cosmos.

Out of *atzilus* a further diminished light emerged, the world of *beriah*, "creation." *Atzilus* experientially is felt as a loss of self-hood. It is called *ayin*, a sense of nothingness. *Beriah* emerged out of it; thus *beriah* is a manifestation of, and the place of, *yesh me-ayin*, something coming out of nothing. In this world, there is a possibility of evil although good is the majority. This world parallels the section of prayers that speak of accepting God's yoke, reciting *Shema* and its blessings. This world is also termed *Olam Ha-Kissei*, "the universe of God's throne." Symbolically the Almighty "sits" there. That is why there is a widespread Jewish custom to sit during the prayers of *Shema*. *Beriah* produced and parallels the *neshamah* part of the soul. The *neshamah* is located in the mind and expressed through thought; in the world of *beriah*, thoughts are tangible and real. The depths of *neshamah* can be felt when all of one's thoughts are holy, centering on Torah knowledge and Mitzvah fulfillment.

Beriah let out a lesser light that became the world of *yetzirah*. *Yetzirah* implies *yesh mi-yesh*, "something from something," to form an item out of a primordial matter. In *yetzirah*, evil has even more presence and is equal to the amount of good. This world is represented by the *Pesukei De-Zimra*—verses of praise—part of the morning prayers. *Zimra* also means to prune, the verses of praise are pruning shears—they cut away the forces of evil and allow man's prayers to enter before God.[175] This universe let off

---

175. See further, *A Call to the Infinite*, pg. 67, quoted from Rabbi Yosef Gikatilla.

the *ruach* part of the soul that it parallels.[176] *Yetzirah* is the world of feeling and man's emotions of holiness reach this world. The ultimate level of *ruach* is felt when one's heart is filled exclusively with the best desires, such as swirls of love for Judaism, or awe and fear of Heaven. Feelings are as tangible in the world of *yetzirah* as objects are in our universe.

Finally, there is the universe of *asiyah*, where the majority is evil, and it parallels the *nefesh* part of the soul, as well as the prayers of *korbanos*, the sacrificial order that purified and provided the spiritual merit for this world.[177] Good deeds performed on this earth reach the world of *asiyah*.

After the spiritual universes stands the physical universe itself, which is joined to the world of *asiyah*.

Man in Hebrew is called *adam*, a word that shares a root with the word *adammeh*, literally, "I will resemble." What is a man? A being that resembles the Heavenly domain. Since man's soul parts constitute a small harp to the great harp of the physical universe's "soul-parts," his actions cause similar results in those realms. Man is the soul of the universe.[178]

---

176. In *yetzirah*, the forces for good and evil are equals. This is why the heart, which contains *ruach*, has two ventricles. The left ventricle contains an advocate for sinful acts and the right ventricle contains a spiritual force that attracts man to Mitzvos.

177. See further, *A Call to the Infinite*, pgs. 74-75, quoted from *Derech Hashem*, 4:613-14.

178. See further *Sichas Malachei Ha-Shareis*, Chapter 3. Rabbi Tzadok explains that the life-forms on our planet are roughly divided into four categories: (1) *domeim*, inanimate materials such as air and water, (2) *tzome'ach*, growing items such as grass and trees, (3) *chai*, living beings like animals, fowl, and insects, and (4) *medabber*, speaking creatures, namely, humans. The world of *asiyah* and the soul part *nefesh* are expressed through righteous deed. If you put a coin into the hand of a poor person without any care for his welfare nor a thought about why it is correct to give charity, then it is exclusively in the realm of *asiyah*. *Domeim* bears a trace of *asiyah*. An act without feeling or thinking is like an inanimate item, the doer was a block of wood during its performance, no better than a machine. The world of *yetzirah* is the source for *ruach* and feelings and resembles *tzome'ach*. Most of what I feel is internal; only a small fraction of my love or hate can be seen by others. I cannot see the tree moving up when it grows. However, I do see a small fraction of the growth process, and by regular monitoring of a plant I can stay abreast of its development. Animals have some intelligence, thus *chai* corresponds to *beriah* and *neshamah*, the sources of thoughts. *Chayah* and *atzilus* is total connection to God, thus corresponding to *medabber*, the human, who, through speech, can experience union with Infinity.

The secrets of creation are hinted in the letters of the Hebrew language. Lesson Ten will show how the spiritual universes and the parts of the human soul are hinted in the four letters of God's name Y-H-V-H.

GOD'S NAME OF CREATION

THE NAME OF God that denotes God as Creator[179] is the Tetragrammaton, Y-H-V-H.[180] The first letter, the *yud*, has an apex, *kutzo shel yud*, a crown with which it begins, that visually seems to stand apart from the letter. The apex is to be considered a virtual letter unto itself. Since the five universes and the five parts of the soul were created with this name they parallel the Name's five letters.

The soul part *nefesh* and the universe of *asiyah* were created from the final *heh* in God's name. In Hebrew the *heh* is a letter of femininity, since a *heh* at the end of a word usually indicates that the word is grammatically feminine. In the process of creating life, the masculine contributes the first seed, while the feminine receives that seed within her. She then hides it within herself for nine months and develops it into a new being. In Jewish thought the masculine represents giving while the feminine represents humility, to be empty, and receive. In conception, after receiving the first spark, the feminine eventually develops it into a child, thus returning something far greater than what she received. Our universe is primarily feminine in that we receive from God life and all

---

179. God created the world with this ineffable name.

180. This name of God also refers to God's love. It was with the name of love that He created the world, for His purpose in creation was love. He loves. That is why he made a world, as a total gift to creation. See Psalm 89, *olam chesed yibbaneh*, "The world is built upon love." See further *Pachad Yitzchak*, Rosh Hashanah, *Ma'amar* 1, Chapter 2. Rav Hutner explains that the blowing of the Shofar is a reminder of the beginning of Creation where God filled an empty space with His essence, as a result, it causes an awakening of love, for God's purpose in creation and His mode of creation was love. See further *Horeb*, Chapter 72.

of its blessings, our mission is to absorb these gifts, develop them, and eventually return to Him a better world.[181]

The soul part *ruach* (emotions) and the world of *yetzirah* emerge from the letter *vav* in the Divine name. Emotions and speech connect the mind (*neshamah*) with the body (*nefesh*). The letter *vav* means "and"; it connects words to each other. *Vav* also means hook, and a hook is an item that pulls together two disparate and different entities, such as a curtain with a wall. The world of *yetzirah* is the world of angels.[182] Angels serve as intermediaries. God is the source of life, and it is the angels who transmit God's blessings to the physical dimension. *Yetzirah* is the world of connecting *beriah* with *asiyah*, and it too emerged from the *vav*.

Neshamah and the universe of *beriah* are represented by the first letter *heh* in the Divine name. *Beriah* is a universe in which the majority is good, pure thought. The *neshamah* usually is good and is thus "mostly" good.

Chayah is experienced as a state of soul in which all of the personality is united with, and attached to, Heaven. It parallels the world of *atzilus* and the first *yud* of the Name. *Yechidah* represents the connection with God that is so powerful that one absolutely ceases to exist independently. It corresponds to the *kutzo shel yud*, the apex and first dot of ink in the formation of the *yud*. This connection is hidden, just as the apex of the *yud* is hidden within the letter.

Another set of terms for body and soul is *chomer* (matter) and *tzurah* (form). An example of these terms is a sculpture where the rock is the

---

181. See further *Innerspace*, Chapter 9, where Rabbi Kaplan writes,

> If you think of male and female biologically, the male is the giver; the female receives and nurtures and then gives forth much more than the man initiated. The man gives over one million sperm cells from which the woman selects only one. From her one single fertilized egg, however, she gives back a complete infant. She receives, but as part of receiving she ends up creating and building something complete. Hence, the essence of femininity turns out to be much more complex. If masculine is giving, femininity is receiving and completing (pgs. 75-76).

182. *Innerspace* pg. 31

matter (*chomer*) while the shape, the form, is its soul (*tzurah*). Matter is the body to its soul, its form. Rabbi Tzadok Ha-Cohen of Lublin[183] defined *chayah* and *yechidah* as matter and form:

> *Chayah* is the *chomer* of the life-source for *neshamah*, *ruach* and *nefesh*. It is the principle of *chelek Elokah mi-maʾal*, "A piece of the Divine from above." This concept provides existence and passion to the *neshamah* [it stimulates holy thoughts that arouse holy feelings that guide saintly behavior]. When you are totally attached and immersed into this thought, feeling that "All of my capabilities, energy, and strength are from He who resides within me." This is the matter that provides life and passion to the rest of the saintly soul.
>
> That is why it is called *chayah*, "living soul." God is an eternally living King, and since my soul is a piece of Him, that piece will live even after all else in the physical world withers....[184]
>
> *Yechidah* is the *tzurah* to *chayah*—it is when you think deeply upon this thought and you feel so connected to God that you unite as one. In other words, all the forces are united in the essence of the One who released them. There, all is One in the most absolute union. [For the human this level is reached through] absolute *deveikus*, "attachment." The piece is so connected to its Source that it is no longer a separate piece of Divinity... total union between the spiritual and physical... this is *yechidah*.[185]

Since *yechidah* is an amplification of *chayah*, its letter, the crown or apex, is subsumed within the *yud*, the letter of *chayah*.

---

183. Rabbi Tzadok was born to a non-Chasidic family in 1823. He was a child prodigy who eventually joined the Chasidic movement and became a follower of the first Izbetzer Rebbe. He was a great expert in all aspects of Jewish law and an extremely prolific and original Chasidic thinker. Many of his writings were lost in the Lublin ghetto during World War II and never published. Fortunately his five volumes of collected writings, and his *Pri Tzaddik*, five volumes of homilies on the Torah portions, were published and are widely used throughout the world of Jewish learning. He passed away in 1900.

184. See *Bereishis Rabbah* 14:9.

185. *Sichas Malachei Ha-Shareis*, Chapter 3.

The letters of the Tetragrammaton tell the story of charity. *Yud* is small and simple representing a coin. *Heh* has a *gematria* of five, and it represents the five fingers of the hand of the giver holding the coin. *Vav* as the letter of bonding signifies the outstretched arm of the giver connecting with the poor man. The final *heh* represents another hand, the hand of the poor man who receives the charity.

Life is charity that God constantly provides. First it exists in a different and spiritual state (*atzilus* and *chayah*), then it enters God's hand (*beriah* and *neshamah*), finally God reaches to give it to us (*yetzirah* and *ruach*). We then receive it, and the ability to receive is also from God (*asiyah* and *nefesh*).[186]

There are four levels of interpretation for every verse in the Torah. These layers of meaning are known by the acronym of their terms, *Pardes*, which stands for *peshat*, *remez*, *derash*, and *sod*. *Peshat* is the literal and simple meaning of a verse. *Remez* is the hinted meaning such as lessons from *gematria* and *roshei teivos*. *Derash* is the homiletical interpretation such as lessons that emerge from the rules for resolving Scriptural difficulties, i.e., grappling with contradictory verses and their resolutions. *Sod* is the secret, mystical meaning.

A parable might amplify the nature of these layers of Divine intent. Imagine that you are a traveler in South Africa. You arrive at a plot of land, and it seems to be a simple field with wheat. What would happen if you took a sledge-hammer and dug in that field? Once you reach a certain depth you might find copper. Take a better instrument and dig deeper you might find deposits of silver. Burrow lower and you might reach gold. If you continue to dig and reach the depths you will discover diamonds.

Torah is the field. The literal interpretation provides the learner with one level of benefit. If one considers all the hinted meanings in the verse, such as the hidden connection between words due to word values, the heart might sense the joy of discovering a treasure of copper. If one then ponders verses that contradict each other, or considers laws and attempts to determine whether they are meant to apply in realms beyond where they are mentioned, one will access enlightenment as precious as silver. If one delves even deeper one will reach the most precious part of Torah,

---

186. *Innerspace*, pgs. 11, 16, and 21-37.

the *sod*, the secret meanings of verses. *Sod* teaches how all is about God, and it attaches the student to Him in a most powerful way. The secret meanings of Torah verses are gold and diamonds.

The Torah is truth. The four levels of interpretation are four layers of truth. They, like the soul and the universes, evolved from the supernal universes and the letters of God's name. *Peshat* corresponds to *asiyah* and the final *heh*. *Remez* corresponds to *yetzirah* and the *vav*. *Derash* corresponds to *beriah* and the first *heh*. *Sod* emerges from the world of *atzilus* and the *yud*.[187] Without the *yud*, God's name would merely be *heh*, *vav*, *heh*, spelling *hoveh*, the Hebrew word for the present, and without the *samech*, the *Pardes* would be *pered*, meaning, "divided." To become truly Godly, to feel how all is One, the Torah learner must also taste the secret interpretations of the Torah.[188]

Some *tzaddikim* have a grasp on the secrets of *sod*; others do not comprehend the depths of *sod*. They focus on the literal truth, such as *peshat* and the knowledge of *halachah*, Jewish law. The reason for this is that the *seder hishtalshlus*, the "Order of Development,"[189] for each soul differs. Each soul passes through the same steps before it appears in this world yet each has a different main stop along that journey.[190] Hence each individual has a different point in Heaven that is the root of his or her soul. The ability to comprehend Torah depends on one's root in Heaven.

The road of the soul is the four spiritual universes, *atzilus*, *beriah*, *yetzirah*, and *asiyah*. After the soul has passed through the four worlds, the soul appears in this world clothed in a body. Some souls are rooted in *atzilus*—these souls were affected greatly by their sojourn in *atzilus*.

---

187. See further Rabbi Dr. Akiva Tatz's *Living Inspired*, pg. 93, and pg. 18.
188. *Razei Ha-Bosem* pg. 17.
189. The term *seder hishtalshlus* was discussed in Chapter 9.
190. Rabbi Tzadok Ha-Cohen of Lublin expressed this concept in the following passage (adapted from his *Sichas Malachei Ha-Shareis*, pg. 21, s.v. *sibbas hevdel*): "Each soul is a piece of the Divine, each personality is a microcosm of all the forces in the world, so how can personalities differ? God desired to create distinct and different characters. So, while each soul has within it all of the forces of life, God arranged that the combinations of strengths should differ from soul to soul. While each soul has all the forces of life within it, in each soul there is one aspect that is primary. Other souls will also have that force, yet it will be secondary within them."

Individuals who are mostly rooted in *atzilus* merit to fully access their *chayah*. *Sod* parallels *atzilus* and *chayah*, and therefore these *tzaddikim* have the feelings that allow them to comprehend *sod*. Other souls were influenced greatly by their time in *yetzirah*. These individuals, if they live a life of devotion, will merit a strong sense of *ruach*, which will be the dominant force within them. Other souls have a predominant element of *nefesh* and *asiyah*, and they stuggle to grasp the abstract and complex sensitivities of Kabbalah. These *tzaddikim* may have "merely" a great grasp in the realm of *peshat* and *halachah*. Secrets of Torah cannot be merely read in a book and organized in the mind. The secrets of Torah must be sensed, and some souls struggle to fully feel these concepts, since they are not strongly *atzilus*-like, and they have a weak attachment to the sensitivities of their *chayah*.

Rav Yosef Karo[191] studied mysticism with Rabbi Isaac Luria. When the Ari would teach classes with very deep lessons in Kabbalah, R. Karo would fall asleep. Rav Karo was very upset about this. The Ari revealed to him that the secrets he was revealing were from a very high point in the Heavenly worlds and Rav Karo's soul was not rooted at that height.

No one should infer from this story anything negative about Rav Yosef Karo. The level of his *nefesh* and *asiyah* was lofty, as he had tremendous mastery of practical *halachah*. There may have been individuals whose grasp of secrets was at a higher point than Rav Karo's yet he was greater due to the breadth of *peshat* that he possessed.

The Chasam Sofer[192] was unique in that he had a grasp in all four levels. Apparently he possessed a full complement of soul (*nefesh, ruach, neshamah,* and *chayah*) and connection to the worlds (*asiyah, yetzirah, beriah,* and *atzilus*). The Chasam Sofer was a giant in practical law indicating a strong and holy *nefesh*. His homilies display great creativity in *derash* (resolving scriptural difficulties) and *remez* (hinted meanings)

191. He was born in Spain in 1488, he later moved to Israel and served as the Chief Rabbi of Safed, and he passed away in 1575. He was one of the greatest experts of Jewish law and authored the authoritative *Shulchan Aruch*, "Code of Jewish Law." He was also a great Kabbalist.
192. Rav Moshe Sofer was born in 1762 and passed away in 1838. He was the Rabbi of Pressburg from 1806 until 1838. He was a great teacher of Torah who wrote responses to questions of Jewish law and wrote voluminously about the five books of the Torah. He is known by the title of his books, *Chasam Sofer*.

revealing a holy *neshamah* and *ruach*. And his original ideas in the realm of *sod* indicate that he possessed a sense of *atzilus* and *chayah*.[193]

We differ because of differences in the influences of our souls.[194] In our prayers we ask, *Ve-sein chelkeinu be-Sorasecha*, "And please give us our portion in your Torah." All we can hope for is the attainment of our part of Torah, our level of understanding based on the capabilities of our soul. Each soul passed through all four worlds so each soul can have some degree of connection to all the levels of Torah: literal, hinted, interpreted, and hidden. Yet the area of your success in Torah learning will depend on where your soul is rooted.[195]

---

193. Rav Wolfson.

194. The *Tanya* asks: How can people be different if we all emerged from God's breath and God is an absolute unity? He answers that the *seder hishtalshlus*, the Order of Development, explains the distinctions. For example, we all emerged from the same source, but some of us spent more time at the third step within *asiyah* and others spent more time at the fourth step within *yetzirah*. At the beginning of any soul's descent, it was an absolute unity indistinguishable from other souls, after its particular journey it has its own unique character that differs from other souls who had a different emphasis in their descent.

195. "Behold in the world of *asiyah* there is far more chaff [waste] than food, and the amount of holiness in *asiyah* is very limited. In the world of *yetzirah* there is less waste, but it is a place of much waste, and it is where good and evil reign together. In the world of *beriah* good rules over evil, and there is very little chaff. *Atzilus* is total and absolute holiness. This is why an individual who emerged from the world of *atzilus* [i.e., the *tzaddik*] has no sin, and no sins occur because of him, for in this universe the *sitra achra*, the forces of evil have no hold. Because of the four universes there are four Torahs: the Torah of *atzilus*, the Torah of *beriah*, the Torah of *yetzirah*, and the Torah of *asiyah*. The simple meaning [*peshat*] is from *asiyah*; the hinted meaning, *remez*, is from *yetzirah*; the interpreted meaning, *derash* is from *beriah*, and the secrets of Torah are from *atzilus*. Corresponding to these, man has *nefesh*, *ruach*, *neshamah*, and *chayah*. *Nefesh* is from *asiyah*, which is why it tends to sin, to physical urges. One must be vigilant and purify one's *nefesh* through avoidance of prohibited food and ritual impurity, and be careful even with Rabbinic prohibitions. One must be very exacting on one's limbs, eyes, and mouth to ensure they do not perform misdeeds in order to attain and preserve the Godly *nefesh*. If one does not preserve one's *nefesh* one will be unable to access *ruach*. One who maintains the saintly level of his *nefesh* might then attain *ruach* and might fully comprehend the hinted meanings of the Torah. If one rises to the next spiritual level one will comprehend *derash*. Only those with the highest level of soul will fully comprehend the secrets of Torah" (*Ma'or Va-Shemesh, Parashas Yisro*).

The Torah has five types of numbers: singles, tens, hundreds, thousands, and ten thousand. These correspond to the five universes and the five levels of soul. Thus, when the prophetic leader Devorah asked for ten thousand Jews to join Barak in battling the Canaanite tyrant Sisra, she was really attempting to arouse the full complement of the Jewish soul. Jews were being asked to reach down to the level of *yechidah* and dedicate all for a war to save the Jewish people. Furthermore, this symbolic number was intended to arouse the merit of all the parts of the soul and all the positive effects that Jews had produced in all the universes. These merits would be reason for a miraculous routing of Sisra's armies (*Resisei Lailah* pg. 48).

The Chasam Sofer explains the reason why in the count of the Jewish nation in the Desert, each tribe's total was completed in the hundreds column (such as 57,400 for Zevulun and 59,300 for Shimon). These groups of Jews had fully perfected their *nefesh* and *ruach*, and they were seeking to perfect that which is rooted in the world of *beriah*, the realm of *neshamah*, which corresponds to the hundreds.

LESSON ELEVEN

THE MEANING OF THE
TALMUDIC TALES IN *BERACHOS* 10A

THE UNIVERSES AND their correlating human soul parts is the deeper meaning of the following Talmudic passage:

The five *Barchi Nafshi*'s ["My soul will bless..."] that David recited, for whom, and in reference to what, did David say them? He recited them for the soul and for God. God fills the entire world, and the soul fills the entire body. God sees and is not seen, and the soul sees and is not seen. God feeds the entire world, and the soul feeds the body. God is pure and the soul is pure. God sits in the innermost chambers and the soul sits in the innermost recesses. Let he who has these five qualities come and praise the One who has these five qualities.[196]

The Talmud is teaching that God's relationship with the world is an exact parallel to the soul's relationship with man. At the lowest level there is *nefesh* in man that is most connected to the body. The world of *asiyah* is the Godliness most connected to the physical universe. "God fills the physical world" through the world of *asiyah*, just as the "soul fills the body" with *nefesh*. Above *nefesh* is *ruach* that connects mind to matter and is the source of emotions. Emotions are in the heart.[197] The heart can sense even what is not seen. It is this aspect that the Talmud refers

---

196. *Berachos* 10.
197. According to Jewish mystics, the ability to speak also emerges from the heart. See further *Nefesh Ha-Chaim* (1:15), *Sichas Malachei Ha-Shareis*, Chapter 3.

to as "God sees and is not seen just as the soul sees and is not seen." This also refers to the world of angels who are not seen while they see (*olam ha-yetzirah*).[198] *Neshamah* is the life of *ruach* and *nefesh*. *Neshamah* is in the mind, and the mind is the source of life for the body; cut off the head and everything will stop. *Neshamah* parallels *beriah*, the source of life for *yetzirah* and *asiyah*, and the Talmud refers to this parallel with the phrase, "God provides life for the entire world and the soul provides life for the entire body." *Chayah* corresponds to the universe of *atzilus*. *Atzilus* is all good, with no evil in it whatsoever. This is the meaning of "God is pure, and the soul is pure." Above *atzilus* is the hidden world of *Adam Kadmon*, and in the person there is *yechidah* of this relationship the Talmud says, "God is hidden and the soul is hidden."

Rav Tzadok Ha-Cohen of Lublin adds that the theme of the five soul-parts is also the intent of the beginning of that Talmudic story:

Said Rabbi Yochanan in the name of Rabbi Shimon bar Yochai, what is the intent of the verse, *Piha*[199] *paschah be-chachmah*, "She opened her mouth with wisdom" (Prov. 31:26)? Solomon intended this verse to serve as a statement about his father David who lived in five worlds and in each, sang a special song to God. He lived as a fetus within his mother's womb and sang, *Barchi nafshi*, "My soul will bless God, and all of my insides will thank His holy name" (Psalm 103). He emerged from the womb and he looked upon the stars and their constellations and said, "Bless God, O His angels, strong warriors who fulfill His word..." (ibid.). He nursed from his mother and sang, "My soul, Bless God! Do not forget all the good that He did for you." This refers, according to Rav Avahu, to the placement of the body's repositories of milk at the place of wisdom [the heart]. He saw the fall of the wicked and he sang, "All sin will disappear from the earth, there will be no more sinners, my soul shall thank God. Hallelujah!" (Psalm 104). He looked at the day of death and sang, "My soul shall bless God, God my Lord, You are most exalted."

---

198. R. Tzadok Ha-Cohen of Lublin, *Sichas Malachei Ha-Shareis*, pgs. 46, 49.
199. The Hebrew word *piha*, "her mouth," can be divided to spell *pi heh*, "the mouth of the letter *heh*," whose *gematria* is five.

The five worlds David lived in correspond to the five spiritual universes and the five parts of the soul. The universe of *asiyah* produced *nefesh* and is felt through the physical performance of a Mitzvah. This was the world of his mother's womb. At this point all the child has is blood and simple physical existence. Looking at the stars was an emotional experience, it corresponds to the world of *yetzirah*, the place of angels where King David's *ruach* sang to God for the wonders that his heart sensed. Nursing from his mother was an experience akin to the world of *beriah* and the soul level of *neshamah*. Food contributes to intellectual understanding, and once the child nurses he or she begins to comprehend. The world of the fall of the wicked corresponds to the sense of *chayah* or an *atzilus*-like experience. In *atzilus* all is good; there is a loss of any bodily sensation. Thus witnessing how wickedness will dissipate and only good remains is an *atzilus*-like experience. David's day of death corresponds to *Adam Kadmon* and the world of *yechidah*; it was an absolute and total connection with God.[200]

The Part Equals the Sum of the Whole

In light of the Talmud's lesson that King David was describing the parts of his soul, why did his verses began with praise for *nefesh*? Shouldn't there have been a mention of the terms *ruach*, *neshamah*, *chayah*, and *yechidah*?

---

200. *Sichas Malachei Ha-Shareis*, Chapter 3. R. Tzadok Ha-Cohen in his book *Dover Tzedek* (pg. 6b) points out that the Talmud calculates that the average individual has twelve and a half years to dedicate to the service of God in his life. The reason for this number is the five parts of the soul. In Jewish law three years are needed to fully acquire title to an item. Each of us must fully acquire the level of *nefesh*, namely, all our deeds should be Mitzvos. We also must internalize the level of *ruach*, that all our feelings should be holy. We must reach the level of *neshamah*, all our thoughts saintly. And we must acquire the level of *chayah*, constant attachment to Heaven, and the level of *yechidah*, to completely lose all sense of self and to become fully one with the Almighty.

Therefore, man should need fifteen years of life to fully attain each level of soul. However, in the spiritual dimension, levels interlock. Once you reach the top of *asiyah*, you are already at the lowest rung in *yetzirah*. That is why once you complete two and a half years of acquisition for a particular level, you then progress to the next level. 2.5 times 5 equals 12.5, the years of life.

The spiritual domain reflects its maker—the single, united, Creator. A close examination of spiritual entities reveals unity. Thus in a broader sense, the soul has five parts and in a detailed sense, viz., if you look at each part, it too has five parts. There is a part of *nefesh* that is *nefesh*-like, called *nefesh de-nefesh*, *nefesh of nefesh*. Then there is a *ruach*-like part called *ruach de-nefesh*, the *ruach* dimension of *nefesh*, then *neshamah de-nefesh*, *chayah de-nefesh*, and *yechidah de-nefesh*.

Nefesh is expressed through action. Instinctual activity with no thought or feeling is *nefesh de-nefesh*. An act performed out of love for God is *ruach de-nefesh*. If one considers the laws of a Mitzvah while performing the good deed one might have accessed *neshamah de-nefesh*. If the good deed is performed with *deveikus*, with attachment to God, for instance, feeling that, "He is moving my hands as I shake the four species during Sukkos," it is *chayah de-nefesh*.

King David was primarily on a level of *nefesh*. That is why he thanked God for the soul parts as they appear within *nefesh*.[201]

DIFFERENT *HEH*'S

The Gaon of Vilna[202] uses the Talmud's explanation *Barchi nafshi* to explain the two instances where the letter *heh* in the traditional Torah text appears in unusual form. In Gen. 2:14 a small letter *heh* appears in the word *be-hibbaram*, "when they [heaven and earth] were created," and in Deut. 32:6 a large letter *heh* is written in the word *ha-la-Hashem*, "for God":

> The soul has qualities that resemble God's attributes. However, relative to God the soul can never reach holiness that truly resembles Him, for who can be compared to God? That is why

---

201. Ibid.
202. Rabbi Elijah of Vilna was one of the greatest geniuses of the modern era. He was born in 1720 and he passed away in 1797. Due to his brilliance, he is called, the "Gaon," literally, the "genius."

in Gen. 2:14 it says *be-hibbaram* [203] with a small *heh*, for the five human qualities are miniscule relative to the Divine's.[204] This explanation corresponds to the interpretation that God created the world with the letter *heh*.[205] There is another explanation to the word *be-hibbaram*. Its letters spell *be-Avraham*, and it teaches that God created the world due to Abraham's merit.[206] These five qualities [of soul] only existed in Abraham [the small size of the letter reflects the rarity of its attainment]. However the *heh* in the verse *ha-la-Hashem tigmalu zos*, "Will you do so before God?" (Deut. 32:6) is enlarged. For the five qualities of God are great in a manner that we cannot fully comprehend.[207]

God's five (His *heh*) are the five supernal universes. Man's five (his *heh*) are the five parts of the soul. The Gaon is teaching that God's universes are beyond our total grasp, and that only Abraham fully internalized all five soul parts.

To understand why only Abraham internalized the full complement of soul it is necessary to better understand the nature and source of *yechidah*, the soul's hidden voice.

---

203. The full verse reads, "These are the genealogies of Heaven and earth when they were created [*be-hibbaram*], on the day that God made earth and Heavens." The section then proceeds to detail the story of the creation of the first man. There are two classical interpretations for the unusual word *be-hibbaram*. One is that God created this world with the letter *heh*, the other is that He created the world for the sake of Abraham.
204. The *gematria* of the letter *heh* is five.
205. See further *Menachos* 29b.
206. See further *Bereishis Rabbah* 12.
207. *Imrei Noam, Berachos* 10a.

LESSON TWELVE

YECHIDAH: THE *PINTELE YID*

A JEWISH BILL of divorce is only valid if the husband willingly delivers it to his wife. If he is forced to write or send the document it cannot dissolve the marriage. Nevertheless, Maimonides rules that when a husband, ordered by the religious court to divorce his wife, refuses to obey, the court may send officers to hit the man until he mutters that he "wants" to divorce his wife. The Rabbis will then execute a divorce in his name.[208]

This ruling raises an inherent question. A coerced bill of divorce is meaningless. If the husband uttered the words, *rotzeh ani*, "I want to [fulfill the mandate of the court]," while being brutally beaten, how can the court accept that he meant what he said?

Maimonides[209] raises this question when formulating the law. He answers that in truth every Jew wants to fulfill the law of Torah and act in the moral way. Subconsciously the husband desired to give the bill of divorce. His evil inclination, however, coerced him and silenced the voice of virtue. The court enforcers with their blows merely silence the loud voices of his body. When the man croaks, "Stop hitting me! I want to," his inner voice is speaking and the bill of divorce is commissioned willingly.

Yechidah is the part of the soul that sends a voice to man stating, *rotzeh ani*, "I want to [fulfill the law of God]."

---

208. This law was also formulated in regards to sacrifices. Sacrifices are only effective if they were offered willingly. If a man is obligated by law to bring an offering and refuses to spend the money and offer the animal, the court can send enforcers to beat the sinner. Once he says, "I want to," they will bring a sacrifice in his name and he will receive forgiveness. See further Maimonides, *Mishneh Torah*, "The Laws of the Sacrifices" 14:16.

209. *Mishneh Torah*, "Laws of Divorce" 2:20.

Yechidah is the hidden part of the soul. Man himself is frequently unaware of it; it is a root motivation underlying much of one's conscious thought. It is deeper than the subconscious, and it is totally united with the Almighty. This soul part is completely pure and constantly advocates virtue.

In Psalms it is written, *Ve-od me'at ve-ain rasha*, which literally means, "A little bit [of time] and there will be no more evil" (Ps. 37:10). However, Chasidim interpret the verse to mean that within every person "there is a little bit that is not evil." Even when one commits many sins and it seems that the person is entirely corrupt there is a little bit that is faultless. A small part of the sinner always wanted and still desires holiness. This *od me'at*, "little bit," is the voice of the *yechidah*. In Yiddish, this is called the *pintele yid*, the small and indestructible Jewish spark of faith.

Isaiah proclaims, *Ve-ammeich kullam tzaddikim*, "[Members of] Your nation are all righteous" (Isa. 60:21). This verse is also understandable in the light of *yechidah*. Since every Jew at his or her deepest level wants to serve God, from that perspective he or she never wanted to perform any sins and is completely saintly. Based on *yechidah*, all of Jewry is guaranteed a portion of eternal reward united in the perfect fellowship of pure virtue and total observance.[210]

The Secret of Lashes

Rava said,

> Most people are so foolish! They stand in the presence of the Torah scroll yet they do not rise to honor the Torah scholar. [The Torah scholar's power is greater than the scroll for] in the scroll it is written that the court will punish the sinner with forty lashes, and the Rabbis [using the tools for interpreting the Torah text] taught that the maximum amount of lashes is thirty-nine.[211]

Rava's point seems to be that Torah scholars are greater than the Torah scroll, for Torah scholars have the power to interpret the Biblical text in

---

210. See further *Sanhedrin* 90a.
211. *Makkos* 22b.

ways that override the literal meaning. There are numerous examples where Rabbis of the Talmud reveal non-literal meanings of Biblical verses. Why did Rava feel that the lesson of thirty-nine lashes instead of forty was the most inspiring?

Lashes are administered by the court to a Jew who openly and brazenly disregards the admonition of witnesses and violates one of the Mitzvos. Why did the Torah seem to require forty blows? Nachmanides explains that forty is the number of days for the formation of a child. According to the Talmud, every human body is formed during the first forty days after conception.[212] The sinner has defiled every aspect of his person so he deserves forty lashes. Furthermore, the Torah was first taught to Moses, while he was atop Mt. Sinai, over forty days. Forty blows symbolize that the sinner has defiled the entire Torah with his brazen disregard for its statutes.

The reason why it takes forty days to create a child is that there are four primary supernal universes, *atzilus*, *beriah*, *yetzirah*, and *asiyah*, that correspond to the letters of God's ineffable name: *yud*, *heh*, *vav*, and *heh*. Each universe has ten levels within it, for God created the world with ten statements,[213] each of which appears in a different form in each universe. For the fetus's body to develop, its soul must first travel through forty stops, four universes with ten levels to each. Hence forty days of formation, for on each day a different level of soul is received. The Torah's multiple layers of meaning were redacted over forty days, so that Moses would understand forty levels of Divine Thought, and every level of Moses' soul and personality would be filled with Torah thought.

The greatness of Torah sages is that they revealed the existence of a hidden voice within the Jew. They taught that even the sinner who proclaimed, "I am sinning even though I know that it violates God's command," is not all bad. He did not defile every day of his formation. He may have seemed to sully all the letters of God's name, but in truth he did not dirty the crown atop the *yud*, the fortieth level, the highest

---

212. Prior to the fortieth day, the developing child is legally considered mere fluid. After the fortieth day it is an embryo and at least a partial life.
213. *Rosh Hashanah* 32a; *Bereishis Rabbah* 17:1. See further *Zohar Vayikra* 11:2, and *Emunas Etecha, Parashas Nitzavim 5758*.

point.[214] The apex stayed pure, and one voice within him always sought sanctity. That day of his formation, or innermost point in his soul, did not agree to the misdeed. This point, colloquially called a *pintele yid* always advocates sanctity. Take the inner voice into account when judging the sinner, and as a result he only deserves a maximum of thirty-nine lashes.

For Rava, this lesson is the most impressive example of Rabbinics because it guarantees hope and consolation. Never feel that you are all bad. That is impossible. There is always at least a small voice of good within.[215]

A superficial glance at the sinner would not see his innermost voice. One who only sees the externals would say that the sinner has fully desecrated his being and deserves forty lashes. Fortunately, God is never superficial. God probes deeply to find merit. In His compassion, God takes the innermost voice into account and declares that the sinner only deserves thirty-nine lashes.

The Torah requires that man emulate His Maker. God hears the innermost voice. Likewise, man should always seek to view others in light of their innermost voice. Noah successfully thought about the hidden good within people. That is why Noah rebuked in the softest and gentlest terms, for no sinner was a demon in his eyes.[216]

There is a Rabbinic custom that when meting out the punishment of lashes the following verse is recited three times: *Ve-hu rachum yichapper avon ve-lo yashchis ve-hirbah le-hashiv appo ve-lo yair kol chamaso*, "And He the Compassionate One will atone for sin and not destroy, He will repeatedly overcome His rage and He will not reveal the full measure of his fury" (Ps. 78:38).

The verse has thirteen Hebrew words. Through threefold repetition a total of thirty-nine words are recited. Perhaps this custom is an expression of the following thought. The sinner seemingly deserved forty lashes, but due to the Almighty's compassion God looked deeply

---

214. Since the supernal realm is constructed as a chain, the highest level of *atzilus* is really also the lowest level of *Adam Kadmon*. Thus the highest point of *chayah* is the lowest level of *yechidah*. This point, the *yechidah* within man, or the world of *Adam Kadmon* within each of us, cannot be defiled. See further *Ma'or Va-Shemesh, Parashas Yisro*.

215. See further *Emunas Etecha, Parashas Ha'azinu 5757*, and *Shem Mi-Shmuel, Parashas Noach* pg. 85 s.v. *be-Zohar ha-kadosh*.

216. See further *Mishbetzos Zahav* on *Parashas Noach*.

and acknowledged the voice of *yechidah*, and the sinner is only to receive thirty-nine blows.[217]

THIRTY-NINE INSTEAD OF FORTY

In addition to *malkos*, "lashes," there are several other instances in Jewish thought and history where the number forty plays an important role.

1) When the Jews were about to enter the Land of Israel, spies were sent to scout out the terrain. They returned after forty days and delivered a devastating report. They claimed that the land was inhospitable and its indigenous nations unconquerable. The people believed the scandalous spies and they cried and complained. As a result of the lack of faith in God's promises to give them the land, God punished the Jewish nation and declared that they would spend forty years in the desert as a punishment for the forty-day mission of sin that the spies carried out.[218] However, it emerges from the writings of the Tosafos[219] that in the fortieth year nobody died. In the end, Jews only died for thirty-nine years.

---

217. The scriptural source for the punishment of lashes contains a warning prohibiting excessive punishment. "He should be hit forty times, no more, lest you increase the amount of blows over these a great deal and your brother will then be embarrassed before you" (Deut. 25:3). Since the Rabbinic tradition revealed that the real limit is thirty-nine blows, the verse is referring to the fortieth blow, warning that forty blows is *makkah rabbah*, excessive. The *gematria* of *makkah rabbah* (65+207=272) is the same as the value of the words *ve-hu rachum* (18+254=272). This indicates that the compassion of God (represented by the words *ve-hu rachum*) is the reason for the liberal definition of *makkah rabbah*.

The Torah introduces the law of flogging with, *im bin hakkos ha-rasha*, "If the guilty party has incurred the penalty of lashes" (Deut. 25:2). The *gematria* of *im bin hakkos ha-rasha* (41+52+431+575=1099) is the same *gematria* as *nefesh, ruach, neshamah, chayah, yechidah* (430+214+395+23+37=1099). This is an indication of the lesson mentioned above. At the moment of flogging all the parts of the soul appear, the blows are then reduced, since the pure *yechidah* is present (*Emunas Etecha*, 5757, pg. 7).

218. See further Numbers 13-15.

219. See further Tosafos at the end *of Ta'anis* s.v. *yom she-bo kalu meisei midbar.*

This historical event is another example of the power of *yechidah*. It seemed that the spies were all evil. It appeared that the Jewish nation was fully complicit in the sin of the spies, and it was decreed that the generation of the desert would die over forty years. However once the fortieth year was reached, *yechidah* was revealed. God looked at the deepest desires and saw that in the innermost recesses there had been a will to be good. Due to the revelation of *yechidah*, in the fortieth year all the Jews were deemed righteous and the community suffered no further punishment.

2) As a result of Adam's sin (eating from the Tree of Knowledge of Good and Evil), he was punished with the world, receiving thirty-nine curses. Due to these curses, there are thirty-nine primary categories of *melachah*—creative work, which parallel the curses. These types of work are performed during the six days of the week and are prohibited on Shabbos.

There should have been forty curses, and the Sabbath too should have been a day of work, yet God looked at Adam's voice of *yechidah*. He saw that within Adam there had always been regrets and a desire to withstand the temptation of the Tree of Knowledge. Shabbos represents the fortieth level. On Shabbos there are blessings, not curses; therefore, no *melachah*. Shabbos returns man to an Eden-like existence.

In our lives we may sink spiritually through our involvement in our mundane activities of this world, the thirty-nine *melachos*. On Shabbos, though, we hit the fortieth level, and we are then liberated from the universe of toil.[220]

3) Yom Kippur is the day of revealed *yechidah*.[221] Rabbi Shraga Feivel Mendelovitz, of blessed memory, would tell his students that on Yom Kippur every Jew has to touch the level of *yechidah* that they have within them for at least one moment.

---

220. See further *Emunas Etecha* (ibid.) and *Shem Mi-Shmuel, Parashas Noach* pg. 85 s.v. *ve-hinneh*.
221. See Lesson Two, where the lesson of the *Sefer Yetzirah* of *olam, shanah*, and *nefesh* was explained.

Why is Yom Kippur connected to *yechidah*? According to some, we are to begin blowing the shofar, which awakens man to repentance,[222] on the first day of the Rosh Chodesh, New Moon festival, of the Hebrew month *Elul*.[223] The shofar is then blown every day after that until Yom Kippur.[224] Yom Kippur is thus the fortieth day after we began to remind ourselves of the need to repent. On the fortieth day there is a revelation of *yechidah*—the innermost will.

Generally, touching *yechidah* is only possible for the very righteous. However, on the fortieth day, through rigorous prayer and repentance, everyone can touch it. That is why Rabbi Mendelovitz said that every Jew is obligated to reach his personal level of *yechidah* on Yom Kippur.[225]

222. See further Maimonides' *Mishneh Torah*, "Laws of Return."
223. *Elul* has a two-day Rosh Chodesh. Blowing the shofar on the first of the two days means that one is blowing on the last day in the Hebrew month of *Av*.
224. Twenty-nine days in *Elul* and nine days in *Tishrei*.
225. Perhaps the most appropriate moment to reach *yechidah*, the fifth part of the soul, is during *Ne'ilah*, the final prayer of Yom Kippur, which is the fifth prayer of the day (ZR).

The Purim holiday that celebrates Jews being miraculously saved from a genocidal decree in the Persian Kingdom is also a day of *yechidah*. The *Zohar* links Purim to Yom Kippur, stating that the Day of Atonement is a *yom ke-purim*, "a day like Purim." The name Purim is a derivative of the term *pur*, "lot," for Haman cast lots to decide when to kill the Jews. Yom Kippur as well is a time of lots, as the key ceremony that creates atonement is one in which the High Priest draws lots to determine which goat is a sacrifice and which is sent to the desert.

On Yom Kippur the innermost will is revealed through a mortification of the flesh, on Purim it is revealed through indulgence of intoxicating alcohol that causes the innate essence of an individual to emerge. The symbolism of drawing a lot and then sending a goat out into the wilderness represents that our sins are not our essence, our sins are our external voices. The innermost "I" is a sacrifice to God, fully committed to His service. This concept transcends logic, hence the lots, a trans-logical means of decision making. Purim too is a day that celebrates the innate nature of a Jew that is fully committed to God, which is why its name is *Lots*.

In fact, the reason why the Talmud requires that the Purim reveler drink alcohol to the depths of a stupor is that the light of *yechidah* is shining on this day. The light of the *yechidah* is far beyond our world, which is why *tzaddikim* would get drunk in order to be able to contain such a powerful life force. Most of us, however, do not sense the light of *yechidah* as it comes to our world. That is why it is inappropriate for us to drink excessively on Purim.

4) According to Jewish law, many forms of ritual impurity are removed by means of fully immersing oneself in a *mikveh*, the immersion pool. A *mikveh* is a gathering of forty *seah* (a Talmudic liquid measure, approximately two gallons) of pure water (either rainwater or spring water that has not been transported in a man-made vessel). The purifying quality of a *mikveh* is *yechidah*. Once one is covered by the fortieth *seah* of water, the fortieth level of the soul, the *yechidah*, is awakened. At that point there was never sin or misdeed, resulting in purification.[226]

THE DEEPER MEANING OF RETURN

Yechidah causes a redefinition of the concept of *teshuvah*, "repentance" or "return." It is generally assumed that sin distances man from God, and *teshuvah* is the process through which man returns to stand before God. However in light of the above, *teshuvah* is not a return to God, rather it is primarily a return to oneself. Once you reconnect with your innermost self, you find yourself in the presence of God.

Even the sinner has an inner point—his *yechidah*—that is perfectly righteous. *Teshuvah* is when he returns to this inner essence and allows it to influence the rest of his personality. Perhaps this is the meaning of the verse, *Ve-hasheivosa el levavecha* (Deut. 30:1), which is literally translated, "Take it to heart," but it may also mean, "Return to your heart."[227]

The Talmud, in *Megillah* 12a, relates a discussion between Rabbi Shimon bar Yochai and his students as to why the Jews of that era were deserving of a genocidal decree. "They bowed to an idol," Rashbi taught, "Yet since they only did it in an insincere manner, since at their essential core they desired to serve God fully, the decree against them turned out to be hollow as well." Purim came about because God looked at the essential core of the Jew, saw his pure intentions, and therefore forgave (Rav Wolfson). See further *Pachad Yitzchak, Purim, Ma'amarim* 6, 8, and 11.

226. Rabbi Tzvi Elimelech of Dinov, the author of the work *Bnei Yissachar*, explained that the days of repentance (the month of *Elul* and the first ten days of *Tishrei*) are in fact a *mikveh* in the dimension of time. Yom Kippur as the fortieth day is the fortieth *seah*, the water that fully covers the body. On that day we are fully immersed in holiness, which results in forgiveness and spiritual cleansing. See further *Emunas Etecha, Parashas Ha'azinu 5757, Shem Mi-Shmuel, Mo'adim* pg. 103 s.v. *be-midrash*.

227. See further *Noam Elimelech, Parashas Vaeschanan,* s.v. *hishamer lecha*, who writes, "A person should constantly consider his Heavenly soul... for if he does not know himself he will definitely not know the Almighty."

The Talmud teaches that when Rabbi Alexandry would complete his prayers he would say:

Master of all worlds! You know that our will is to fulfill Your Will. Who prevents us from listening to our will? The leaven in the bread [a symbol of the evil inclination] and the yoke of foreign governments [who enact decrees prohibiting Jewish practices]. Please save us from their hands and we will return to serve you with full hearts.[228]

Here too is a Talmudic reference to *yechidah*. *Yechidah* is "our will that desires to fulfill Your will."

One of the ways to calculate a *gematria* is to turn each letter into a word (the name of the letter) and calculate the numeric value of the "filled out" word. For example, the word *lev* (heart) in its filled out form would be *lamed, mem, dalet*, and then *bet, yud, tav*.

The filled out form of *lev* (74+412=486) equals the phrase, *Veammeich kullam tzaddikim*, "And your entire nation is righteous" (136+96+254=486). For in the depths of the heart, once you fully fill out the heart, the entire nation is righteous.

Yom Kippur is the day of return, when Jews are to return to their innermost will. The *gematria* of the phrase *rotzeh ani*, "I want to," (301+61=362) is the same as the term Yom Kippur[229] (56+306=362).[230]

Lessons Thirteen and Fourteen will further clarify the power of the *yechidah* soul part.

---

228. *Berachos* 17a.
229. If *kippur* is spelled with a *yud* (כיפור).
230. *Emunas Etecha, Parashas Ha'azinu* 5757.

Lesson Thirteen

Yechidah and Love of Fellow Jews

Love of fellow Jews is one of the most important principles of the Torah. Unfortunately, such love is a difficult task. Thinking about *yechidah*, the hidden innate virtue each soul harbors, enables this love. Frequently, we are alienated from each other due to judgementalism. We decide that others are sinners or that we are better than they are, and as a result we do not love them. If we would truly internalize the fact that every Jew has a point of *yechidah*, if we would look at them and only see their *yechidah*, we would have to respect and adore them, for they would be perfectly righteous.

There were righteous individuals who insisted on seeing the *yechidah* part in their fellow Jews and as a result only saw goodness in their Jewish brethren.

Rabbi Levi Yitzchak of Berditchev once saw a man smoking a cigar on Yom Kippur. The Rabbi approached the Jew and said, "Perhaps you are unaware, but today is the holiest day of the year when we Jews are not supposed to light fires."

The man responded, "I know that today is Yom Kippur."

Rabbi Levi Yitzchak then said, "Perhaps you do not realize that you have a cigar in your mouth?"

The man answered, "I know that today is the holiest day and that I should not smoke, but I like smoking."

Rabbi Levi Yitzchak then turned to Heaven and said, "God, see how holy your children are! They know that You do not approve of their smoking on the holy day. Yet they will not lie."

It is told of R. Levi Yitzchak that he never allowed visiting preachers to address his congregation. These itinerant speakers were wont to rebuke the general populace. The Berditchever felt that we may not mention any sins about the Jewish people, for Israel has no sins. Once a preacher came and promised not to say anything negative. In the middle of his speech he got carried away and started to criticize the community for its failings. At that point the Rabbi interjected, "God, don't believe him. He is only saying that because he gets paid for his sermon. He has no credibility!"[231]

Rabbi Levi Yitzchak would serve as the cantor for the High Holiday prayers. One year, he returned home after Yom Kippur and burst into unceasing sobs.

"Woe to you, Levi Yitzchak!" He screamed. "What did you do? Today you recited, *Chatu, avu, pashu amcha Yisrael*, 'Your nation Israel sinned, transgressed, and was iniquitous.' What Lies! Can you find any sins amongst the Jews?"[232]

The former Belzer Rebbe, Rabbi Aharon Rokeach, of blessed memory,[233] was once told that Jews in secular Kibbutzim in the holy land were raising pigs. The Rebbe immediately responded, "These Jews are so holy, they are certain that the Messiah is coming soon. According to the *Zohar* when the Messiah will come there will be a part of pig that will become kosher (the pig's nature will change, and it will then chew its cud). These people are preparing the pigs in honor of Messiah's imminent arrival."[234]

---

231. *Ma'asei Hashem* pg. 138.
232. *Imros Tzaddikim*, Klausenberg, pg. 196 number seven.
233. He was born in 1880 and passed away in 1958. The Belzer Rebbe was very attached to the legacy of Rabbi Levi Yitzchak of Berditchev. Like Rabbi Levi Yitzchak, he constantly found merit in the deeds of Jews. When the Rebbe of Boston, Rabbi Levi Yitzchak Horowitz, met with the Belzer Rebbe, R. Aharon asked him for his name. He responded, "Levi Yitzchak ben Sarah Sasha." When the Belzer Rebbe heard those words, he gripped Rabbi Horowitz's hand a little tighter, and his entire body began to shake. After a long while he again asked, "What is your name?" Rabbi Horowitz did not understand the commotion over his name. The Belzer Chasidim then explained to him that his name, Levi Yitzchak ben Sarah Sasha, was identical to the name of Rabbi Levi Yitzchak of Berditchev. The Belzer Rebbe felt a great attachment to Rabbi Levi Yitzchak, so when he heard the name he was deeply moved (*Admorei Belz*, Volume 4, pg. 132).
234. *Admorei Belz*, Volume 4, pg. 138.

Yechidah leads to a sense of love, unity, and equality among all Jews. Feelings of love, unity, and fellowship with all other Jews lift an individual up to reach the *yechidah* within his or her soul and to hear its voice in a clearer manner.

There is a custom that before the performance of any Mitzvah, a statement of intent is recited. The statement, called *Le-sheim Yichud*, declares that the act will be performed because God commanded it, and through this act more holiness will fill the world. The introduction closes with a phrase that declares, "this deed is being performed *be-sheim kol Yisrael*, in the name of all of Israel." R. Elimelech of Lizhensk[235] explained this custom in light of *yechidah*:

The reason why we say before all of our service to God and our prayers *Le-sheim Yichud* [and conclude with] *be-sheim kol Yisrael* is that there is no man who has no flaws. Therefore how can we perform a service of holiness with our limbs? We have performed sins with these same body parts and they have been damaged [spiritually], so how can we cause the holiness of a Mitzvah act to reside on our grossly impure physical body? The solution to this is joining the collective of Israel. There is a spiritual universe named *Kol Yisrael*, "All of Israel." This universe is pristine and cannot be defiled through sin. The collective of Israel are all *tzaddikim*, as in the verse, *Ve-ammeich kullam tzaddikim.* Therefore, even if individuals sin at times, the community of Israel maintains its sanctity, and there is no evil within it. This [universe] is called in the holy books, *Adam Kadmon*, and there, sin has no authority. Man connects himself to that transcendent holiness through feelings of fellowship with the entire community. Therefore, before the Mitzvah, connect yourself to that world, be filled with radiant holiness, and then you will be able to perform a Mitzvah.[236]

235. Rabbi Elimelech was born in 1717, and he passed away in 1787. He was one of the great students of the Maggid of Mezeritch, and he brought Chasidic practice to Poland and Hungary.
236. *Noam Elimelech, Parashas Devarim*, s.v. *od ba-pasuk hana"l*. Rabbi Aharon Belzer would encourage his Chasidim to follow the words of the *Noam Elimelech* and perform good deeds for the sake of all of Israel so that the entirety of the Torah would be fulfilled by the entirety of Israel.

As we learned in Lesson Twelve, Yom Kippur is the day of *yechidah*. The author of the *Tanya* found a hint to *yechidah* in the verse about Yom Kippur. Yom Kippur is described in the Torah as the day of spiritual purification, *Ki ba-yom ha-zeh yechapper aleichem mi-kol avonoseichem lifnei Hashem tit'haru*, "For on this day He will atone for all of your sins, before Y-H-V-H, God, you will become pure" (Lev. 16:30). The *Tanya* explained this verse to mean that the purity you will receive will come from before the Tetragrammaton, from the apex of the *yud*, from the point before the first letter, from the level of *yechidah*.

Since Yom Kippur is a day of reaching *yechidah*, is it any wonder that Rabbi Yosef Karo records a law that on the eve of Yom Kippur all Jews should ask forgiveness from each other and bond together in love and unity?[237]

There are only several laws in *Orach Chaim* Chapter 606, and perhaps *yechidah* is their common denominator. This chapter records that prior to Yom Kippur one is obligated to patch up relations with all those whom one may have slighted or hurt during the prior year. He instructs how to ask forgiveness from the deceased. Finally, he teaches that there is a custom to immerse oneself in a *mikveh*, a ritual bath, and to undergo thirty-nine symbolic lashes prior to Yom Kippur. As mentioned earlier, the thirty-nine lashes and the *mikveh* represent the fortieth level—the point of *yechidah*. Perhaps the law of asking forgiveness is also to enable

---

The Rebbe once heard that an individual had discovered a lost object and was about to return it to its owner. He then requested, "Please return the object with the express intent that the Mitzvah of *hashavas aveidah* is being performed for the sake of all the members of Israel." The Rebbe then explained that not everyone merits fulfilling the Mitzvah of returning lost objects, for some Jews never merit to find the lost object of another Jew. Therefore, there are probably some Jews who are missing this Mitzvah; for the sake of helping all Jews, this Mitzvah should be performed for the sake of all of Israel (*Admorei Belz*, Volume 4, pg. 119).

237. On Purim as well there is a special obligation to unite the members of the Jewish people. On Purim union is achieved through the obligation of sending gifts to fellow Jews, thus bonding each one to the other. Esther asked Mordechai to gather all the Jews together to pray that her mission to the king succeed. Perhaps Esther realized that there was a need for an arousal of *yechidah* to save the nation; that is why she asked that all Jews come together and pray for her.

attaining *yechidah*. For only through a sense of oneness with all Jews can *yechidah* be accessed.[238]

The Aftermath of Yom Kippur

A mere five days after the holiday of Yom Kippur, Jews celebrate the holiday of Sukkos. During Sukkos we have the opportunity to lift the four species.[239] On each day during the seven-day holiday, four species of agricultural products[240] are lifted and waved around in praise to the Almighty. Rabbi Isaac Luria taught that these four species represent the four letters of God's name. The *hadas*, "myrtle branches," represent the *yud*. And the *aravos*, "willow branches," represent the letter *heh*. The *lulav*, "palm branch," represents the *vav*. The *esrog*, "citron," is the final *heh*. Bringing all four species together is a symbolic unification of God's name and a symbolic discovery of the Divine in all realms. Waving the four species in all directions indicates that God's name fills all the

---

238. *Emunas Etecha, Parashas Ha'azinu* 5757. Rav Wolfson also notes that 606 (the number of the chapter) is the sum of the phrase, *Be-rachamim gedolim akabtzech*, "I will gather you in with great compassion" (300+93+213=606). The final redemption will cause a revelation of *yechidah*, and it is God's compassion that causes Him to consider the *yechidah* within the soul. Perhaps that is why the chapter of the laws of *yechidah* equals *be-rachamim gedolim akabtzech*. It is God's great love and compassion that cause Him to acknowledge the *yechidah* within man, and He will reveal that good to man during the ultimate redemption.

239. The four species are a palm branch, three myrtle branches, two willow branches and the citron fruit.

240. See further *Horeb*, Chapter 31. Rabbi Hirsch explains that the four species represent the different parts of the natural world. The willow is plain wood that does not have a special scent or taste; it represents those items in nature that are merely raw materials, and human effort is needed to transform them into something useful. The palm branch represents food without smell, namely items in nature that have inherent benefit to man, yet he must expend some effort to release that benefit. Food is the symbol of these items for most food must be processed out of its natural form (e.g., grinding wheat to produce bread). The myrtle branches have a beautiful smell but have no taste. They represent the parts of nature that are perfectly suited for human consumption even without any human effort. Air, sweet smelling roses, and water are prime examples of those parts of nature that provide benefit to man even before he changes them at all. The citron fruit represents total perfection as it is both a food and a fragrance.

dimensions of reality, and the Almighty can be found everywhere.[241] This raises a question; the letters in God's name parallel the parts of the soul, and there are really five parts of the soul, for there is also *yechidah*. *Yechidah* is represented by the apex of the *yud*. What part of the four species parallels the apex of the *yud* and the *yechidah* part of the soul?

On Yom Kippur each Jew discovers within himself a bit of his personal *yechidah*, and Sukkos is a continuation of Yom Kippur.[242] On

---

241. See further *Innerspace* pg. 109.

242. See further *Horeb* 23:170. Rabbi Hirsch points out that Yom Kippur has two qualities: *kapparah* (atonement) and *taharah* (purification). The day brings atonement—namely a defense against physical punishment due the sinner—and purification—spiritual cleansing of the soul that was sullied with sin. Sukkos and its concluding holiday of Shemini Atzeres emerge from these two qualities. Sukkos is a celebration of physical survival and completes *kapparah*; Shemini Atzeres is a celebration of spiritual survival and thus completes *taharah*.

See further the Vilna Gaon's commentary to Song of Songs 1:4, s.v. *ve-daled pesukim elu*, and *Avodas Ha-Gershuni* on Song of Songs 3:4, s.v. *ve-shamati mi-dodi ha-gaon he-chasid me-vilna*. The Gaon answers the *Tur*'s question why the holiday of Sukkos, meant to commemorate the clouds of glory with which Israel exited Egypt, is observed during *Tishrei* and not *Nisan*, the time of the Exodus. He explains that the full exit from Egypt was when the Jews merited having the Divine presence (the *Shechinah*) among them. Initially they had the Divine presence, and the intimate relationship between Creator and His children was symbolized by Heavenly clouds that surrounded the people. However, once the nation worshipped the Golden Calf (on 17 *Tammuz*), Moses broke the stone tablets of the commandments, the Almighty distanced Himself, and the clouds disappeared. The people engaged in a massive *teshuvah* campaign that started on the first day of *Elul*. They prayed for thirty-nine days, and on the fortieth they fasted. God forgave them, and on the fortieth day Moses returned to the people with a second set of tablets. Ever since then, the fortieth day (Yom Kippur) became a day of fasting, prayer, and forgiveness (*Pirkei de-Rabbi Eliezer*). To complete the process of forgiveness and Divine reconciliation, on Yom Kippur Moses told the people that God had commanded the erection of a sanctuary. Its construction and inauguration would bring the Divine Presence into the camp for a permanent stay. On 11 *Tishrei* an appeal for gifts needed to construct the sanctuary was made. On the twelfth and thirteenth, the people brought all the raw materials necessary for the building. On the fourteenth, Moses announced that the community had donated sufficient materials and no further donations were needed, and he apportioned raw materials to different craftsmen. On the fifteenth, the construction began and the Divine presence returned. Thus, the fifteenth of Tishrei is the day when we celebrate the return of the clouds of

Yom Kippur each Jew touches the depths of his or her heart (*yechidah*). On Sukkos, the apex of the *yud* is the heart of the Jew that joins the four species in completing God's name.

This may be an added meaning to the verse about the four species. The Torah writes, *U-lekachtem lachem ba-yom ha-rishon*, "And you should take for yourselves on the first day...." Perhaps it also means take yourself along with the species, for the depths of your soul complete God's name.[243]

There are five books in the Torah: Genesis, Exodus, Leviticus, Numbers, and Deuteronomy. Rabbi Isaac Luriah taught that these books parallel the parts of the Tetragrammaton. Genesis is from the apex of the *yud*, Exodus the *yud*, Leviticus the first *heh*, Numbers the *vav*, and Deuteronomy the last *heh*. Genesis deals with the foundation of the Jewish people, with our patriarchs, and it does not detail many laws that we must obey. Our patriarchs are the source of the apex of the *yud* within every Jewish heart. The other books of the Torah that deal with law can be violated and defiled, just as other parts of the soul can be sullied. But the book of Genesis cannot be harmed, and the *yechidah* within can hardly ever be silenced.

We begin reading Genesis at the end of Sukkos during the holiday of Simchas Torah. Perhaps it is due to our having reached *yechidah* on Yom Kippur, and then having further grasped *yechidah* throughout Sukkos while waving the four species, that allows us to learn the book of Genesis that also parallels the apex of the *yud* and *yechidah*.[244]

---

glory. It emerges from this analysis that Sukkos is really a celebration of the completion of the forgiveness attained on Yom Kippur. See further *Zeman Simchaseinu*, Article 1.

243. *Emunas Etecha, Shemini Atzeres*, 5757.

244. Ibid. Rav Wolfson also suggested that the phrase, *Nagil ve-nasis be-zos ha-Torah*, "We will rejoice and celebrate with this Torah," which is sung on Simchas Torah, may be referring to *yechidah*. After having expressed the inner love that is within us, we rejoice. Pointing to our heart we shout, "This Torah is right in our bosom, how fortunate we are!"

YECHIDAH AND THE FUTURE

The Talmud states:

> Ula Biraa taught a lesson in the name of Rabbi Elazar: In the future
> the Almighty will arrange a dancing ring for the righteous in the
> Garden of Eden, and God will sit in their midst. Each and every
> one of the righteous will point with his finger [at the Divine]. This
> is the meaning of the verse, "And it will be said on that day, here
> is this God of ours, we placed our hope in Him and He saved us.
> This is God whom we have hoped for, let us celebrate and rejoice
> in His salvation."

What is the symbolic meaning of all the righteous around a circle with
God in the center? R. Tzadok Ha-Cohen of Lublin explained that in a
circle each point along the circumference is equidistant to the center.
A circle of righteous individuals with God in the center symbolizes
total equality. There will be no distinctions among the righteous in the
World-to-Come. Each one at his point on the circle will be as close to
God as all the other righteous individuals.

This equality stems from a revelation of *yechidah*. At the level of
yechidah, everyone is perfectly righteous. In the future, God will reveal
the *yechidah* within each and every one of the righteous, thus they will
be equals in the fellowship of virtue.[245]

Another image that the Rabbis use for the final glory is found in the
Talmud in *Berachos* 17a:

> Rav would regularly say: the World-to-Come is not like this world.
> In the World-to-Come there is neither eating nor drinking; no
> procreation and no business dealings; there is no jealousy and

---

245. Chasidim have a tradition that the Messiah will be an individual who
will find good in every Jew. He will reveal how each Jew, even the seemingly
complete sinner, is really extremely righteous. Through finding merit for every
Jew, he will return all the Jews to observance and bring about the redemptive
era and its blessings (*Admorei Belz*, Volume 4, pg. 132, quoting the work *Pe'er
La-Yesharim*).

no hatred, no hate nor competition. Rather the righteous sit with their crowns in their heads and they enjoy the glow of the Divine Presence [*Shechinah*].

This may also be a reference to *yechidah*. The future world will be a permanent Yom Kippur, which is why there will be no eating or drinking. Yom Kippur is the day we touch *yechidah*. In the next world we will be fully attached to *yechidah*, and that is the meaning of the crowns in the head. *Chayah* and *yechidah* are parts of the soul that are *makkifin*. They are not internalized within the person; rather they envelope him. They are symbolized as crowns since a crown sits atop the head and is not in the person. In the World-to-Come the crowns of the righteous will be **in** their heads, for *chayah* and *yechidah* will be internalized. We will then completely and permanently express these levels.[246]

Lesson Fourteen will explain why every Jew has a *yechidah* part of the soul.

---

246. *Innerspace* pg. 18 in the name of Rabbi Nachman of Breslov (*Likkutei Moharan* 21:4).

LESSON FOURTEEN

THE SOURCE OF *YECHIDAH*

WHY DO JEWS have a hidden inner voice that loves God, believes in the Divine, and always pulls a Jew toward virtue?

We are all descendants of our father Abraham, who was completely permeated with love of God. Abraham willingly sacrificed all he had for the sake of fulfilling God's directive. Even before Abraham had spoken with God, he willingly gave his life in defense of monotheism.[247] Abraham transformed his personality so that he was totally connected to the Almighty.

It was at the moment of his final trial of faith[248] that he fully internalized the level of *yechidah*. That is why his last test mentioned the word *yechidah*: *Kach na es bincha es* **Yechidcha**, "Please take your son, your only one, and offer him as a complete offering" (Gen 22:2).

Abraham had waited one hundred years for the birth of Isaac, the son who was suitable for the continuation of Abraham's mission. When

---

247. See *Shem Mi-Shmuel, Parashas Lech Lecha* pg. 86 s.v. *be-midrash rabbah*. The Rebbe of Sochatshov explained that the Midrash compares Abraham's jumping into the furnace in Ur Casdim to the sacrifice of Chananya, Mishael and Azaryah (see Daniel 3) because both had no hope of salvation. Abraham had never seen a supernatural miracle, and when he was willing to give his life in defense of his monotheistic beliefs he did so without the slightest hope of miraculous intervention. Chananya, Mishael, and Azaryah also fully gave their lives when they entered a blaze instead of bowing to Nebuchadnezzar's idol, for they had been told by Ezekiel the prophet that God was not about to miraculously save them. Thus Abraham and Chananya, Mishael, and Azaryah represent the most perfect examples of total dedication to God.

248. Abraham was tested with ten trials of faith. For the final test, God commanded that Abraham bind his son Isaac to the altar and offer him as a sacrifice. See further *Ethics of the Fathers* 5:3 and Genesis 22.

the Almighty asked for the sacrifice of Isaac, He was requesting that Abraham take all of his dreams and hopes and sacrifice them joyously for God. Abraham was not to merely give up his most beloved son; he was to perform this task with ecstatic joy, devotion, and a sense of connection to the Divine.[249] Abraham fulfilled the challenge. Despite losing all sense of spiritual inspiration,[250] Abraham reached to his depths and performed the binding of Isaac with joy. As a result *yechidah* entered him fully.[251] In Abraham, *yechidah* was an *or penimi* (inner light) and not merely an *or makkif* (a transcendent light). Our patriarch bequeathed this level of soul to all of his descendants—the Jewish people.

The inner point within every Jew, in which he or she believes in God and loves God, is a genetic inheritance from Abraham, and God Himself protects this point and does not allow it to be sullied and destroyed. In the prayer liturgy, the Divine protection of the *pintele yid*, the small spark of faith, is appreciated in the first blessing of the silent devotions. The first blessing of the silent *Shemoneh Esreh* prayer thanks God for serving as the Shield of Abraham. The blessing is not merely thanking God for having protected Abraham in the ancient pagan world; according to the *Chiddushei Ha-Rim*, it is an offering of thanks to God for protecting the piece of Abraham that is within each and every one of us.

Generally, *yechidah* is a hidden voice, an innermost point, while in Abraham it was revealed because his entire personality was *yechidah*. Abraham was the first individual to internalize *yechidah*. This is the meaning of the Vilna Gaon's teaching that the small *heh* in the word *be-hibbaram* teaches that only Abraham (and *tzaddikim* like him) had all five levels of soul. Others might hear *yechidah* on special occasions, but they have not fully internalized it within.

---

249. God never told Abraham where to offer Isaac. Abraham, as a result, had to be in a state of mind that would allow for prophecy in order to hear from God where to bind his son. A prophet must be overwhelmed with ecstatic joy in order to commune with the Divine. Since Abraham had to be ready for prophecy, God was demanding from him ecstatic joy. See further *Shem Mi-Shmuel, Mo'adim* pg. 13.

250. It is written, *Va-yar es ha-makom me-rachok*, "He saw the place from afar" (Gen. 22:4). The *Zohar* explains that *ha-makom* is really a reference to God. Abraham saw God from a distance because he lost all sense of inspired spirituality.

251. *Shem Mi-Shmuel, Mo'adim*, pg. 13.

THE HIDDEN LOVE

Abraham was filled with *ahavah*, love of holiness. He loved humanity, Jewry, and most of all, God, with every possible ounce of passion.[252] In fact, in scripture God named him *Avraham Ohavi*, "Abraham who loves Me" (Isa. 41:8). Since every Jew has a connection to a little piece from Abraham, there is a hidden love in the hearts of Jews. Deep within stands *yechidah*, a voice within the Jewish soul that is totally attracted to God. This part of the person would willingly sacrifice his most precious wishes,[253] his life, for God's sake.

Every Jew has this hidden love and faith.[254] Even the worst sinner or the most obnoxious atheist, in the depths of his heart, has an undying passion and loyalty to God and His Law. When the Jew is challenged to keep his faith, when he is placed on a stake and offered a choice, "Death or idolatry?" Almost always, the Jew will choose martyrdom. Even the sinner who scoffs at the faithful will willingly give his life. For at the moment of supreme challenge, the deepest depths of the heart are awakened; the Jew realizes that idolatry means disconnecting from God, and his *yechidah* voice calls the Jew to sacrifice and he joyfully obeys.

Udel, the daughter of the Baal Shem Tov, would regularly say, "Jews have done well. God Almighty is our patron. But God also has done well. See, even a man like Feivish, a thief who cared little for Torah and observance, when he was placed in the supreme challenge, he chose martyrdom over converting to a faith that was not monotheistic."

---

252. See further *Nesivos Shalom, Parashas Vayeira* pg. 107, s.v. *ve-ha-Torah ha-kedoshah*.

253. The word for life in Hebrew is *nefesh*. Sacrifice of one's life is called *mesiras nefesh*. In the Bible *nefesh* really means desire or will, as in the verse, *im yesh es nafshchem*, "if you so desire." Life is called *nefesh* because continued living is our strongest and most powerful desire.

254. The Hebrew term for "faith," *emunah*, really means, "hold." Faith is the feeling of holding God's hand and trusting Him. See further *Horeb*, Chapter 10, where Rabbi Hirsch writes, "*Emunah* means to hold fast to God." Abraham was the person of love and the teacher of faith. Our piece of Abraham fully believes in God just as it is fully willing to express its love of God.

Two centuries later, Udel's words still ring true in light of the following account from Rabbi Israel Spira.[255] In the Janowska concentration camp,[256] there was a notorious Jewish policeman, a Kapo, whose name was Schneeweiss. This man was known to have no consideration for his fellow Jews who were in a less fortunate position. In fact, some prisoners felt that the Nazis were more understanding than Schneeweiss.

Before Yom Kippur a group of Jews approached Rabbi Spira, the Grand Rebbe of Bluzhov, with a request. They begged him to approach Schneeweiss and ask for a special work assignment for Yom Kippur. They did not want to perform any *melachah*, Biblically prohibited forms of work, and they wanted to pray the special prayers of the holiest day. The Rebbe was afraid to ask Schneeweiss but he could not disappoint Jews who wanted to observe Mitzvos in the midst of the Nazi inferno. The Rebbe approached the Kapo and begged him to assign this group of Jews to work that would not entail a Biblical sin. Something was touched in the heart of the hard man; he promised the Rebbe that he would try to help.

Mr. Schneeweiss arranged that on the morning of Yom Kippur the Rebbe and his followers were assigned to clean barracks. He gave them

---

255. I have paraphrased Rabbi Spira's account titled, "Even the Transgressors in Israel," that can be found in Y. Eliach's *Hasidic Tales of the Holocaust*, pg. 155. Rabbi Spira said of this story, "This particular story is one of those stories that deserves to be published in a book."

256. The Janowska Camp was a notorious place of suffering and pain. Y. Eliach described the camp in note 1 of *Hasidic Tales of the Holocaust*.

> The Janowska Road Camp was situated near the cemeteries and sand mountains outside the city of Lvov, in the Ukraine. It was established in October-November 1941 by Dr. Wechter, the governor of the district of Galicia, and S.S. Major General Katzman, police chief of Galicia. Officially a forced labor camp, it was in reality a place of torture and death which was eventually taken over by the S.S. economic administrative main office (WHVA), the agency that controlled concentration camps. The camp was notorious for the cruelty of its German commanders and their Ukrainian and Russian collaborators. In many instances, inmates were brutally murdered for the entertainment of the camp officials. Tens of thousands of Jews, mainly from Eastern Galicia, met their deaths there. The Germans, because of the threat of possible resistance, liquidated the camp in a surprise action on November 20, 1943.

rags, and the students did not use any cleaning agents so as not to violate the holiness of the day. Around midday, two Nazis entered the room pushing a cart laden with delicacies never seen in the camp. There was steaming meat and white bread instead of the watery filth that was usually served as "soup."

"Quick, get up and eat lunch!" One of the Nazis ordered.

None of the men moved.

Schneeweiss stepped forward and said, "Today is the holiest day of the year, we Jews fast on this day."

The Nazi was shocked at the insolence, "You are all working for the Whermacht. If you starve yourselves you are guilty of sabotaging our war effort. Whoever does not eat is a traitor! Tell them to eat!" He screamed.

Schneeweiss drew himself up a little straighter and said, "We Jews do not eat on Yom Kippur."

The Nazi took out his revolver and shot Schneeweiss. He ordered the remaining stunned Jews to clean up the martyr's blood and he left the room.

Mr. Schneewiess, of blessed memory, had not kept Yom Kippur for years, but at the moment of ultimate trial he gave up his life for the sake of God's honor. His *yechidah* expressed itself.[257]

The *Tanya* is a work written by the first Lubavitcher Rebbe to explain how every Jew can easily reach perfect observance of all of the commandments. His most powerful argument is based on the hidden love of *yechidah*.

Every Jew has a hidden love for God. In moments of supreme test you and I would willingly give up our lives so as not to harm our connection with the Almighty. In truth, every misdeed, in a certain sense, harms the

---

257. Purim is also a day of the revelation of *yechidah*. *Yechidah* is revealed through sacrifice. We all received our *yechidah* through Abraham's sacrificing of his own desires during the binding of Isaac, and for all of us moments that call for supreme sacrifice trigger a revelation of *yechidah*. Mordechai's willingness to sacrifice all for the sake of God's honor, when he refused to bow to a human despite Achashveirosh's command, caused the revelation of *yechidah*. Mordechai is called *ben Kish* in the Scroll of Esther. The Talmud teaches that this was his name because *hekish*, "he knocked," on the gates of prayer. *Kish* is an acronym for *kutzo shel yud*. Mordechai knocked on the gates of prayer through arousal of the hidden apex of the *yud*, his *yechidah* (Rav Wolfson).

bond with God. Every sin is really a form of idol-worship; it is a denial of the reality that God is the absolute Master and the One who sees, judges, and punishes. If we are willing to give up our lives so as to maintain the health of our relationship with Him, shouldn't we be willing to sacrifice whatever lusts are attracting us to the sin? For instance, if a store-owner has a temptation to deceive a customer, in essence it is a desire for a small pleasure (money). If the shopkeeper is conscious of the fact that he would give up all pleasure, his life, in order to stay connected with God, wouldn't he easily forego a few ill-gotten pennies in order to maintain the bond?[258] [259]

THE PLACE OF *YECHIDAH*

According to *Sefer Yetzirah* our world appears in triplicate form: space, time, and person, as discussed in Lesson Two. Within a person there is *yechidah*. In time there is Yom Kippur. What is the place of *yechidah*? The Western Wall.

Yechidah is the part of the soul that is never sullied. Even the worst sinner cannot destroy *yechidah*'s call to holiness. Similarly, while the

---

258. See further *Tanya*, Chapters 18-20.
259. Perhaps the hidden voice of *yechidah* is the meaning of the following Midrash in *Shir Ha-Shirim Rabbah*. In the Song of Songs, the *Shulamis* woman (the symbol of the Jewish nation) remarks that she is asleep yet her heart is awake. The Midrash explains the verse in the following paragraph:

"I am sleeping"—the Jewish nation said to God, "Master of the world, I am sleeping from the commandments but my heart is awake to perform acts of kindness; I am sleeping from charities but my heart is awake to perform them; I am sleeping from the sacrifices but my heart is awake for the recital of *Shema* and prayer; I am sleeping from Jerusalem's Temple but my heart is awake for synagogues and houses of study; I am sleeping from the *ketz*, the set time for redemption, but my heart is awake for salvation; God's heart is awake to redeem me."

Perhaps the Midrash is saying that externally we are sinners, who neglect our obligations and historic mission, yet internally our hearts are filled with a Godly soul—*yechidah*—that seeks to fulfill as many obligations as possible and it yearns for redemption.

Temple in Jerusalem was burnt by the Babylonians and later the Romans, the Western Wall was never destroyed, and the Divine presence never left its environs. Thus, it represents holiness that cannot be destroyed.[260] This was also the symbolism of the *ner maʾaravi*, the Western candle in the menorah (the candelabrum in the Temple). According to our tradition this western flame would miraculously always stay lit, and all the other flames would turn toward it. It symbolized innermost holiness, the internal flame in Jewish hearts that even the worst sinner cannot extinguish.[261]

THE REALM OF EVIL

God's light takes on different forms, each progressively more physical, as it evolves through different stages. This process is called the *seder hishtalshalus*. The five different parts of the soul are different points along a personal *seder hishtalshlus*.

God's world is perfectly balanced. In order to maintain the harmony that allows for free choice the entire *seder hishtalshlus* has a polar image of evil forces. Therefore, there are parallel soul parts that are physical and pull towards evil.

---

260. See further *Tzion Ve-Arehah* pg. 115 s.v. *kotel ha-maʾaravi*.

261. See further *Tzion Ve-Arehah* pg. 115-116. *Maʾavar Yabok* explains that the four directions east, west, north, and south parallel the four faces on the Divine Chariot: the face of man, the face of an eagle, the face of an ox, and the face of a lion. The four groups of Jewish tribes during the forty years in the desert (the nation was split into groups of three tribes each for the sake of camping and traveling) also parallel these concepts. East represents the face of man (in the chariot) and the group of tribes led by Judah, the holiest members of the Jews. West represents the face of an eagle and the lowest level in the Jewish nation, the group of tribes led by Dan. The lowest Jews do not have their own deeds; all they have is their *yechidah*, an innate goodness. On the west, there is the Western Wall and the western flame, representatives of *yechidah*.

See further *Emunas Etecha, Parashas Kedoshim* pg. 70. Rabbi Shimon bar Yochai is the personality who revealed that there are secrets to the Torah. There are also secrets in every Jewish soul. Even the soul that seems fully evil has a hidden point, its *yechidah*, through which it is fully righteous and beloved to the Almighty. This secret cannot be broken. *Lag Ba-Omer*, the day when Rabbi Shimon revealed the *Zohar*, is a day of *yechidah*. It, like Purim, is a holiday even the lowest Jew can relate to. On this day the innermost secrets within our souls glow, and we all sense a bit of the hidden *tzaddik* that we all are.

There are five soul parts that are from the realm of evil—the physical. For example, the *Tanya* teaches that the Godly *nefesh* is concentrated in the blood and in the right ventricle of the heart, and the physical, animalistic *nefesh* is in the left ventricle of the heart.[262] Thus, just as there is *yechidah*—a hidden soul part that pulls to virtue—there is also a hidden voice of physicality that pushes a person toward sin and hate.[263]

When the Jewish nation left Egypt the various forces of evil, represented by the Egyptians and their deities, were smitten. There was one idol that did not fall initially whose name was *Baal Tzefon*. The root of *tzafun* is *tzadi, peh, nun*, which means, "hidden." The evil urge is also called *tzefon* in the verse, *Ve-es ha-tzefoni archik mei-aleichem*, "I will distance the *tzefoni* [the hidden evil urge] from you" (Yoel 2:20). The symbolism of *Baal Tzefon*'s survival was that the revealed forms of evil had been defeated, yet the hidden, subconscious evil had not been destroyed.

When the Red Sea split the hidden form of evil crumbled. Rabbi Isaac Luriah explained that the splitting of the Red Sea and the revelation of a dry sea floor represented an emergence of the *Alma De-Iskasya*, "the hidden world." The waves of an ocean are always visible and they represent the revealed dimension, while the sea floor that is usually covered with water represents the hidden realm. Apparently, when Jewry arrived at the Red Sea, we found our inner voice of virtue, we revealed our *Rav tuvcha asher tzafanta le-yereacha*, "the great amounts of Your good that are hidden away for those who revere you" (Ps. 31:20). We revealed *yechidah*, and then the hidden evil force that had broadcast anti-Jewish hate and sin collapsed.

The Jewish reaction to the revelation of the hidden was a musical one as the entire nation sang *Shiras Ha-Yam*—the Song of the Sea. There is a simple psychological explanation for this response. When they saw the hidden world and discovered their own hidden soul they glimpsed an entirely new perspective. A vast, exciting new world appeared before them. When you see a magnificent new universe you become a new person and the only possible response is song.[264]

---

262. *Tanya*, Chapter 1.
263. Perhaps this is the subconscious voice that Freud discovered and discussed (heard from the Stitchiner Rebbe). See further *Emunas Etecha, Parashas Kedoshim* pgs. 67-71.
264. Heard from the Stitchiner Rebbe.

LESSON FIFTEEN

WHY EVIL IS CALLED A *KELIPPAH*

THE *NEFESH HA-BAHAMIS*, the animal-like life of the body, emerged from the realm of the *kelippos*, the shells of evil.[265] There are several reasons why Chasidic literature refers to all evil entities such as lustful urges, sinful deeds, wicked individuals, tragedies, suffering, and painful experiences, with the term *kelippos*.

EVIL IS A VEIL

Imagine a magical kingdom with a king who sought to determine the dedication of his subjects. He built a magnificent palace and surrounded it with seven steep walls. The regent then publicized an edict, "Whoever scales the barriers I constructed will be richly rewarded."

Thousands of loyal subjects converged on the royal compound and attempted to climb the first wall. For most, it was an impossible feat. The wall's height was stupefying; there were few ledges to grab, and the crevices that existed harbored hidden knives submerged in dirt. Only a few hundred hardy souls reached the other side of the wall.

Behind the barrier they discovered a garden filled with numerous rewards. Musicians were playing enchanting songs, gourmet chefs were

265. The *Tanya* first describes the part of man that came from the *kelippah*, and only afterwards does he discuss the heavenly soul. The reason for that is that in our world evil precedes holiness. For example, according to Jewish law, night precedes day, one is first born with the body and only later does the heavenly soul enter, and the Jewish nation were initially idolators, and it took time until we arrived at the truth of monotheistic practice. The *Tanya* is a guide to virtue in this world, so he too first discussed the realm of evil and only after conquering the world of darkness does he reveal the realm of light (the Stitchiner Rebbe).

cooking exquisite cuisine for each climber, and fresh water flowed from natural springs. Many decided to stay in the king's garden and satiate themselves with its pleasures. Only a few attempted to scale the second wall.

The second wall was steeper, taller, and more violent. In addition to hidden knives, it had soldiers stationed on its top firing arrows and throwing spears at all who approached. The wall claimed its victims, and only several dozen climbers reached the other side.

Behind the wall was another paradise. In addition to all that the first garden contained, butlers of the king stood with piles of gold coins that they distributed to the climbers. A large percentage of the seekers decided to end their pilgrimage.

This process was repeated at each wall. Each barrier was a greater challenge than its predecessor, behind each wall stood better rewards, and the number of climbers drastically fell.

Only two people, an idealistic teenage boy and the bravest warrior in the country, succeeded in mastering the fifth wall. Behind it they discovered all the possible pleasures the king could award. His royal treasury was opened wide, and the climbers were given free rein to take whatever they desired. The knight decided to stop. He reasoned that the king could not give anything else so there was no reason to bother with the trouble of the most difficult barriers. The teenager announced that he was continuing onward.

The warrior turned to the boy and attempted to talk sense into him. "Why risk your life?" he asked. "The place we have reached provides us with every possible delight. What more could you want?"

"You do not understand." The boy answered, "I am not seeking reward. I am the king's son. I want to see my father."

The boy battled the last two walls and prevailed. He arrived at the king's palace and found his father. He seized him, locked his arms around the king, and started to cry. "Why did you make it so hard? Why are there so many walls preventing us from seeing you?" he wailed.

The king took hold of his son's shoulder and gently turned him around. The boy looked back to where he had come from. All the walls were gone.

The Baal Shem Tov related this story as a parable.[266] God is the king. The Jewish nation, or the *tzaddik* who represents it, is the teenage boy. The seven walls hiding the king represent all the forms of evil: evil desires and deeds (sins), and evil events (tragedies).[267]

In Chasidic literature an evil force is called a *kelippah* (pl., *kelippos*). These are the same Hebrew words for "shell" and "peel" that surround fruits and nuts, since evil functions like the husk surrounding the grain. A shell conceals the essence of the item, the edible part. Evil is a shell inasmuch as it hides God, who is the true life of the universe. In the parable, walls hid the king; those walls are the forces of evil that obscure sight of the Ultimate King, God, who in truth directs all.

The physical world has a trace of evil. Consider pursuit of excess material wealth, or the physical desires of man, they are the paths to evil deeds, such as theft and adultery.[268] *Chomrius*, "physicality," obscures God's light, causing it to be ignored. The Hebrew term for "world" is *olam*. This word derives from the same root as the words *he'elem*, and *ne'elam*, that mean "hidden" or "concealed." One reason for this confluence of terms is that the physical world conceals the Almighty. Consider success in business: it seems that success is the fruit of human toil and failure the result of cunning competitors. Such a perspective is an excessively physical point of view; it hides the truth. In reality, God's grace is the only cause for blessing or its opposite. Consider, God sometimes showers wealth on the laziest fools and He sometimes denies material blessing to the most industrious laborer. Once you don the lenses of a spiritual perspective you will peer through the lattices of evil and find the hand of God in all that occurs.

---

266. See further *Degel Machaneh Efraim* on the *Haftarah* of *Parashas Ki Savo*.
267. Judaism believes in a Just God. Therefore, suffering and tragedy are usually the results of our misdeeds. "The punishment of sin is sin," the sages say (*Avos* 4:2). This means that each misdeed creates a spiritual force. This spiritual agent is what reappears in the form of a tragedy that the transgressor might suffer (See further *Sichas Malachei Ha-Shareis* of Rabbi Tzadok Ha-Cohen of Lublin, and *Shem Mi-Shmuel* on *Parashas Vayechi* pg. 320). Thus moral evil (sin) and historical evil (suffering) coalesce into a single category.
268. See further the earlier lessons where biological and "this-worldly" life was categorized as the *nefesh ha-bahamis* and *yetzer hara*, "the evil urge."

In the Besht's parable, "The king was hidden behind seven walls," God is hidden in the physical universe that was created in seven days. "To approach the king, challenging obstacles had to be surmounted." To approach God, walls must be scaled; to use the terminology of *kelippos*, the shells must be shattered. Observance is a battle. Consider lust— if I lust for a piece of property that is not my own, it is a wall I must scale. I have to battle my desires and transform the selfish fantasy into a Heavenly urge to give generously. When I try to improve my moral behavior I will often feel that I am slipping off of an impossible wall and that the goal is unattainable. I have to remind myself of the parable of the king's walls, then I might hear a voice that insists, "Keep fighting!"

In Genesis, the path to the tree of life was blocked with an angel wielding a revolving sword; this angel represents the *kelippah*. If you want to taste from the tree of life you must battle, let no one stand in your way, not even a *seraph*! Remember, holiness is like the fruit, to enjoy it you first must tear apart the peel. This lesson is a source of comfort to us all. Do not be dismayed by difficulty and failure. The path to feeling Divine holiness is characterized with initial challenge.[269]

"After every wall there were rewards." Mitzvah observance is innately rewarding, and every step along the path to the Divine brings added blessings. "Each wall was progressively more difficult." The Talmud

---

269. Rav Tzadok Ha-Cohen of Lublin teaches, "The Midrash states that *tzaddikim* initially suffer afflictions and at their end arrive at tranquility. The reason for this process is that entry into a good behavior or emotion entails suffering, as it said, 'All beginnings are difficult,' and, 'A scholar will only know a discipline once he has first stumbled about in error within that field' (*Gittin* 43a). There are three great gifts that God has given to the Jewish people: Torah, the Land of Israel, and the World-to-Come, and they are all given through suffering and travails (*Berachos* 5a). The world was created in a manner in which darkness was created first only afterwards light appeared (*Shabbos* 77b). For this world (that is linked with the spiritual world of *asiyah*) is mostly evil (*asiyah* is mostly evil with a minority of holiness, *yetzirah* has an even split between the forces of holiness and their opposite, *beriah* is mostly pure and holy with a minority of evil, and *atzilus* is all good with no evil at all) that is why initially what one sees is the evil, the sorrows and difficulty, yet if one perseveres one will see the tranquility, the good" (*Tzidkas Ha-Tzaddik*, note 170). See further *Sfas Emes* on *Parashas Yisro* (5637) s.v. *ba-midrash*, and Rabbi Nachman of Breslov's *Likkutei Moharan* version one, Chapter 62, letter 5.

teaches that one who has a greater level of virtue has more challenging temptations. As climbers scaled more walls they achieved higher and more powerful feelings of holiness thus becoming greater. Hence, the more trying next step. "The king's son felt an inner calling to overcome all the barriers and reach his father while the knight stopped after the fifth wall." The Jewish nation is named in the Bible, "Children to God your Lord" (Deut. 14:1). All of us innately, and *tzaddikim* actually, sense that the King is behind the walls, and we are to struggle with all the seemingly insurmountable mountains to embrace our Father. The knight represented individuals who pursue a life of virtue due to desire for reward and fear of punishment. "The knight scaled five walls." Motivations of suffering and benefit may lead to a high level of spiritual achievement, but at some point before the apex such a seeker will stop climbing. "The King's son insisted on scaling all of the walls." Those who feel that they are children of God are motivated by love and as a result will scale all the barriers to arrive at God's door. "The king responded to his son's complaints by showing him that the walls were gone." Once the righteous individual reaches the heights of spiritual attainment, he turns back and all the struggles vanish. After years of challenge, virtuous behavior becomes second nature. Furthermore, moral behavior becomes immensely rewarding and pleasurable, thereby denying material concerns the ability to tempt.

Our attitude toward the struggle of life can be greatly enhanced by consideration of this parable. Is observance difficult? Yes. There are walls in our lives, periods when we are tempted or when God seems to be missing. But the King is waiting for us to scale them, and once we succeed, all the pain will melt away. Apply this lesson to human suffering, evil in history; it is a wall hiding the Creator. Break the wall. Realize that God is causing the moment of suffering and trial, and He is with you even during trials. You might feel the burden lifted and your pain alleviated.[270]

---

270. The *Sfas Emes* writes, "And Yehudah stepped forward to him (Gen. 44:18): this is the advice to surmount any moment of travail or when God seems to be hiding His face, accept the will of God and acknowledge that it is God's doing. Clarify to yourself that what you are experiencing is coming from God, and that while He is hidden His life force is what sustains the predicament you are in.

The young grandson of Rabbi Boruch of Mezhibuzh[271] once burst into his study with rivulets of tears flowing down his cheeks. "Zaidy, I was playing hide-and-go-seek with my friend," he stammered, "I went to hide and no one came to look for me." Rabbi Boruch nodded with understanding and then sobbed uncontrollably.

The students in the Rabbi's room were shocked. They appreciated the grandfather's empathy but they could not understand why Rabbi Boruch shed hot tears for a minor event. When the Rabbi calmed down he explained his sadness, "Every experience is a direct encounter with God. My child cried to me with this complaint because God wished to direct his words to me as a message, 'God is hidden in this world and He is crying because no one is trying to find Him.' I cried when I realized that I am causing Divine tears with my neglect."

When playing hide-and-go-seek, one hides in order to be found. God is hiding in the material world for the same reason. He wants each of us to seek and find. We have found God when we constantly feel that our financial security is a result of His blessing and that it is His support that sustains us during moments of trial and pain. We are not looking for Him if we arrogantly presume that success is a result of our own effort and that He is not in charge. Children in hiding cry when their friends decide not to seek them. God might be crying if we do not search for Him. Dare we allow those tears to continue to fall?

Abraham and Isaac were moved by the Divine sobs. They were inspired to expend much time and energy in well-digging. The Torah spends enormous amounts of ink detailing the efforts of Abraham and Isaac to discover wells in the desert. The Torah is a very exact document, so why did it talk so extensively about an ancient and seemingly irrelevant historical fact? Their well-digging was a symbolic act. To discover a well they had to remove many external layers of sand to uncover water, the source of life. This symbolized the struggles with the shells of evil, removing them to reveal the source of life, the Divine.

Yehudah stepped forward to Him, he accepted that his difficult trial came from God.... Once it is clear to you that all comes from God, that essence is revealed, disaster is averted, the stresses relax, and you sense God's grace in a revealed manner" *Parashas Vayigash* (5631) s.v. *Vayigash*.

271. Rabbi Boruch was the grandson of the Baal Shem Tov.

Abraham and Isaac engaged the walls around the king in combat, they battled temptation, and at times of tragedy declared with faith that God was with them, even when it seemed that He was not. Their life of battling *kelippos* is symbolized by their life-long endeavors to reveal water underneath scorching sand. Their efforts paved the way for the Jewish nation; since their descendants are inspired and encouraged through their example, we seek to continue their ways and remove the veils that hide God from us.[272]

EVIL IS DISTANCE

Another explanation for the term *kelippah* as "evil" is that sin creates distance from the Divine as shells separate the eater from nourishment.[273] We only perform sins when we feel estranged or alienated from God. Someone who feels a deeply joyous bond with the Divine will never violate his "Best Friend's" wishes. Even one who does not relate to God with love, but merely fears God as the Divine Judge who punishes infractions, would not commit misdeeds were he to feel that the Judge is near. The mistake of imagining Divine distance facilitates sin.

R. Zhisha of Anipoli,[274] before he was famous as a righteous man, was once the lone traveler in the buggy of a simple peasant. Along the way, the wagon passed an orchard filled with ripe fruit. Noticing that there was no guard nearby, the peasant stopped his wagon. He hopped off and told R. Zhisha, "Keep watch, if you notice someone observing me, yell." He then ambled over the fence that surrounded the orchard and began

272. See further *Sefer Ha-Zechus* on *Parashas Toldos*, "The purpose of the wells that our forefathers dug was for our benefit. Prior to their efforts, the Divine Light [feelings of closeness to Him] was hidden in the dust. Material matters concealed the Divine while the goal of creation was that man would feel the Divine in all matters. They dug deep, they removed the dirt, until the waters emerged. This was all for our benefit, so that we would be able to dig and find God even during moments of His Hiddenness." See further *Beer Mayim Chaim* on *Parashas Toldos*.

273. Just as sin distances men from feeling Divinity, tragedy, which is the force of the sin in another form, also causes one to feel detached from the Almighty.

274. R. Zhisha was the brother of Rabbi Elimelech of Lizhensk. He too was a student of the great Maggid of Mezeritch. He was born in 1718 and passed away in 1800.

to pick fruit. After a few moments, R. Zhisha started to scream, "They see you! They're after you!" The startled driver dropped the stolen apples, jumped into his wagon, and quickly snapped his whip to set the horses into gallop. After ten minutes he realized that no one was following him and the entire region seemed deserted. He slowed his wagon, turned to R. Zhisha and said, "Who saw me? There is no one here." R. Zhisha smiled and pointed his finger toward Heaven as if to say, "He saw."

Pride and egocentrism are the foundation of the *kelippah*. The *kelippos* are sometimes called *eser kisrin de-misaavusa*,[275] "the ten crown of impurity." They are called a crown, for their source is a sense of privilege and a large ego, as if they were kings.[276] Evil's root is a self-aggrandizement that causes one to imagine that God is not the absolute authority and to imagine the thought, "I control my destiny." Ego is what creates the distance between man and God that causes sin.[277] *Chametz*, leavened dough, is the symbol and embodiment of this arrogance.

Commentators are troubled with the many prohibitions surrounding leavened dough on Passover. It may not be eaten. Nor may any enjoyment be derived from it. Furthermore, it cannot be left in one's residence. Nor may one own it in any location. The night before the holiday of Pesach there is a Rabbinic law mandating the owner of the house to conduct a thorough search of the house to find and then destroy all *chametz*

---

275. See further *Tanya*, Chapter 6.

276. The *kelippah* says, *Ana emloch*, "I will rule," while holiness states, *Attah hu Melech Malchei Ha-Melachim*, "You, God rule over all kings."

277. Consider the following explanation of the Maharal of Prague: "Akavia ben Mehalel's advice addresses the root cause of sin. God placed in mankind a drive for sin, which is personified as the *yetzer hara*…. The power of the *yetzer hara* arises from arrogance. All desire, jealousy and other causes of sin originate from a heart that swells in pride…" (Maharal of Prague on *Pirkei Avos* 1:1, pg. 142-143).

Evil will always try first and foremost to overcome man by making him prideful, for nothing is more fundamentally destructive of man's spiritual life than pride. This is part of what King Solomon meant when he said, "Pride comes before the fall" (Prov. 16:18): a man's pride is what precipitates the fall of the soul into the dark prison of materialism (*The Juggler and the King*, pg. 37).

crumbs. Why is eating *chametz* on Passover such a delicate prohibition that there are so many fences to prevent its violation? The Radbaz[278] answered that *chametz* represents the evil urge. The Talmud calls the evil urge "leaven in the bread"[279] because evil is essentially hubris. Leavened dough rises, and evil is when I allow my ego to rise. In truth, the dough has no reason to feel arrogant; it is merely water and flour that are sitting still. Similarly, there is no legitimate basis for arrogance. The source of the evil urge must be treated with utmost caution, hence all the prohibitions that surround *chametz*.

In the *Zohar*, the realm of evil is called *alma di-prodah*, "the world of separation." Evil deeds stem from a feeling of separateness, the sense of a multitude of disconnected strands. Arrogance and ego spawn that emotion. The sinner deludes himself into thinking that God is divorced and disconnected from this world. If one can imagine that God is detached, then one might imagine that people are detached and that we do not share a common soul that unites us. Furthermore, this divisive thought leads to a fragmentation of life suggesting a lack of an overarching single purpose to life. As a result, one will sin. A life of holiness is achieved through a sense of oneness. The attitude that the Almighty inheres within all, that all mankind partake of a common soul and their acts influence each other, and that there is a single goal and purpose to all of life's activities, ensures that no sins will be performed.

There are very few Mitzvos that call for an act to be performed exclusively in the public street, the *reshus ha-rabbim*. According to Jewish law, the public street belongs to many different owners, thus it represents the realm of *kelippos*, the arrogant disconnected peels, *alma di-prodah*. Mitzvos are primarily performed in the *reshus ha-yachid*, the private domain that belongs to a single owner symbolizing oneness.

The ancient pagans fully accepted the premises that foster evil. They worshipped many gods. They saw a world filled with millions of different and disconnected forces. Due to this fractured world-view, within their community there was a sense of alienation and differentiation. Esau

---

278. Rabbi David ben Solomon ibn Avi Zimra was born in 1479 and he passed away in 1573. He emigrated from Spain to Safed in Israel and later to Cairo, where he headed the local Jewish community.
279. *Berachos* 17a.

(Hebrew, *Esav*), according to traditional commentary, was an idol-worshipper. The Torah describes the six members of Esau's family as *nafshos beiso*, "the souls of his home," indicating that even a group of six could not forge a single unit.

On the other hand, the Jewish nation's *weltanschauung* is pure monotheism. We see the One everywhere. As a result, the seventy members of Jacob's family are referred to in the Torah as *ha-nefesh le-bais le-Yaakov*, "the soul to the house of Jacob" (Gen. 46:27). Seventy different bodies were all parts of one soul.[280]

Distance is not only what leads to sin; it is also the fruit of misdeed. A sinner loses his sense of spirituality and becomes estranged from his innate Godly voice that advocates holiness.[281] As it is written, *Avonoseichem hayu mavdilim beinchem le-vein Elokeichem*, "Your sins separated you from God" (Isa. 59:2).

Since sin causes a distance in the inner world of man's personality, it fosters distance in the external realm of physical reality.[282] For example, when Adam was first created he resided in God's garden. After his sin, he was banished from God's presence. Similarly, the land of Israel is a miniature Garden of Eden. It is the place where *Tamid einei Hashem Elokecha bah*, "God's eyes are constantly focused upon it" (Deut. 11:12). Due to national sins the Jewish nation was exiled from the land, and we lost the sense of closeness to the Divine that a life in Israel endows.[283]

---

280. Rashi ibid. See further *Da'as Tefillah* pg. 155.

281. In the earlier lessons this voice was identified as *chayah* or *yechidah*. This part of the personality is the *tzaddik* aspect within each person.

282. The inner spiritual universe of man is a perfect parallel to the external physical universe.

The Talmud in *Berachos* (17a) records that in truth we all wish to serve God. "What impedes us is the leaven in the bread and the yoke of foreign governments." Rabbi Tzadok Ha-Cohen of Lublin explained that the two powers mentioned in the Talmud parallel each other. The evil inclination is an internal foreign power, just as oppressive foreign rulers are powers in the external world. If we allow our internal evil urge to be our ruler then the same will occur in the external universe, and foreign governments will overwhelm us and promulgate laws to lower our spirituality.

283. The nation of Amalek is the paragon of evil. They are called *reishis goyim*, the "first of the multitudes." They embody the principles and foundations of all the negative ideologies that can be found among the many nations. Since they are so evil, the Torah demands that Jewry wage eternal war against them.

EVIL IS NOT ALL BAD

In the Besht's parable of scaling walls, the barriers provided many benefits. In addition to the sense of satisfaction that the climbers must have felt once they scaled the walls, the walls strengthened the climbers' bodies and character, and for every successful scaling they entered gardens stocked with rewards. The walls also successfully ferreted out the insincere, preserving a relationship with the king for those who truly deserved it. A shell has many benefits—it preserves the fruit. Without the shell one would never have been able to enjoy the fruit, for the elements or the animals would have consumed it first. Evil is a shell, and it too has beneficial qualities.

Evil is like physical therapy. It hurts but it helps. A physical therapist must push a patient through painful exercises in order to restore muscle strength. Similarly evil is a barrier that pains us for our ultimate good.

In the *Zohar* the role of evil temptations is symbolized with a tale of a hired harlot:

A king loved his son with abiding passion. He knew that if his son frequented houses of ill repute he would have to disown the child. He warned the boy to never succumb to a harlot's temptations. The boy swore to his father that he would maintain his chastity.

Amalek embodies arrogance and distance from God. The *gematria* of the name *Amalek* (240) is the same as the word *ram* (240), "high and arrogant." Amalek is arrogant. This consideration of self leads them to create distance between man and God. Amalek also equals *safek*, "doubt," for they create alienation and distance between the created and the Creator through raising questions and doubts about His existence. In all the sections about Amalek in the Torah, the words *karcha* or *karahu* appear. These terms shares a similarity with the word *mikreh*, "happenstance." Ego leads to distance from God to doubts about His supervision to a claim that the indications of His presence are mere coincidences and no more. See further *Worldmask*, Chapter 17, pgs. 193-205. Entrance to the Land of Israel, the place of closeness to the Divine, also requires that the scourge of Amalek be confronted. "The Jews are commanded in three obligations upon entry to the Land, to appoint a king, to destroy Amalek, and to build the Temple in Jerusalem." (See further *Sanhedrin* 20a, *Shem Mi-Shmuel*, *Parashas Shoftim*, pg. 113, s.v. *Be-Midrash Rabbah*).

Later, the king desired to enjoy a display of his son's loyalty. He hired a woman and paid for her cosmetics, jewelry, and dress. He then sent her to seduce his son. The immoral woman fulfilled the king's directive by tempting the prince. The prince fulfilled his father's innermost wishes when he withstood her affections.

The king was so excited with his son's loyalty that he rewarded him with a state dinner. Who caused the rewards? The harlot did. As a result, she too entered the royal banquet when the prince was honored.[284]

The harlot helped the prince, since she enabled his special dinner and his ascension to the throne. Without her tempting him, he might never have revealed his father's affection. Similarly, *kelippos* are from God, sent for us to resist their tempting. when we ignore their claims, we benefit, thus they are good for us, and not fully evil.[285]

When we withstand evil's attractions we give God great joy.[286] He then rewards us in the next world. According to the above cited passage from the *Zohar*, since Evil caused our reward, the evil urge is allowed entry into the Garden of Eden.

In the book of Genesis, after every day of God's creation, He examined His handiwork and declared that it was good. On the sixth day He reviewed all and declared, *Ve-hinneh tov me'od*, "And behold it is very good" (Gen. 1:31). The Midrash[287] explains the phrase "very good" as referring to *Gehinnom*, death, and the evil inclination. How can the Midrash call these disasters "very good"? The answer is that deep down even the worst evils are good. A *kelippah* (a shell) fulfills an important function, it preserves the fruit. *Kelippos* in the moral sense, such as evil desires, help maintain the pleasure that is slated for man.[288]

---

284. *Zohar* 2:163a.
285. "Once the prince realized that the harlot was sent from his father, he remembered his oath (to maintain his virtue) and withstood her charms. Similarly once we internalize that evil comes from God to be rejected, we will not lose ourselves in the allures of passion and our good will shall prevail" (*Innerspace*, pg. 84, and footnote 40).
286. We are fulfilling our commitment to him that we accepted with birth when we swore to be a *tzaddik*. See further *Matok Mi-Devash* on the *Zohar* 2:163a.
287. *Bereishis Rabbah*, Chapter 9.
288. *Innerspace* pg. 71.

In a world with no *kelippos*, God is apparent. If God is apparent then man deserves no reward for following God's commands. There would be no free choice were man to constantly feel that the Divine is close as long as he observes His commands. If God were not hidden at all, we would be unable to appreciate God's gifts, for we would not have been able to do anything to deserve reward. *Kelippos* hide God. It is not easy to be observant. As a result, those who battle and draw near to God earn Divine pleasure. Without the shell, we would not enjoy the fruit; and without a temptation we would never enjoy Divinity, for we would be embarrassed since it would be given to us without any effort on our part. The embarrassment of receiving pleasure without earning it is called *nehama de-kissufa*, "the bread of shame."

On a deeper level, the *kelippos* enable us to resemble God. Resemblance causes spiritual closeness. Closeness to God is the greatest pleasure imaginable. God wants us to be like Him and to feel the deepest possible sense of fulfillment. The Almighty is independent and creative. When we exercise our free choice and pick the good, we resemble Him. Through that decision we are creative since we fashion our character. Furthermore, we display independence by listening to conscience instead of lust. Without the option of evil, there would be no choice, we would be neither creative nor independent, and we would not truly enjoy what God has in store for us.[289]

A shell keeps the fruit from flies and harsh winds that might damage it. In the Garden of Eden story, the tree of life was guarded by an angel with the revolving sword. That *kelippah* prevented Adam, who was no longer deserving, from eating of the tree. Similarly, the *kelippos* hide God's light so that only the righteous will reach it and the wicked will not use it.

THE MESSIAH WILL BREAK THE *KELIPPOS*

At the end of the Besht's parable, the "King turned his son around and all the walls were gone." This means that in the future, during the Messianic era, the Almighty will reveal how there really never was evil.[290]

289. See further *Innerspace* pgs. 155-156, 9-15, 84-91, 71-73.
290. Perhaps another explanation for the end of the parable is that once we

Consider lustful urges. Evil desires are referred to as *Shav she-barasi be-olami*, "the emptiness that I created in My World."[291] It passes and dissipates. Furthermore, the prophet promised in God's name that in the messianic era, *Ve-es ruach ha-tumah a'avir min ha-aretz*, "I will remove the spirit of impurity from the land" (Zech 13:2).

One of the barriers hiding God is the theological problem of evil. Many ask, "Why do bad things happen to good people and good things to bad people?" The final redemption will bring answers to these questions. We will then see how in truth the righteous were rewarded and the wicked individuals were punished.

Mizmor shir le-yom ha-Shabbos, "A song for the Sabbath day," (Psalm 92) was composed by Adam and is recited on Friday nights during the prayers that inaugurate the Shabbos. The psalm does not really describe Shabbos; it details the future age, the *yom she-kullo Shabbos*—an era that will be totally Shabbos.[292] The psalm explains that presently fools are plentiful; they see the transient successes of evildoers and they deny God. However in the Messianic age it will be clear that *Bi-froach resha'im kemo eisev*, "The flowering of sinners was like plants" (it was temporal), and it was allowed, *Le-hishamdam adei ad*, "To destroy them for eternity" (Ps. 92:8).

True pleasure is the joy of partaking in the World-to-Come. True pain is experienced by those who do not appreciate that world. Evildoers

---

appreciate the joy of redemption the evil and the sorrows of the past will be forgotten and viewed as merely a passing dream. Perhaps this is the intent of King David when he wrote in Psalm 126, "When God will restore the returnees to Zion, we will be like dreamers." The past will be a mere dream because the joy of the present will be tangibly real. Perhaps this is also the reason why God revealed to Abraham the exiles that his descendants will undergo while Abraham was in a sleeplike trance. Abraham's trance symbolized that exile and suffering is a dream and the ultimate redemption will be so real that it will cause the sorrows of the present to fade like dreams (see further *Emunas Etecha, Parashas Lech Lecha* s. v. *vayehi*, pg. 23).

291. *Bereishis Rabbah* 63 s.v. *va-yikra'u shemo eisav*.

292. According to Jewish tradition just as the world was created in six days and the seventh—Shabbos—was a day of rest. Similarly, humanity will have six thousand years to create a more wholesome world and then the seventh thousand will be a *yom she-kullo Shabbos*, a time of Shabbos (*Sanhedrin* 97a). Shabbos can be accepted early, and the Messiah can come before the end of the six thousand years.

might receive physical blessings in this world, yet those gifts reduce whatever merits they have and in the next world they are denied the real pleasure. Righteous individuals partake of the pleasure in the World-to-Come. Their suffering in this world removes all their sins and in the next dimension they enjoy the infinite pleasure of Divine reward.

Armed with this insight, the psalm continues, *Le-haggid ki yashar Hashem*, all will be able "to testify that God is just" (Ps. 92:16).[293]

When we merit the final redemption God's hidden secrets will be revealed and we will see the good within the *kelippah*. We will then understand how all the suffering we personally experienced—evil in history—was ultimate good.

There was a childless couple that lived near the Baal Shem Tov. Once the Baal Shem's fame as a miracle-worker spread, they approached him and requested that he bless them with a child. The Besht promised to pray for their cause and a year later a boy was born to them. Filled with gratitude they brought the baby to him and the Rabbi served as the baby's *sandak* (the man who holds the baby during the circumcision). The couple moved away from the Baal Shem, and the child developed to his parents' unceasing delight.

The boy was special. He rarely cried, and he showed signs of great intelligence and ability. When he was one year old he started to speak

---

293. The Hebrew *yashar* is here translated as "just." In truth, *yashar* means "straight" and "orderly." The meaning of "straight" will also bring us to a conclusion similar to what was advanced in the text.

God's name of being, Y-H-V-H, is the source of existence. The letters in this name can be rearranged in twelve different ways: YHVH, YHHV, YVHH, HVHY, HVYH, HHVY, VHYH, VHHY, VYHH, HYHV, HYVH, and HHYV. These letter arrangements correspond to the twelve months and the twelve tribes of Israel. Different letter arrangements represent distinct spiritual influences. Some months are times of blessings; others are times of harsh justice. The nature of the month is hinted in its letter pattern. The month with the most Divine blessings is the first month, *Nisan*. *Nisan* begins springtime when nature is reborn, its weather is usually pleasant, and Jewry was born (through the exodus from Egypt) during that month. The letter arrangement of *Nisan* is Y-H-V-H; the letters of this name are in their straightest and most fitting order. Other months were times of Divine harshness—their letter arrangements are relatively disorderly. In the future we will say that God is *yashar*, "straight," for we will then see how all experiences were blessings like the exodus from Egypt (Rav Wolfson's classes on prayer).

and learn words of Torah. On his second birthday he suddenly died. The parents were heartbroken. The father ran to the Baal Shem and asked him, "Why did you torture me with such pain? We waited twenty years for a child. Why raise our hopes with a boy only to dash them with his death?"

The Baal Shem answered with a story:

There was once a childless Russian nobleman who owned lands, serfs, and Jews. His personal priest was a vindictive Jew-hater who claimed that the nobleman was barren as a punishment for permitting Jews to live unmolested in his territory. The nobleman therefore decreed that all non-Christians must leave his land within two weeks.

The Jews were shocked by the sudden decree and they sent an eminent delegation to beg the nobleman to change his mind. The nobleman's heart was touched by the emotional pleas. He announced that the exile would be deferred for a year, and if he and his wife had a child during that year the decree would be rescinded entirely.

Once they heard the news, the Jews were relieved but also quite apprehensive. As a response, they organized a day of public fasting, penitence, and prayer. The entire community gathered in the Synagogue and prayed with utmost devotion, begging the Almighty to send a child to their nobleman and save them from financial ruin.

In Heaven, these prayers caused a tumult. One group of angels claimed that God should miraculously allow the noblewoman to conceive in order to save guiltless Jews. A different group of angels insisted that the nobleman did not deserve a son and God should not change the rules of nature to help a wicked man.

The argument was not resolved by God. A soul in the Garden of Eden heard the commotion and volunteered to descend to earth and enter the nobleman's family.

All the celestial beings were awed by the soul's generosity. A sojourn on earth entails great risks for a soul because listening to the evil urge could cause a forfeit of eternal pleasure. What a soul—

its very birth was an act of sacrifice for the welfare of others! The nobleman had a boy within the year and the decree was annulled.

The child grew up and from a young age he stood out. In grade school he displayed an interest in questions of theology instead of sports and hunting. The priest tried to inculcate his hate into the child but the boy was too good to accept drivel.

When the child was fifteen he met a Jew and began to ask about the Jewish faith. Inspired by the truth, he converted to Judaism and ran away from home to avoid the priest and his ilk. The teenager studied at *yeshivas*, married a righteous woman, and lived a life of simplicity and virtue. His death caused a tumult in Heaven.

On the one hand, there were those who claimed that the soul deserved the greatest possible reward, its birth saved a community and its life was holiness. Others claimed that, while the soul deserved reward, it should not ascend to the highest levels because for two adult years this soul ate pork, mistreated servants, and discriminated against Jews.

The decision of the High Court of Justice was that the soul should reenter the physical world for a short period. Were it to live a full life it might lose all the good it had earned, so it was sent for a life of two years to a home of supreme holiness, which deserved such a rarefied creation. For this *tikkun*, rectification, period it was to ingest kosher food, imbibe an atmosphere of respect, and be influenced with a spirit of love of Jews. Afterwards it would receive the highest levels of pleasure and reward.

The Besht then concluded to his neighbor, "That soul was your son. Do you still have complaints?"

Initially the neighbor of the Besht perceived the short life of his son as a painful curse, it was an insurmountable wall. After the Besht's revelation it was perceived as a great blessing. Similarly when the Messiah will come he will reveal to us secrets that will shed light on the darkest periods of our lives and we will realize how they were really blessings.[294]

---

294. In Rabbi Paysach Krohn's book, *Around the Maggid's Table*, there is a story that exemplifies this principle:

This principle is also true in regards to sins. When the Messiah will come the inner will of good will be revealed, and all our evil deeds will be seen as not the real personality and thus fixed.[295]

Raising *Nitzotzos*

Nothing can exist divorced from God. Even evil has a bit of Him in it to sustain it; this little bit of Godliness is called a *nitzotz*, a spark of Divine light. When a *kelippah* is broken, when I break a wall and find God behind it, then I am causing the spark of God that is hidden to be revealed, I am raising the sparks. For instance, the material world is a

---

Moshe Rabi was a Jewish refugee from Nazi Germany who had escaped to London. As the British began to suffer defeats, at the onset of the war, Moshe was deported with other refugees. He was placed on a ship, the *Dunera*, to Australia. Along the way the crew members would torment the passengers. Once a Nazi torpedo was fired at the ship and miraculously it just missed hitting the ship. The crew members were enraged. They took the last family heirlooms of the passengers and threw them overboard. Moshe was distraught since his family heirlooms were now forever lost.

Several years ago, the diary of the Nazi captain who had fired the torpedo at the *Dunera* was published. It turns out that after he missed the ship, he saw papers floating in the ocean. He sent divers to retrieve the materials since he thought they might be valuable for his nation's intelligence. When the materials were brought to his ship he discovered that they were letters and diaries written in German. He realized that the ship was carrying German nationals. He radioed all the Nazi ships in the area to take care not to torpedo the ship since it carried their countrymen. After the passengers disembarked in Australia, he tracked the *Dunera* on its return home and he sank it with a torpedo blast.

When the letters and heirlooms were thrown overboard Moshe had thought it was a horrific tragedy. Years later he realized that it was a blessing. When the messiah will come we will all merit similar revelations. We will see how all of our tragedies were blessings (see further *Around The Maggid's Table*, pgs. 194-197).

295. See the lessons about *yechidah* and the next world. Rabbi Aryeh Kaplan explains that even Adam's first sin stemmed from a good intention. He thought that acquiring an innate attraction to evil and then overcoming that attraction would give God the greatest joy. In the future the Almighty will reveal all those good intentions and show how they caused blessings.

kelippah. Imagine a hot summer day; my body is sweating as it desires a bar of cool and refreshing ice cream. If I eat for the sake of my body then the act will be one in which I too become ensnared in the shell. My arrogance and sense of self-importance might be strengthened. However, if I resist the physical urge and eat in order to have the peace of mind in order to study God's Torah, then I have broken the shell and redeemed the Godliness, the *nitzotz,* that was trapped.

The same is true for historical evil. Tragedy enervates, frightens, and isolates man. Yet if one realizes that within the evil event there is a *nitzotz,* there is Godliness, and He is all good, then traces of that goodness must exist in this ordeal. If you focus on that good, if you begin to feel that good, you are raising the spark to the Ultimate source, it will reveal itself fully, and the experience will become revealed goodness and blessing.[296]

To determine which *kelippos* can be engaged with and broken and which are to be avoided, it is necessary to detail the different types of *kelippos.*

---

296. See further *Sfas Emes, Devarim* pg. 6, s.v. *ba-pasuk be-sinas Hashem.*

Lesson Sixteen

Four Primary *Kelippos*

When the prophet Ezekiel experienced the vision of God's chariot, he first encountered obstacles that clouded the Divine light:

Va-ereh ve-hinneh ruach se'arah ba'ah min ha-tzafon, anan gadol, ve-aish mislakkachas, ve-nogah lo saviv.

And I looked, and, behold, a stormy wind came out from the north, a great cloud, a fire flashing up, and a bright sheath around Him (Ezek 1:4).

The four barriers that Ezekiel mentioned are the primary veils in our world, and they encompass the various *kelippos* that we experience.[297] The first *kelippah* was *ruach se'arah*—a stormy wind. The second was *anan gadol*—a great cloud. The third was *aish mislakkachas*—a fire flashing up, and the fourth was *nogah*—a translucent curtain.

All *kelippos* hide God and prevent the prophet from reaching the Divine, yet there is a difference in degree of opaqueness among the four. The first three are total veils that fully conceal sight of the Divine; however, the fourth is translucent. *Nogah* is like a thin sheet of cloth used as a curtain. One sheet will not hide what occurs behind it, while many such sheets together will cloud sight through them.

Similarly, three categories of behavior contain irredeemable sparks. God cannot be seen through these walls, and one should avoid them.

---

297. The world was created with God's name of *Havayah* (see earlier lessons). That name contains four letters. Evil's four categories correspond to them, and conceal the fact that the life in our universe stems from those four letters.

The fourth category, *kelippas nogah*, has a spark that can be raised through correct use while incorrect use will hide God.[298]

The lower three *kelippos* are the spiritual source of all foods and acts the Torah prohibited, while *nogah* is the source for permissible physical pleasures. The Hebrew term for forbidden acts is *asur*, which also means "tied" and "in bondage." In the forbidden foods and forbidden acts, God's sparks are tied in bondage and meager man cannot release them. Permitted foods are called *muttar*, which literally means, "untied," or, "released." These foods and acts contain Divine sparks that are untied and through proper behavior and context the sparks are liberated. Most physical items in our world are permitted. That is why Chasidim teach that our world derives from *kelippas nogah*.

The *Zohar* explains the verse, *El ginnas egoz yaradti*, "I went down to the walnut garden" (Song of Songs 6:1) in light of the lesson of the four *kelippos*. A walnut has four shells. When it first grows and is still on a tree, it is covered with a velvety thick green peel that surrounds its hard shell. This peel is totally inedible. Behind the peel is the "wooden" shell that is also indigestible and requires a nutcracker to crack it open. Once the walnut is opened one finds that it has slight brittle walls that seem to shape the walnut into a nut consisting of four parts. These walls are inedible. Finally, surrounding the fruit there is a thin filament. If the filament is on the nut it will be eaten together with the fruit and the sweetness of the nut will overwhelm its bitterness. However, if it is separated from the nut it will not be eaten and most of us will not even consider it food.

The walnut is a parable for our entire physical world. God created the world with the four letters of his name, Y-H-V-H. Traces of these four letters are to be found on the walnut fruit, which is why it seems to have four parts. It is difficult to get to the fruit because the fruit is covered with four shells. The four letters of God's name, and the special lights they produce, are hidden by the four *kelippos*. The first three barriers of the walnut represent the *shalosh kelippos ha-teme'os*, the three incorrigible evils, which is why they are inedible. The filament represents *kelippas nogah*. The filament is edible when attached to the fruit. Similarly, when

---

298. *Tanya* Chapter 1 pg. 10, and Chapters 6-7. See also *Chasidic Masters* pg. 74.

kelippas nogah is connected to holiness it adds sanctity; however when it stands alone, it connects with the three lower *kelippos* and is evil.

According to the Talmud, there are two parts to the Mitzvah of circumcision, *milah* and *periah*. *Milah* occurs when the *mohel*, the individual who performs the circumcision, cuts off the foreskin from the eight-day old baby boy. In *periah*, the *mohel* lifts a layer of skin to ensure that the crown atop the male organ remains revealed. R. Tzvi Elimelech of Dinov[299] pointed out that three layers of skin are cut during *milah* while a fourth layer of skin is pulled for the sake of *periah*. These parallel the *kelippos*. The three lower *kelippos* are irredeemable and as a result are cut off entirely. The fourth layer of skin is a representative of *nogah*; it can be rectified if it is appended to holiness, which is why this skin is lifted up and connected to the holy.

Perhaps it is these two classes of *kelippos* that are referred to in the following verse: *U-maltem es orlas livavchem, ve-arpechem lo takshu od*, "And you shall circumcise the foreskin of your heart and you should not harden your stubbornness any further" (Deut. 10:16).

The foreskin of your heart refers to manifestations of the three lower *kelippos*, they must be removed entirely. *Arpechem*, "your stubbornness," refers to *nogah*—that which does not have to be eradicated but rather redirected hence the instruction, "Do not harden it any further."[300]

The prayer against heretics states: *Ve-hazeidim meheirah te'akker u-sishabber u-simagger, ve-sachni'a bi-meheirah bi-yameinu*, "May you speedily uproot, smash, whittle away, and subdue the wanton sinners, speedily in our times."

This prayer employs four terms of destruction: uproot, smash, whittle away, and subdue. The first three connote total annihilation, for they address the three totally impure *kelippos*. The fourth term is *sachni'a*, "subdue," which implies overcoming yet not destroying. This refers to *kelippas nogah*, expressing the hope that it will be channeled towards good.

According to the Torah, the fruit from the first three years of a newly planted tree in Israel is prohibited. This produce is termed *orlah*. The

---

299. He was a student of the great Seer of Lublin. He was born in 1783 and he passed away in 1841. His most famous work is his book *Bnei Yissachar* about the twelve months of the year.
300. Heard from the Stitchiner Rebbe.

fruit of the fourth year, *neta revai*, may only be eaten in Jerusalem, and outside the holy city it is forbidden. *Orlah* is from the three forbidden *kelippos*, while *neta revai* is from *nogah*; if it is in Jerusalem there is a Mitzvah to eat it, when the fruit is outside of Jerusalem it is prohibited; man determines whether ingesting this fruit will increase or decrease his spirituality.

PERMITTED VERSUS PROHIBITED

A prohibited act like worshipping idols is from the three impure *kelippos*. Conversely, permitted pleasures such as enjoying comedy is from *nogah*. *Nogah* can be raised, and the Talmud records that Rabbis would introduce their lessons with jokes. Their humor was attached and subordinated to a Torah goal, relaxing students to facilitate more effective learning of Torah. As a result their jokes caused an increase in Divine feelings within the students and the sparks within the *kelippah* were redeemed. However, for those who use comedy to waste time, or to consider inappropriate thoughts and ignore Torah study, their *nogah* act is being utilized in a way that renders it evil. The act is then like the three impure *kelippos*—it will increase a sense of arrogance, coarseness, and physicality.

Eating pig is very different from enjoying comedy. Pork belongs to the class of the three impure *kelippos* and its *nitzotz* cannot be raised. Even if one eats from the pig, the energy the pork provided will inevitably lead to misdeed, not holiness. On the other hand, kosher meat is in the category of *nogah*. One can recite a blessing before eating and thus raise the sparks in the food through turning the moment of eating into an occasion to acknowledge the Almighty.[301] Even if one did not sanctify

301. There is a Chasidic custom that on the Yahrtzeit (the date of a person's passing) food that was purchased from the deceased's money is served, and those that eat it say, "Let the *neshamah* [soul] have an *aliyah* [ascent]." The explanation of this custom is that within a person's property are special *nitzotzos*, sparks, that relate to that person's soul. When a blessing is recited with correct intent prior to the eating of food, its spark is raised. On the day of the soul's passing, its level in Heaven is reevaluated by the Heavenly court. Eating food that belonged to the soul, and reciting a blessing beforehand to raise the spark, can serve as a merit for the deceased and the soul will then ascend to a higher level of enjoyment in Heaven.

the act beforehand, after one eats, it is possible to use the strength gained for study of Torah. In such cases, after the eating, the sparks within the food are raised and the *nogah* becomes holy. According to the Jewish tradition, after one enjoys food a blessing thanking the Almighty is recited. This reflects the fact that the *nitzotz* in the food can be raised after the eating. On the other hand if one eats a forbidden food, one may not recite a blessing before it nor after its ingestion, because the sparks are tied and they cannot be released.

A student of the *Tzemach Tzedek*[302] once asked his teacher, "Why are there so many types of food that the classic halachists permitted, yet modern custom is not to eat them?"

The Rabbi answered that within all permitted food is a *nitzotz* that can be raised through virtuous ingestion. He then added, "As we grow more distant from Sinai and the Temples of Jerusalem the spiritual level of the generation decreases. We have less spiritual strength than our ancestors. They could raise the sparks in those foods, we cannot, and that is why God guided our custom to develop a prohibition forbidding those foods."

The *Tzemach Tzedek* was teaching a perspective on life. The forward march of history is a downward slide of spirituality.[303] We have reached a low level; as a result, even items in *nogah* that were redeemable in the past are now prohibited by Jewish law and are treated as if they belong to the three lower *kelippos*.

---

302. *Tzemach Tzedek* is the name of the book of Rabbi Menachem Mendel, the third Lubavitcher Rebbe. He was born in 1789 and he passed away in 1866.
303. In Chasidic literature, our era is called *ikvasa di-meshicha*, "the heels of the Messiah." In a body, the head is the highest point while the heel is the lowest. All Jewish souls can be viewed as a single body. The generation that left Egypt and received the Torah was the head. That is why they were called *dor de'ah*, "the generation of understanding." The generation of King David was the heart of the Jewish body. King David was the epitome of his generation. In Jewish literature, King David is called the sweet singer of Israel, for he was the greatest master of emotional expression in Jewish history. Our present era, since the sixteenth century, is the heels of the body. We are at a very low spiritual level. Yet we will play the most momentous role. Our meager spiritual accomplishments are to be added to the great achievements that earlier generations wrought. Our service to God will complete all the merits needed to usher in the world of Redemption. Thus we are a heel, but this heel will bring the Moshiach. We are *ikvasa di-meshicha* (Rav Wolfson).

THE ELEMENTS AND THE FOUR *KELIPPOS*

Ancient science divided the physical world into four elements: *aish* (fire), *ruach* (wind), *mayim* (water), and *afar* (dirt). Modern science also has these categories, yet it has different names. Today, the scientist speaks of solids (*afar*), liquids (*mayim*), gasses (*ruach*), and energy or electricity (*aish*).

The physical world is what leads to sin for the spiritual is all Godly.[304] The four elements of the physical world therefore represent concepts that resemble the four *kelippos*. Water, dust, and wind (which can be felt in a balloon) are physical, tangible items and they parallel the lower three *kelippos*. Energy or electricity is qualitatively less tangible, for there is a strong spiritual streak in energy. Thus *aish* parallels *nogah*,[305] the *kelippah* that is a tree of evil and good.[306]

It is no wonder that four is such an important number in this world, for this world was created with the Tetragrammaton, the four-letter name of God. All fours evolved from those four letters.[307]

304. The physical world also has more tragedy and evil than celebration and virtue. Calculate the days of your life, the days of joy are the minority. There are more impure (unkosher) animals than pure ones. There are more animals than men, and more evildoers than saints. It is a world where the majority is evil, sadness, and tragedy.

305. Heard from the Stitchiner Rebbe.

306. The Tree of Good and Evil was in fact *kelippas nogah*. While God prohibited its consumption to man on the sixth day, the *Or Ha-Chaim* (Rabbi Chaim ben Attar) explains that it was a grape vine and God intended for Adam to use its wine for *Kiddush* (the sanctification blessing) on Friday night. Like all *nogah*, the tree of good and evil had the option to be bad or good. Adam was impatient and he ate from it on Friday afternoon when it was prohibited, instead of exercising patience and using it that evening for Shabbos. The Jewish nation had an opportunity to rectify Adam's sin when we received the Torah at Sinai. Receipt of the Torah entailed spiritual heights, the Evil Urge was silenced and all Jews reached an exalted level of prophecy. Then Moses was late returning from the mountain. The nation lost patience; they despaired, and constructed a Golden Calf. Instead of rectifying Adam's sin we repeated it.

Judaism seeks to lead us to correct Adam's failing. That is why patience is so important in our tradition. We wait patiently for the coming of a better age, even though this wait has lasted millennia, for we will correct Adam's sin. See further *Tomer Devorah* Chapter 1.

307. Energy (*aish*) emerged from the letter *yud*. Wind (*ruach*) emerged from the first *heh*. Water (*mayim*) emerged from the *vav*. The final *heh* developed into solids (*afar*). (*Anatomy of the Soul*, pg. 34.)

One God created this multifarious world. A deep look at reality will find many common denominators. Therefore, within every item, even though it is classified as a solid or a liquid, all four elements are to be found.[308] For example, a log of wood is classified as *afar*, a solid. A deeper look reveals more to the wood. Light the log, why does it burn? Because the fire element (energy) within it is unlocked when it nears revealed fire. While burning, it will cackle due to the water element (liquid) in it. Smoke and steam will emerge from it due to the *ruach* (gasses), within the log, and it will turn into ash because of the *afar* (solid) element within.

In Lesson Ten, we learned that due to the apex of the *yud* there are five parts to the Tetragrammaton. Therefore, there is really a fifth element that is hidden in the world like the apex is hidden in the *yud*. The ancients called this element the *koach ha-galgalim*, the spheres that caused planets to rotate. Today's science identifies this fifth element as the *koach ha-moshech*, the force that attracts, gravity. Gravity is a hidden element that causes all the other forces to move. Thus, it parallels the apex of the *yud* out of which a hidden life force that animates others emerged (heard from the Stitchiner Rebbe).

308. Our world is a series of repeating patterns. A broader perspective reveals one pattern, but within each individual element the same pattern is revealed. A good illustration of this is the stones from Mount Sinai. All stones from Sinai have a unique rock structure whereby a picture of a bush, a main branch with twigs emerging, is on the stone. Cut the stone and try to only have offshoots, you will have a smaller picture of a bush. No matter how small you cut the stone you will still have a bush. Or, consider the fern tree. The fern is broad at its base and it narrows as it rises. Cut the tree at the narrow top and the piece one might hold will also be wide at its base and narrower at its top. Wherever along the fern you cut, you will have the same structural pattern. Similarly, while there are four elements in the broader sense, in the narrower sense each of the elements has all four elements, and within that it is repeated again and again. This principle is also true in regards to generations. From the perspective of all of Jewish history, the first generation was a head and our generation is a heel. Yet if one cuts a piece off of the picture, if one considers our generation by itself, one will find individuals who are the head-souls, others who are heart-souls, and others who are heel-souls. Within the era of *ikvasa di-meshicha*, the times of the Ari were the head relative to our times which are clearly the heel part (see further *Anatomy of the Soul*, pg. 34).

The technical term for this concept is *bechinah*, "relative value." Wood compared to water is *afar* to *mayim*, yet when the parts of wood are compared to each other there is a *bechinah* of *mayim* in wood and a separate *bechinah* of *afar* in wood.

The entire physical world can be understood in terms of the four elements.[309] Even personality traits can be seen as expressions of the elements. For example lusts and desire for pleasure stem from the liquid element. Water is the source of all pleasure in this world; in the personality it becomes a desire for pleasure. Wind is empty, and it can fill a balloon with nothingness; similarly the desires for meaningless prattle, cynical laughter,[310] and false glory emerge from *ruach*. Dust and solids are stationary. The desire to laze about or to be depressed[311] is an expression of *afar*. Fire and energy leap ever higher and the desire for haughtiness and anger stem from that part of the personality.[312]

Some people have a physical soul that emerged from the lower *kelippos*. These people can never elevate their physicality. Within such people the physical urges for haughtiness, anger, and wasteful speech are evil and fully selfish. Even human mercy and empathy that they naturally feel is tinged with self-interest and is not fully for God's sake. For example, they will give charity so that when they eat at night they will not feel guilty at

---

309. Rabbi Nachman of Breslov (*Likkutei Moharan* 1, Lesson 4, Paragraph 8) points out that the physical world can be divided into four types of items, inanimate beings such as wood or air (called *domeim*), growing items such as fruit and trees (called *tzome'ach*), living creatures such as animals, fish and fowl (called *chai*), and humans who speak (called *medabber*). These four groups display the same pattern as the four elements; in fact the spiritual root for the four elements (the four letters Y-H-V-H) is also the spiritual cause for the four classes of physical items. The energy element (that has within it a strong spiritual streak) corresponds to humans (who possess a soul), the wind element to living beings, the water element to growing items (who all need water to grow), and the earth element is the source for the inanimate items. See further *Razei Ha-Bosem* pg. 177, Paragraphs 7-8.

310. Cynicism states that no matter is important, no person is sincere, and no activity is meaningful. It is like wind, it is all about emptiness and nothingness. See further *Pachad Yitzchak, Purim, Ma'amar* 1.

311. Depression is a state of minimal energy and life, it stems from the urge to be caught in place.

312. Ancient science felt that the human personality is determined by the four liquids ("the four humors") within the body. These too correspond to the four elements. The black liquid (foul fluid) corresponds to inanimate items and the earth element. The green bile corresponds to the growing class or the water element. The red blood corresponds to the wind element and living creatures. The white liquids correspond to the energy element and the human class (*Anatomy of the Soul*, pg. 34, and *Likkutei Moharan* Lesson 4, Paragraph 8).

their own luxurious lifestyle. These individuals can attain great spiritual heights through destruction of the physical, but their four elements and the personality they spawn are irredeemable. Others have physical souls from *kelippas nogah*. They too have a desire for pleasure, anger, prattle, and laziness, and physical empathy and concern for others, yet these desires have an admixture of selflessness within them that is virtually apparent. These people will sometimes give money to the poor solely for the poor man without thinking of themselves. Such individuals can direct the parts of their personality in the holy way, and their physicality can become holiness.[313]

The Talmud mentions four different ways to destroy *chametz*: burning, crumbling and scattering it to the wind, throwing it into the ocean, and *bittul* (nullification) whereby the owner of the bread declares that he does not value the bread at all, renounces ownership, and declares that it is like the dust of the earth. These examples are representatives of the four elements (burning = fire, throwing to the ocean = water, crumbling into the wind = wind, nullification = dust). *Chametz* represents arrogance, the foundation for the entire world of *kelippah*; as a result, it must be destroyed in all the four elements of the physical world.

The Strongest Weapon against the *Kelippah*

The most effective way to legally rid oneself of possessing *chametz* is *bittul*. According to Jewish law, nullification affects even the *chametz* that is unseen and beyond the reach of the owner. This law can be understood with our analysis. Since the essence of evil is arrogance, when one recognizes its emptiness, one has directly confronted it and it can be overcome. Peels might think that they are important, yet in truth relative to the fruit they are worthless. Similarly, evil thinks it is something, but if you recognize its emptiness, you will undoubtedly overcome its charms.[314]

---

313. See further *Tanya* Chapter 1, pg. 6.
314. There is a tradition that Abraham's war with the four kings occurred on Passover. The *Midrash Rabbah* on *Parashas Lech Lecha* (43:3) teaches that Abraham had a unique way of battle—he would throw dust. The earth he threw would miraculously turn into spears, arrows, and swords that pummeled the

Rebbe Nachman of Breslov expressed this thought in the following parable: The Evil Urge is like a prankster running through a crowd, displaying a tightly closed hand. No one knows what he is holding, and he accosts each one, saying, "What do you suppose I have in my hand?" Each one imagines that the closed hand contains just what he desires most. They all hurry and run after the prankster. Then, when he has tricked them completely, he opens his hand, and there is nothing in it. The same is true of the Evil One. He fools the world, tricking all into following him. People think that his hands hold what they desire most, but in the end he opens it, and it is empty. No desire is ever fulfilled. Worldly pleasures are like sunbeams in a dark room. They may seem solid, but one who tries to grasp a sunbeam finds nothing in his hand. The same is true of earthly matters.[315]

---

enemy. Perhaps the symbolic import of Abraham defeating the four kings with dust was the following lesson: The four kings represented the four *kelippos*, they sought to encourage a life of sin, and the most effective way to combat them is dust. Consider how empty evil is, recognize how its pleasures are so transient and its claims so spurious, and you will defeat evil.

The four *kelippos* stem from what *chametz* represents. Abraham implanted through his act the ability within his progeny to do as he did, we too, can declare that the evil is nothing, we will then overcome it (Rav Wolfson).

315. Rabbi Nachman of Breslov, *Sichos Ha-Ran* 6 quoted in *Chasidic Masters* pg. 111. See further the Vilna Gaon to Prov. 6:25, where he explains that lust is a form of deceit since the evil urge presents its urgings as a source of benefit to the individual while in truth they are a trap that will ensnare the individual in eventual pain and suffering.

Lesson Seventeen

Transforming the Physical into the Spiritual

THE SPARK WITHIN *nogah* can be raised in several ways. On the lowest level, one enjoys the physical for the sake of the spiritual. For example, if you are hot and thirsty and cannot concentrate on learning Torah and you then eat an ice cream cone and enjoy its cool refreshing smoothness so that you will be able to learn Torah. A higher level of spark elevation entails ignoring all physical pleasure. A *tzaddik* eats with special meditative intent. The only reason why he puts the morsel of food in his mouth is to raise sparks with the act. Such a person was Rabbi Avraham Yehoshua Heschel from Apt:[316]

> It is well known that the Rebbe from Apt would eat a great deal. He once said, "Believe me, with every bite I chew I feel a taste that is as bitter as the bitterest herbs." When he would complete his meal he would apologize to those foods that he had not succeeded in consuming. [The explanation of all this is that] his eating was exclusively for the sake of holy sparks that are within the foods.[317]

---

316. See Lesson Three. He was born in 1755 and he passed away in 1825. He was filled with overflowing love for all Jews, and he was a student of R. Elimelech of Lizhensk.
317. The Rebbe of Klausenberg, *Imros Tzaddikim*, pg. 18.

Another example of a *tzaddik* who turned a physical act into a spiritual act is our forefather Jacob. The Torah relates that after Laban agreed with Jacob, that our forefather would serve Laban for seven years to earn Rachel's hand in marriage:

Va-ya'avod Yaakov be-Rachel sheva shanim va-yihyu be-einav ke-yamim achadim be-ahavaso osah.

And Jacob worked for Rachel seven years, and they were in his eyes as a few days, due to his love for her (Gen. 29:20).

Jacob's feelings seem unusual. If someone desperately wants something, being forced to wait for it is torture. Every minute becomes an eternity. If Jacob loved Rachel, shouldn't the seven years have been seven thousand years in his eyes? The answer is that Jacob's love was unique.

When we desire an item, we want it for selfish pleasure. You may hear someone say, "I love fish. Whenever I go to a restaurant, I order salmon." Then he does not love fish. Were he to love fish, would he kill them and eat them? The real meaning of his statement is that he adores himself, and his eating fish is an example of how he indulges in self-gratification. Since we are focused on ourselves, when we have to wait for hedonistic attainment it seems like an eternity.

Jacob never thought of himself. According to the Midrash, Jacob was a *merkavah* of the *Shechinah*; his body was a throne that God's Presence resided upon. He achieved this degree of devotion because he fully emptied himself of all egotism.[318] If Jacob desired someone or an item he only sought it in order to benefit God's service.[319]

The Torah emphasizes the uniqueness of Jacob's feelings in the words *be-ahavaso osah*, "in his love for her." He loved her, not himself. When one of us tells someone, "I love you," we usually mean, "I love myself, I enjoy what you do for me, therefore I want your company." Jacob was

---

318. Arrogance causes God to be pushed away, to be filled with God implies a total renunciation of all ego.

319. Even his service of God was in no way linked to desiring reward or avoiding punishment, for he did not think of himself. He performed Mitzvos for God's sake, because they furthered the Divine purposes of Creation.

unique. He fully loved Rachel and did not consider himself at all. Since the items we love are means to further our ego, when we have to wait for them, every moment hurts. Jacob had no ego, which is why it was not an eternity for him to wait for Rachel.

He desired Rachel because the marriage of Jacob and Rachel would cause the appearance of powerful streams of spiritual blessings. He wanted to marry Rachel in the same way a *tzaddik* wants to perform a Mitzvah. He endeavored to cause a Heavenly flow of blessing, through the seemingly physical act of uniting with Rachel. When one truly wants to perform God's service, one becomes inspired, rising over the dimension of time, one rushes to do the act with *zerizus*, "industrious speed," and the moments pass quickly.[320]

Alternatively, for Jacob each day of work for Rachel was a Mitzvah, for he was walking along the path to an act that would bring enormous blessings to God's world. The search for Mitzvos and the preparatory steps to enable Mitzvah observance are themselves Mitzvos. Since he was a *tzaddik* all the Mitzvos that he performed were pleasurable, as a result his days of work passed quickly.

On a deeper level, we can suggest that the Divine motivation of Jacob was the desire to reveal the spark of *Yovel*—the Jubilee year—which Rachel contained.

YOVEL RESTORES BRANCHES TO THEIR ROOTS

In the land of Israel, after every forty-nine years, during the fiftieth year, a special Heavenly spirit descends into the world. This *shefa*, abundant flow of blessing, has a unique characteristic; it returns all to their root. In the Torah, the unique character of the fiftieth year is expressed in the following passage:

Ve-kiddashtem es shnas ha-chamishim shanah u-krasem dror ba-aretz le-chol yoshveha, Yovel hi tihyeh lachem, ve-shavtem ish el achuzaso ve-ish el mishpachto tashuvu.

---

320. See further *Pachad Yitzchak, Pesach, Ma'amar* 1.

And you shall sanctify the fiftieth year, proclaim liberty throughout the land to all its inhabitants, it shall be a Jubilee for you; each of you shall return to his ancestral lands and every man will return to his family (Lev. 25:10).

What is the meaning of the name *Yovel*? Rashi suggests that this name refers to the fact that the year's special laws are set in motion through blowing the ram's horn. Nachmanides however offers a different explanation, "In my opinion, Scripture does not call the year *Yovel* because of the blowing [of the horn], but with reference to 'the liberty' [that it brings the inhabitants of the land]." Nachmanides then quotes many sources for his contention that *Yovel* means "to bring." He closes his argument by stating, "By the way of truth [we learn]... *Yovel* means that every being will return [be brought back] to the source [*yoveil*] where his roots lie."[321]

Nachmanides quotes as a source for his explanation of the name *Yovel* a verse in Jeremiah, *Ve-al yuval yishallach shorashav*, "And its roots will be sent forth" (Jer. 17:8). *Yovel* is when spiritual roots spread out to return their offshoots home. *Yovel's* nature is further reflected in its two defining laws.

The first law of *Yovel* is freedom. *Yovel* frees the *eved ivri*—the Jewish servant. Who is the *eved ivri*? A thief who was sold. Why is a thief punished with servitude? And why does *Yovel* free him?

The material possessions you own contain *nitzotzos*, sparks of light from your soul. Those sparks need you to elevate them. You are given possessions that are related to your soul for only your correct usage will redeem those sparks. When someone steals your possessions he is taking a part of your extended person and preventing you from fulfilling your mission. To rectify his misdeed, he must return the stolen object. If he cannot return the object then he must give you its monetary equivalent. If he cannot afford to pay, the court will sell him as a servant, an *eved ivri*. Theft removed items from their rightful place, as a punishment the thief must leave his domain, and he is separated from his family and subjugated.

---

321. Nachmanides, commentary on Lev. 25:10.

Spiritually, the *eved* falls to a wretched state. Prior to his sale, he was a fully vested member of the Jewish community; after his theft and sale he loses much of his spirituality, and he may marry the Gentile maids in his master's home.[322] *Yovel* brings all to their roots and it returns the Jewish servant to his appropriate spiritual condition. As a result, during *Yovel* he returns home to his family and spiritual level.

Most servants do not need a full-fledged *Yovel* to effect freedom. The usual term of service for a Jewish servant is six years, and in the seventh he goes free. The seventh year shares a quality with Shabbos, the seventh day. The light of Shabbos[323] also pulls all to their root, and thus it lifts the slave back to his root. Only the servants who insist after six years of work that they do not wish to leave their master need a full *Yovel*. These men were inducted into eternal servitude when the master pierced their ear lobe. Yet, once *Yovel* occurs even these servants go free, for *Yovel* pulls all to their root.

All returns to the source emerge from *Yovel*. For example, the *eved* who leaves in the seventh year tastes freedom because of the *Yovel*-aspect within the seventh year. *Yovel* as the fiftieth year is a display of the spirituality symbolized in the number eight. Seven times seven represents the most complete form of seven. The fiftieth year represents the number eight, a number above sevens. In the spiritual domain every higher level extends into the lower level, the level of eight can be found in the seventh. Thus, even the seventh day and the seventh year that return offshoots to their source stem from *Yovel*, the *Yovel* that is in Shabbos.

---

322. The word for family and wife in Hebrew is *mishpachah*. The thief has defiled the forty days of his formation and the forty days of Torah instruction at Sinai. The letter *mem* has a *gematria* of forty. Since he has lost his forty days, he is left with *shifchah* (*mishpachah* without the *mem*), the Hebrew word for a Gentile maid (Rav Wolfson).

323. The word Shabbos shares a root with the word *shav*, "return," for on Shabbos we all return to our root. Adam committed his sin and ate from the tree of knowledge on Friday afternoon. The punishment due for that misdeed was banishment from the Garden of Eden. However, God allowed him to spend Shabbos in the garden because Shabbos restored his soul to its root, which had not tasted sin.

The second law of *Yovel* is the return of land. When the Jewish nation first entered the land of Israel, Joshua divided the land among the families within the nation. The portion one received was an eternal inheritance, it could not be lost. Even if someone in a family sold that land, when *Yovel* arrived, the land would return to the family that had initially received it from Joshua.

Land has a root-quality. Every nation is attracted to their homeland and countries of origin are frequently called fatherland or motherland because they are viewed as a source for national life. Since *Yovel* returns branches to the root, it returns the individual to his or her land.

The Place of *Yovel*

Spiritual concepts appear in the dimension of time, person, and place.[324] In time, *Yovel* is the fiftieth year. The place of *Yovel* is Bethlehem. In Hebrew, this is *Beis Lechem Yehudah*, whose first three letters are the same as the word *Yovel*.[325] Bethlehem is famous for its role in the book of Ruth.

The book of Ruth is the story of Naomi and her daughter-in-law Ruth. Naomi and her husband Elimelech were the gentry of Bethlehem. They left the town to avoid the hordes of poor who were begging for their help during years of famine. The family moved to the land of Moab, and Naomi's two sons married Moabite women. After Elimelech and his sons died and much of the family's wealth was lost, Naomi decided to return to Bethlehem. Ruth, Naomi's former Moabite daughter-in-law, followed Naomi and joined the Jewish nation. According to the Chida,[326] Ruth always possessed a Jewish soul; it had been born into a Moabite family though. Ruth's conversion was really a return of a spark to its rightful place, *Yovel* effected that process. In God's plan, Naomi left Bethlehem in order to return Ruth to her rightful fold. Perhaps Bethlehem as the place of *Yovel* caused this story of a return to its root.

---

324. See further Lesson Two.
325. The *roshei teivos* of *Beis Lechem Yehudah* (בל"י) are the same as *Yovel* (יבל) spelled without the *vav* (ו). It is spelled without the *vav* in Lev. 25:54.
326. Rav Chaim Yosef David Azulai (1724-1806) was one of the great Sephardic Kabbalists; he is known by the acronym *Chida*.

Yovel Personalities

Maimonides explains that the hallmark of the Messiah is that he will return the dispersed Jews to the Land of Israel, their homeland. This aspect of the Messianic mission is the force of *Yovel*. The Messiah will have within him a bit of the spirit of *Yovel*, and that will cause the nation to return to the Land of Israel, our root. He will be a descendant of David, and a *gilgul*, a transmigration, of David's soul.[327] David is named in the Prophets, *Ben Yishai beis ha-lachmi*, "Son of Jesse the Bethlehemite." David is a descendant of Ruth who lived in Bethlehem, and he was born in Bethlehem. Perhaps the fact that he is the personality of *Yovel* emerges from his birth in the place of *Yovel*.

Rachel is buried in Bethlehem, because Rachel is a personality of *Yovel*. When the Jewish nation went out into exile the souls of our ancestors interceded with the Divine on our behalf. Rachel's prayers were answered in the affirmative.

Koh amar Hashem, kol be-ramah nishma, nehi bechi tamrurim, Rachel mivakkeh al baneha me-anah le-hinnachem al baneha ki einenu. Koh amar Hashem min'i koleich mi-bechi ve-einayich mi-dimah ki yesh sachar li-feulaseich neum Hashem ve-shavu me-eretz oyeiv. Ve-yesh tikvah le-achariseich neum Hashem ve-shavu vanim li-gvulam.

So says God, a voice is heard in Ramah, it is the wail of travails, Rachel is crying for her children, refusing consolation for her children are missing. So says God, remove your voice from sobs and your eyes from tears; there is reward for your good deeds, by Lord, they will return from the land of the enemy. There is hope for you! Your children will return to their land (Jer. 31:14-16).

---

327. *Adam* (אדם) is the acronym for the names of a single soul that appeared in *Adam* (א), the first man, *David* (ד), the first Jewish king, and *Moshiach* (מ), the final human king.

God promised to return us to our root in her merit for she has the personality of *Yovel*. God promised that return in the words, *neum Y-H-V-H ve-shavu vanim li-gvulam*. The first letters of the last four words spell *Yovel*, for *Yovel* returns the children to their land.[328] Perhaps the reason why when the Jews left Israel, they passed by her grave was to convey this message to the exiles, "Do not despair, the force of *Yovel* is in your nation, Rachel is your mother and she is the person of Bethlehem, the place of *Yovel* and redemption. *Yovel* teaches that at some point even the lowliest will return to their root. You too will someday return home to your rightful place."[329]

JACOB, RACHEL, AND *YOVEL*

Jacob spent seven years working for Rachel, and then Laban had him marry Leah. Once he found out that he had been tricked he waited seven days and then married Rachel in return for promising to work for another seven years (see Gen. 29:27-28). These two sets of seven, first years and then days, represent the full complement of seven. Jacob spiritually accomplished what seven times seven regular years usually accomplish. After the two sevens of forty-nine years, we have *Yovel*, and after Jacob's two sevens he too received *Yovel*, the light of Messiah, through marriage with Rachel.

According to the *Zohar*, Rachel's death was an unparalleled calamity for Jacob. Perhaps it was because Rachel contained within her the spark of *Yovel* and redemption that her loss was so devastating to Jacob.[330] After Rachel died, Jacob traveled to Migdal Eder.[331] Targum Yonasan[332] explains that Migdal Eder is the place where Messiah will be revealed.

---

328. *Tzion Ve-Arehah* pg. 59.
329. *Tzion Ve-Arehah* pg. 58.
330. The Baal Shem Tov once traveled on a Friday afternoon to visit a simple Jew in the forest. After spending some time with that Jew, the Besht insisted on leaving even though it was late Friday afternoon and he would not reach the next Jewish village before Shabbos. After he left, his students asked him, "Rebbe, why did you insist on leaving this Jew?" To which the Besht responded, "The man I was visiting contained the soul of the Messiah. I know that due to the unworthiness of our generation he will die this Shabbos. I cannot stand to see the loss of a spark of the Messiah." Witnessing the loss of great hopes is heartrending.
331. See Targum Yonasan to Micah 4:8.
332. See *Megillah* 3a.

Migdal Eder literally means "tower of the flock." The reason for this name is that Messiah will collect together the dispersed Jews of exile, the many flocks of sheep, and unite them into a single flock. Perhaps God was comforting Jacob by showing him that the light of Messiah was not fully lost, and it will yet be revealed in Migdal Eder.

When Jacob kissed Rachel he did not view the act as a physical act. It was like kissing *tefillin*, or more accurately kissing the Torah scroll, for the Torah is also the root of the Jewish nation. Since Rachel personified *Yovel*, the years that Jacob worked for her flew by.

A parable might help explain why Jacob's years of labor seemed to be short days. Imagine if you could see the light of redemption at the end of a tunnel. With every step along the tunnel you see the light a little clearer. As you move forward, you can constantly measure progress and frequently feel the fulfillment of goals nearing accomplishment. The brighter the glow the more excited you get. Even if it took years, wouldn't the years seem like a few moments?

Lesson Eighteen

Times of *Yovel*

Yovel Moments and the Three Impure *Kelippos*

In our world, the Godly sparks caught within the three lower *kelippos* are irredeemable. *Yovel* is a revelation of a new World. In the world of *Yovel* all Godly sparks may return to their holy roots. Thus, when the light of *Yovel* glitters, even items of the three lower *kelippos* might become permitted. Sometimes, the atmosphere from a *Yovel*-like dimension might enter into our realm of existence.

According to Jewish law, when forbidden foods are mixed with permissible edibles, there is a law of *bittul*, "nullification." This law states that if the mixture is found to contain sixty times more permitted material than forbidden, the entire combination is allowed. Apparently, through the preponderance of good, the evil is neutralized. Perhaps some of the principles we have discovered in earlier lessons help explain this law. Nullification means that an item loses its identity. We have learned that evil is predicated on arrogance. Loss of identity represents annihilation of ego, hence its ability to remove the strong *kelippah* quality that surrounds a prohibited food item. *Bittul* takes a member of the three lower *kelippos* (prohibited food) and transforms it into a display of *nogah* (permissible food). In *nogah*, the spark is closer to its source in holiness. Thus *bittul* is a light of the final redemption, the time of *Yovel*—return to Source.

Jewish law states, *ein mevatlin issur lechatchillah*, "One may not deliberately cause a *bittul* of forbidden foods." Perhaps the reason for this is that we may not coerce God to bring the redemption; He will send it at the time He deems right.

Yovel Holidays

Some of the holidays contain emanations from the light of *Yovel*. The holiday of Chanukah is a time when the hidden light of redemption shines. Chanukah is an eight-day holiday, thus it is connected with *Yovel*, which is above the natural limits of seven. *Yovel* breaks through all *kelippos*, returning sparks and souls to their rightful place; similarly, the light of Chanukah pierces the darkest corners and frees sparks that are usually trapped. This is why even though Mitzvos are usually performed in the home, the Chanukah candles are to be lit in the *reshus ha-rabbim*, the public domain, which parallels the *alma di-prodah*, the realm of separation.[333] Ideally, the Chanukah menorah is to be placed on the outside of a door to a dwelling, its message declaring that the private domain really extends into the public street. Where there seem to be many, in truth, it is all One. This is an echo from the final redemption when good will reach everywhere.

A group of Chasidim once asked the Seer of Lublin[334] to curse a Jewish informer who was causing much hardship to his community. The rabbi asked them to write the name of the troublemaker on a piece of paper. When he saw it, he screamed, "I cannot curse this man! His soul is shining in the highest realms of Heaven." The Chasidim were shocked and they made a shamefaced exit.

Life with the informer was intolerable. He continued to prey upon the Jewish community. He had no mercy. He would even report widows and indigent individuals to the authorities. He constantly demanded hush payments of money and honor. After a few months, the Chasidim decided to ask the Rabbi again to do something about the informer.

This time they gave the name to the Rabbi, and he immediately cursed it. The Rabbi explained, "When you first came, it was Chanukah, and at the moment I looked at his name he was lighting Chanukah candles.

---

333. See Lesson Fifteen for an explanation why evil is represented by the domain of the many.

334. Rabbi Yaakov Yitzchak Horowitz was born in 1745 and he passed away in 1815, He was called the *Chozeh*, the Hebrew word for "Seer." Due to a childhood injury he lost physical sight out of one eye, yet due to his great spiritual level he had the ability to spiritually see that which was hidden physically.

When one lights the menorah, even the worst sinner of the world, his soul shines in the highest points of Heaven. On Chanukah, there is a light from the ultimate age. Then there will be no evil and even the worst will be exceedingly righteous for their *yechidah* will be revealed. However, now it is a regular day, therefore, the informer is judged on his present level. Today, he does not deserve life."

The holiday of *Lag Ba-Omer*, the thirty-third day of the *Omer* count, is also a time when the light of *Yovel* appears. Rabbi Shimon bar Yochai's birthday and Yahrtzeit, day of passing, is *Lag Ba-Omer*. Rashbi[335] revealed that there was a secret dimension to Torah.[336] *Chayah* and *yechidah* are the parts of the soul that correspond to the *sod*, the secret part of Torah. His revelation caused the hidden part of Jewish souls to be revealed as well. Once the hidden soul emerges, all are united in a fellowship of perfect virtue.

Rashbi had a spark of the soul of Messiah. That is why in the Messianic era, *halachah* will follow his rulings.[337] His lessons raise souls and reconnect them with their Root in Heaven. Rashbi's day, *Lag Ba-Omer*, contains his light, the light of *Yovel*. That is why all types of Jews come to Meron[338] to celebrate at Rashbi's grave on *Lag Ba-Omer*. There are observant and non-observant Jews there, for all souls sense that Rashbi is the one who restores them to their Source.

The holiday of Purim also contains a light from the world of *Yovel*. Purim celebrates the downfall of Haman, the wicked Persian Prime Minister, who sought to exterminate the Jewish race. Haman had a great hatred toward Mordechai, the leader of the Jews. To hang Mordechai, Haman constructed gallows that were fifty *ammos* (cubits) tall. The

335. The acronym of his name.
336. The *gematria* of the phrase *sod Hashem li-yire'av*, "The secret of God is [revealed] to those who fear Him" (353) corresponds to the *gematria* of the phrase *Adoneinu bar Yochai*, "Our master the son of Yochai" (354). The discipline of *gematria* allows for a discrepancy of one, for God comes to complete the numbers (*Tzion Ve-Arehah* pg. 141).
337. The *Tiferes Shlomo* to *Parashas Shoftim* writes that even though presently *halachah* is not in accordance with R. Shimon's views, in the future when the world will be filled with the knowledge of Heaven, we will fully realize how correct his views are and *halachah* will follow his positions (*Tzion Ve-Arehah* pg.140-141).
338. Meron is the town in Israel's Galil region where Rashbi is buried.

Maharal[339] explained Haman's behavior with the concept of *Yovel*. Haman sought to arouse the fiftieth gate of impurity, a display of an impure parallel to *Yovel*. Hence a gallows fifty *ammos* tall, just as *Yovel* is the fiftieth year. When God caused Haman's downfall and Jewry's salvation, we merited that on the holiday commemorating these events, light of the fiftieth gate of holiness, *Yovel*, would shine in our world. According to the tradition of the Jewish calendar, in every year, the day of the week on which Purim takes place is identical to the day of the week on which we celebrate *Lag Ba-Omer*. Perhaps the reason for this link is that both days reveal the light of *Yovel*.[340]

THE *KELIPPAH* COPIES THE HOLY

Evil attempts to externally copy the realm of holiness. Lesson Seventeen taught that Bethlehem is infused with the spirit of *Yovel*. The Messianic era will display an awesome revelation of *Yovel*. That time will be revealed through a descendent of King David, a child of Bethlehem, the place of *Yovel*. The souls of Gentile nations sense that Bethlehem contains the spark of redemption and that is why they claim that their leader was the Messiah and that he was born in Bethlehem. In truth, the real Messiah is a reincarnation of King David, a true child of Bethlehem.

In the book of Isaiah the prophet revealed that every single human possesses two souls (Isa. 57:16). What is the meaning of two souls? One soul is the breath of God. Lesson Five called this life force the *nefesh Elokis*. The other soul is the biological soul. It emerges from the *kelippos*, and in Lesson Five it was called the *nefesh ha-bahamis*. Since the *kelippah* copies the domain of the holy, we learned in Lesson Fourteen that the *kelippah* soul has parts that parallel the five parts of holiness, *nefesh*, *ruach*, *neshamah*, *chayah*, and *yechidah*.

Perhaps one can apply the concept of evil as an imitator in the following manner: The essence of life is the Heavenly soul. True life is the experience of serving God. The *kelippah* apes that concept. It presents physicality as the sum total of existence. To live a life of exclusively physical concerns is like buying a poor imitation of a master painting and paying the price of the original drawing.

---

339. Quoted in *Afikei Mayim, Binyanei Chanukah U-Purim*, pg. 192.
340. See *Emunas Etecha*, Volume 3, pgs. 50-52.

THE HOLY PATH

Lessons Six through Eighteen have revealed that the body can be transformed into holiness. The physical *kelippah* soul usually emerges from *kelippas nogah*. *Nogah* is a mixture of good and evil. The good within *nogah* is the reason why a *tzaddik* can transform his body into pure saintliness.

All of us can achieve some level of *tzaddik*-hood. The road map to success in the struggle for virtue is a strong understanding of the human personality. That knowledge can be achieved through defining the *Sephiros* and their function. Lesson Nineteen will attempt to explain the concept of *Sephiros* and how they are reflected within man.

LESSON NINETEEN

THE *SEPHIROS*
AND MAN'S PERSONALITY

MAN HAS TEN components to his personality. These ten parts appear in the soul piece of *nefesh*, reappear differently within *ruach*, and they assume another form within *neshamah*. Why ten parts? The physical universe was founded with ten spiritual elemental forces and man is a small universe. The spiritual sources for the physical world were miniaturized into the ten parts of human character. The initial primal powers are Godly lights called the ten *Sephiros*.[341]

There are many connotations to the term *Sephirah*. It shares a relationship with the word *sefar*, "border." It also recalls the words *sippur*, "story," and *sefer*, "book." Lastly, in the Torah, the word *sappir* refers to a glittering, light filled, crystal, related to the English word "sapphire" (see Exod. 24:10).

God Himself is an infinite light. He is so overwhelming that He would incinerate any human or physical creature that would directly approach Him. God desired to create a material world populated with frail human creatures. He desired that meager men, despite their infirmities, would experience Divine essence in some measure. To enable such a world, God limited His light by placing borders on the emanations that He released out of His essence.

Imagine an individual who desires to appreciate the sun; can he look directly at a blazing midday sun? To look at such a bright light he must don a pair of thick, colored lenses. The sunglasses limit the light to a degree that makes it appreciable. The reduced light might still be too bright, so he might add more pairs of sunglasses to his nose.

---

341. *Tanya*, Chapter 3.

God's light[342] was too bright, so He fashioned ten tinted lenses, each with a different color, to allow for the light to be appreciated. Examine the light out of the first window pane. It is the light of the first *Sephirah*. This glow is still too intense; hence the need for more window panes. God pulled out of the first light a more constricted radiance,[343] and out of the second a third, still lesser ray, emerged. In total, God set up ten barriers to limit His infinite light. These veils are the ten *Sephiros*, the limited lights of Divinity. The process of limiting His lights was repeated millions of times. It is called *seder hishtalshlus*, the orderly chain of progressive revelation. Each stage along the emanation chain contains the same ten steps. After each limitation the light became less Heavenly. Eventually out of lights that bordered on the physical a material world emerged. The ten *Sephiros* are represented in the ten primary colors,[344] for God's Light was limited with panels of different hues.

The bordered lights enable the telling of the story of God. Absent these limitations, no words would be able to describe Him or instruct man as to the way to approach Him.[345] Varying colors represent the idea that there are different paths to feeling Divinity. For instance, some

342. God does not have any light, for there is nothing physical to the Creator. Yet, the imagery of light is used to help convey lessons that relate to more abstract spiritual concepts.

> It is important to warn the reader that in order to describe certain Kabbalistic notions such as the *Sephiros*… it is necessary to use metaphors to express abstract concepts, due to the limitations of human language. The reader should understand these descriptions as complex poetical symbols rather than focusing on the imagery as such (Foreword to *Innerspace*).

343. In earlier lessons, the limited lights were called universes (*olamos*). Now we are calling them *Sephiros*, yet both points are true. Limiting Divinity is the process of *tzimtzum*, "limitation," and *hishtalshlus*, the world's progressive evolution. The general view of this process reveals five worlds; if you look closer within those worlds you will discover the ten *Sephiros*. The *Sephiros* display, in greater detail, the same pattern as the universes.

344. According to Jewish mystics there are only ten primary colors; other colors are composites and shades of the ten.

345. "It is through the *Sephiros* that God limits His infinite essence and manifests specific qualities that His creatures can grasp and relate to. As such, the *Sephiros* act variously as filters, garments, or vessels, for the light of *Ain Sof* (Endless Light) that fills them" (*Innerspace* pg. 40).

reach God through acts of love to His creatures, while others experience the Divine through study of His Torah and feeling the harmony of His judicial laws. The different paths a man will choose are usually a reflection of his personality. Some individuals are very kind. Within their temperament the Divine force of kindness is paramount. Such individuals will experience God when giving charity. A woman who is very demanding, for whom the Divine force of restraint and self-control is the dominant strand in her character, might feel true spirituality when she meticulously observes every detail of Jewish law.[346]

The Heavenly lights are themselves extension of God's very essence.[347] God is a source of illumination, and the *sappir*-concept indicates that the *Sephiros* glitter with Divine incandescence. In our world it would be inappropriate to call anything a *Sephirah*. A *Sephirah* is a Heavenly, Godly Light. Material items bear meek similarities to the Godly forces that are their source.

"The universe was created through ten statements."[348] This Mishnah is based on the ten appearances of the word *Va-yomer*, "and God said," in the first chapter of the book of Genesis,[349] which are the ten Divine decrees that produced the world. What the Mishnah called ten statements, the

---

346. This idea is sometimes presented as the lesson of the structure of the first man. Adam was the first human, and as a result, all the future souls of mankind were incorporated in his soul and its parts. Some individuals are very generous. They attain a sense of Divine experience through giving charity. These souls were in the hands and fingers of Adam, that is why their innate nature is generosity, and they reach God through charity. Other souls were in the heart of Adam. These are the singers of Israel, those who pray with extra devotion and reach God through the service of the heart, prayer (Rav Wolfson). See further *Wellsprings of Faith* pgs. 46-47, *Shem Mi-Shmuel* on *Parashas Vaeschanan* pg. 31 s.v. *u-va-zeh yuvanu*.

347. See further *Innerspace* pg. 40, note 27.

348. *Ethics of the Fathers* 5:1.

349. In truth, the Talmud teaches that there are nine commands of creation and the tenth was the first word of the Torah, *Bereishis*, "In the Beginning." Perhaps this lesson teaches that the first "statement" was the creation of speech, while the other statements were expressions of speech. According to the *Zohar*, there is a different list of ten. The first statement is "And God said, 'Let there be light,'" and the final statement is (Gen. 2:18) *Va-yomer Hashem Elokim lo tov heyos ha-adam le-vaddo e'eseh lo eizer ke-negdo*, "And God, the Lord, said 'it is not good for man to be alone I will make for him a helpmate opposite him'" (Rav Wolfson).

mystics termed ten *Sephiros*. Human speech is a limitation of breath, the essence of human life.[350] The ten *Sephiros* are the limitations of God's essence; hence they are symbolically called ten statements.

Items in the physical world display traces of their roots, the individual *Sephirah* they emerged from. Man is *be-tzelem Elokim*, in the image of the entire spiritual realm. Man resembles all of the spiritual roots, and he has within him traces of all ten statements (*Sephiros*).

Within the name of man is the lesson of his ten components. The numeric value of the Hebrew word for man, *Adam*, adds up to 45, which recalls the name of God in its fullest form which also equals 45. The full *gematria* form was discussed earlier, where each letter is spelled out and then totaled. The full *gematria* of God's primary name, Y-H-V-H is 45. The spelled out form of the name is ten letters. The ten letters represent the ten *Sephiros*. Man has innate traces of those ten forces. A life of righteous deeds leads man to become a *merkavah*, "chariot," for revealed manifestations of all ten Heavenly forms of holiness.

Since man has all ten distinct forces he can choose how to react to a stimulus. If a lion appears before him and roars, man will decide whether to arouse the force of fear and flee, or to arouse the force of dominance and fight. Other creatures, since they only have one spiritual source, will always respond instinctually, in the mode of their spiritual root, to a given situation. A lion that is suddenly threatened will never respond with generosity and compassion. A lion will always fight when he is attacked. An attack dog will never respond to a threat by fleeing like a mouse. With only one root, they cannot choose what modality of behavior to employ.

Man might have within him traces of all ten *Sephiros*, yet he will probably have one force as the dominant part of his personality. The other forces lie dormant as latent parts of his persona. Some people are very tough and withdrawn. These individuals have, as their primary force, the attribute of restraint or fear. That is why they restrain themselves and engender fear in others. Usually, they will act in accordance with the characteristics of fear. For example, when faced with a perceived

---

350. The word for soul, *neshamah*, shares a relationship with the word *neshimah*, "breath," for respiration is vitality.

infraction they will get angry and cause others to withdraw. However, as humans, they have latent within them all the Divine forces including, for instance, Heavenly love. Sometimes they will summon forth love and treat the violator of the rule with tenderness. Other individuals are very intellectual because the forces of wisdom and understanding are the dominant motifs to their personality. Even the intellectual can arouse passionate feelings, for as a human he has traces of all ten forces, and he can call any of them forth.

The ten statements are a creative pattern that keeps repeating itself. Each universe has a different expression of all ten *Sephiros*, for to be a universe it must be an arena that has all of the primal forces.[351] They appear in different forms in each world. In the world of *beriah*[352] they appear in a virtually entirely spiritual form.[353] In *yetzirah* they take on a slightly more corporeal form; they then progress to a more physical state in the world of *asiyah*, and out of these spiritual lights all the physical items in our world appeared. Even within each *Sephirah* in each universe there are component parts that correspond to the full array of ten *Sephiros*. Within each component part of each *Sephirah* there is another reflection of the full ten *Sephiros*, for this pattern appears a myriad of times within the world.

Earlier lessons taught that the parts of the soul emerged from the different supernal universes. Each part of the soul has within it the full ten forces that animate its corresponding world. *Neshamah* has ten forces that resemble the ten *Sephiros* in *beriah*. *Ruach* has ten forces that share similarities with the *Sephiros* of *yetzirah*, and the ten forces of *nefesh* correspond to the ten *Sephiros* of *asiyah*.

To describe the *Sephiros* themselves and to attempt to define them is not the goal of Chasidus. Kabbalah teaches how the *Sephiros* appear in different worlds. Chasidus seeks to use the *Sephiros* concept as a means to understand the nature of man.

---

351. The technical term for a complete array of forces is *Shiur Komah*, which literally means, "the full measure of height."

352. See Lessons Eight through Twelve for discussions about the spiritual universes and their corresponding soul parts.

353. The *Sephiros* appeared in the realms of *atzilus* and *Adam Kadmon* as well. However, those levels are so exalted that Chasidim hardly speak about those concepts (Rav Wolfson). See further *Innerspace* pg. 41.

DEFINING THE PATTERN:
THREE SOURCES, SEVEN OFFSPRING

If you examine the creation account, the first three statements detail spiritual items that do not fully exist in our dimension of reality: "In the beginning,"[354] "Let there be light," and, "Let there be a divider between [spiritual] waters above and the waters below on earth."[355] The fourth statement, "Let the waters gather and reveal the dry land," and all the subsequent creative demands deal with the earthly realm. Evidently, in our dimension of reality, God appears through the seven lower *Sephiros*, and the first three lights are only fully realized in Heavenly worlds.[356]

Our dimension of reality has seven points that correspond to these seven *Sephiros*: south, north, east, west, above, below, and the point

354. The words "and God said" are missing from this statement, because this creative power is the hidden root. With it, God created speech and the incipient forces that would later become material existence (Rav Wolfson).

355. The first statement created an initial existence, one which could not be fully verbalized. This does not exist fully in our world, where items are relatively completed. The second statement created a light that according to our sages was too holy for mere man so it was hidden away for the righteous in the World-to-Come. The third statement created a spiritual barrier that will never be touched by man.

356. Later on it is taught that the deeper meaning of seven days of creation is that they refer to the seven lower *Sephiros*, or the seven revelations of God's light that animate the seven days of the week—each day has a different revelation. The Temples that stood in Jerusalem and the mobile tabernacle the Jews constructed in the Desert were places that were filled with these seven Lights. That is why Betzalel, who constructed the tabernacle, knew the secrets of creation, because he had to bring down the same influences that fill the physical world (See further *Innerspace* pg. 57). This is also the meaning of the verse about Solomon's temple, *va-yivnehu sheva shanim*, "And he built it seven years" (1 Kings 6:38). It does not say, "he built it for seven years," rather "he built *it* seven years," for the building was a manifestation of the seven emanations that are symbolized with the term, seven years. We mourn for the destruction of Temples of Jerusalem on the ninth of *Av*. During the subsequent seven weeks, on each Shabbos, we read a different prophecy of consolation. The seven prophecies of consolation correspond to the seven lower *Sephiros*. During each of those seven weeks, a different *Sephirah* light appears. Since the Temple was a display of the full seven, re-experiencing the seven *Sephiros* is a partial rebuilding of the Temple and a consolation for its loss (heard from the Stitchiner Rebbe).

of reference, which is the inner point that all the directions surround. Our world bears traces of the seven lower *Sephiros*, which is why most physical items in our world have these seven directions and not eight or nine directions. According to the Talmud[357] the section of the Torah, *Va-yehi Bi-nsoa*, "And when the ark traveled" (Num. 10:35-36), is a separate book of the Torah. According to that classification, there are seven books to the Torah instead of five. Rabbi Tzadok Ha-Cohen of Lublin[358] explains that there are seven books in the Torah to correspond to the seven lower *Sephiros*. Each book of the Torah is a reflection of a different one of the *Sephirah* lights. The Torah is the means through which God is revealed in this world. Since our world, primarily, only accesses the seven lower *Sephiros* there are only seven books and not eight. At special times, forces and atmospheres from another realm enter our world, and then we too might taste a product of the first three *Sephiros*.

Within man, the *Sephiros* became two sets of forces. The first three are called *mochin*, "intellects," and the lower seven are *middos*, "emotions," or "behaviors."

Lesson Twenty will further detail the meaning of the forces within man.

---

357. *Shabbos* 115b-116a.
358. See *Pri Tzaddik* to *Parashas Devarim*.

Lesson Twenty

The Components of Thought

There are two approaches as to the identity of the three *mochin*, "intellects." From one perspective, the three intellects that enable all meaningful abstract thought are *chochmah* (wisdom, intuition), *binah* (understanding), and *da'as* (knowledge, internalization). If one looks at these forces from a different vantage point they would be called *keser* (essential will), *chochmah* (wisdom, intuition), and *binah* (understanding). The highest possible level of the personality is *keser*—essential will.

Keser literally means, "crown." A crown sits atop the head. It represents levels of a person that transcend the logical and the rational.[359] There are items that I want, I have a will for them, and I cannot explain why I desire them. These wills are an expression of the crown of my personality. This point is higher than the stages of wisdom, understanding, and internalization, so the mind cannot comprehend the reason for these urges. In truth, will is an extension of essence.[360] I want certain behaviors or items because they are true and good for my truest self. When I experience the fulfillment of those wishes I feel, at my core, that I have experienced my essential identity.

An example of essential will is the love between a groom and a bride. Why did the groom choose this bride? Why did the bride agree to marry this groom? Is each one absolutely certain that they could not find someone else in the world a little wiser, prettier, or nicer? Why did they decide to commit to each other?

359. The *yechidah* part of the soul is another name for the aspect of *keser* that is within man.
360. Heard from the Stitchiner Rebbe.

The real answer is that their innate will is being expressed. The will to link their lives stems from a point that is beyond rational explanation. Will is an extension of essence. Each feels that their very essence is linked with that of their spouse. They sense, in a hidden manner, that they are each a half of the other's soul. That is why they are attracted to each other, and it is why they will commit to each other wholeheartedly.

Beneath will stand the forces of *chochmah* and *binah*, which enable acquisition and comprehension of knowledge. *Chochmah* literally means, "wisdom," and *binah* means, "understanding." *Chochmah* is a spark of light, and *binah* is the enlargement, development, and application of that beginning. The spark is the start of intellectual thought, what we commonly call "intuition."

Picture a student studying Talmud. He reads a difficult passage with his study partner and discovers an intractable contradiction. He and the study partner knit their brows in concentration. He paces the floor of the study hall, thinking, delving into the depths of the topic, desperately seeking a resolution. Then his forehead clears, a small smile appears on his lips. "Aahh! I know the answer," he exclaims. "Tell me," his partner says. He cannot. After a few minutes of clarifying what he is feeling, he details the answer.

Chochmah was the flash of inspiration, the feeling of intuition, when the student sensed that he knew the answer. When the student pulled out of his initial illumination the components that explained the resolution it was *binah*, "understanding." The word *chochmah* spells two words: *koach mah*, "the force of something." However, the word *mah* can also mean, "nothing."[361] Thus it is initial existence with a connection to the force of nothingness. First thoughts, that are not yet defined, seem to come out of nowhere. The next level of the intellect, *binah*, reveals details and implications. *Binah* recalls the phrase, *meivin davar mitoch davar*, "Comprehending one matter from another," and the word *binyan*, "building." Understanding builds upon the inspiration of intuition and develops a complete system of thought.

Chochmah and *binah* can be symbolized in the stages of construction. *Chochmah* is the bricks, the basic pieces. *Binah* is putting one brick on

---

361. For example, Moses said, *Va-nachnu mah ki talinu aleinu*, "We are nothing, so why do you complain about us?" (Exod. 16:7).

another, dividing bricks that are too large, and arranging the materials into a meaningful edifice. The basic postulates in any field of study are the *chochmah* element. How principles interact, such as resolving contradictions between them, and determining when the principles are to be applied, is the force of *binah*. When I place my hand on a table and say to myself, "I am touching a table," it is *chochmah*. When I realize the properties of the table, such as the facts that it occupies space and is made out of wood, those realizations are *binah*. You will rarely find *chochmah* and *binah* divided. Immediately when I know of something I also realize some of its details. Their linkage causes the mystics to term them, *Terei reyin de-lo misparshin*, "Two friends that do not separate."[362]

In the process of creating life the male's seed is *chochmah*, it is a small point. The mother's womb is the arena of *binah*. She develops the initial spark, actualizes all its potential, and a fully developed child emerges.[363]

362. Heard from the Stitchiner Rebbe. Rabbi Aryeh Kaplan writes, "One of the Biblical sources for *chochmah* and *binah* is the verse: "God founded the earth with *chochmah*, 'wisdom,' and established the heavens with *binah*, 'understanding' (Prov. 3:19). The Bible states here that *chochmah* and *binah* are the basic components of creation. In a divine sense, *chochmah* constitutes the axioms which define the world while *binah* is the logical system that connects these axioms. All the laws of nature are essentially axioms, and the simplest axiom contains several levels. For example, the fact that the shortest distance between two points is a straight line means that a point exists, straight lines exist, space exists, the concepts of existence, of shortness and length exist. All of these categories exist in *chochmah*. In *binah* they interplay logically and emerge as a coherent system of laws."

The Stitchiner Rebbe explained how *chochmah* is the foundation of the world in the following manner. *Chochmah* is the grasping of a concept. When God conceived the need for an item He thought of the entire item and the need for it, as a result of having arisen in Divine thought, the item then immediately appeared.

363. "The relationship between *chochmah*, 'wisdom,' and *binah*, 'understanding,' can be grasped in terms of the relationship between male and female. In a human relationship, the male essentially provides the sperm and the female takes it, holds it in her womb for nine months, after which she delivers a fully developed child. In the same way, *chochmah*, 'wisdom,' is a series of facts which we can put into the womb of *binah*, 'understanding,' in order to develop an entire logical structure. The paradigm of this is mathematics. If we take ten digits from zero to nine and a few axioms, put them in the womb of *binah*, and let them gestate, we can obtain the whole corpus of mathematics" (Aryeh Kaplan, *Innerspace* pg. 58-59).

The Kabbalists refer to *chochmah* as *abba*, "father," and to *binah* as *imma*, "mother."[364]

Man's body parts perform tasks that bear traces of the spiritual roots (the *Sephiros*). The spirit of Elijah the prophet once taught a lesson in the academy of Rabbi Shimon bar Yochai in which he detailed how the parts of the human body represent the *Sephiros*. The lesson is known by its first words, *Pasach Eliyahu*, "Elijah began." Some Chasidim recite it every morning before their first prayers. According to his teaching, *chochmah* is in the right brain, the seat of thought. *Binah* is in the heart, and it is the power of the heart to understand. *Chochmah* and *binah* are the parents. Once *da'as*, "internalization," is employed, they produce offspring: emotions, feelings, and behaviors.

Da'as implies connection and separation. *Da'as* implies connection, as the attachment between husband and wife is called in the Torah a *da'as* relationship.[365] It also connotes a separation as evidenced in the statement of the Jerusalem Talmud, "Without *da'as* how could distinction be drawn?"[366] *Da'as* means focusing upon and blending together the ideas from intuition (*chochmah*) and understanding (*binah*). To focus on a thought, I must separate my mind from other concepts and attach it exclusively to a single topic.[367] Feeling fully connected to the ideas that

---

364. Perhaps the idea in the Talmud that women have added *binah* relates to this analysis. The feminine intellect is one of comprehending details, while the masculine intellect is inclined to sweeping generalizations and flashes of intuitive inspiration. See further the Vilna Gaon's commentary to Prov. 6:20.

365. The initial intimate closeness between Adam and Eve is called a connection of *da'as*: *Va-yeda adam es chavah ishto*, "And Adam knew Eve his wife" (Gen. 4:25).

366. *Da'as Tefillah* pg. 401.

367. See further *Da'as Tefillah* pg. 402, who applies this focus to internalization of a sense of holiness and quotes the following source: "The concept of holiness requires two stages. Initially, it is a struggle and its end is a gift. Initially, man sanctifies himself, and at the end, God dedicates man."

The effort entailed in man's sanctification is that he detach himself entirely from materialism, and he must attach himself fully, at every moment, to His God. This level caused the prophets to be called angels, as was written in regards to Aaron, "For the lips of the priest preserve *da'as*, and Torah will be sought from his mouth, for he is an angel of the Lord of Hosts" (Mal. 2:7). Even at moments when he is involved in material acts that are needed for his body, he feels a sense of attachment with the Divine.

are father and mother (wisdom and understanding) causes them to fully enter one's personality and to create emotions.

The following scenario is an example of the intellects producing emotions. The other day I was sitting at the table and I felt my stomach growling. I then looked up, a picture entered my mind, I saw a jar with brown circles in it, and each circle contained small black dots (*chochmah*). I then delved into the details of the snapshot. I realized that I was seeing a cookie-jar filled with chocolate chip cookies, my favorite snack (*binah*). When I concentrated on the import of the scene and internalized what it meant (*da'as*) my emotions were aroused. I felt love, a desire to reach out and take a cookie (the attribute of *chesed*). If I were to have been on a diet, I might have realized that the jar was a clarion call to the horrors of obesity. Concentrating on thoughts of premature death from heart failure would have caused recoiling and loathing toward the unhealthy sweets (the emotion of *gevurah*).

Love and loathing are examples of attributes that the intellects produce. In total, the intellects produce seven basic emotions. These seven types of feelings bear traces of the seven lower *Sephiros*.

Both approaches reveal only three intellects. Why is there no system that counts four intellects: *keser, chochmah, binah,* and *da'as*? The deeper wisdom reveals that *da'as,* "internalization," and *keser,* "innate will," are two forms of the same force; *da'as* is an externalization of *keser.*[368] To understand this point more fully, we must first study the attributes. After describing what the seven behaviors and feelings are, it will be possible to explain the link between *da'as* and *keser.* Lesson Twenty-One will explain, and provide examples of, the seven emotions.

"It is impossible for man to reach this level on his own. Man is a material being composed of flesh and blood, which is why I said that the end is a gift. Man can attempt to pursue *da'as* of truth and constant appreciation of the saintliness of deeds. However, successful attainment of these levels comes from God who will lead man down the path he has chosen and He will place upon man His holiness and He will sanctify man" (excerpted from Rabbi Moshe Chaim Luzzatto, *Path of the Upright*, Chapter 26).

368. Heard from the Stitchiner Rebbe.

LESSON TWENTY-ONE

THE SEVEN EMOTIONS: *CHAGAT NEHIM*

THE SEVEN EMOTIONS are divided into two categories and are known by the acronym of their names, *Chagat Nehim*. The first class contains *chesed*, "love," *gevurah*, "restraint," and *tiferes*, "harmony." The second group is composed of *netzach*, "dominance," *hod*, "submissiveness" or "empathy," *yesod*, "continuity" or "foundation," and *malchus*, "kingship."

THE FIRST EMOTION IS "GIVING"

The most powerful human emotion is *chesed*, the desire to love. *Chesed* is the desire to give of oneself, to extend outward and empty myself into another person. The key word for this feeling is *hispashtus*, which means, "spreading out." The seven days of creation are in truth manifestations of the seven lower *Sephiros* that are the roots of the seven emotions within man. On the first day God created light. Light spreads. Enter a dark room and turn on a flashlight, the light will instantaneously move from the bulb throughout the darkness.

Ahavah, "love," is an amplification of *chesed*, as in the verse in Jeremiah.

Koh amar Hashem zacharti lach chesed neurayich, ahavas kelulosayich.

So says the Lord, I have remembered for your sake the *chesed* of your youth, [it is] the *ahavah*, "love," of your marriage (Jer. 2:2).

Ahavah has at its root the word *hav*, "give," for love is the desire to give to someone else unconditionally.[369] Giving is when I spread myself out into the recipient and feel a part of myself within the recipient.[370]

The Jewish nation has been blessed with seven great shepherds, or leaders, who helped frame our national consciousness, According to the *Zohar*, the spirits of these men visit the Jewish *sukkah* on the different

---

369. Rav Wolfson in *Emunas Etecha* to *Parashas Naso* (pg. 120) explained Rashi's lesson that an individual who withholds the payments he owes the priest will eventually bring his wife to the priest for the straying wife test, in light of the linkage between love and giving. "A man who refuses to give the gifts to the priest is displaying a self-centeredness; all he cares about is his own benefit. He does not wish to give to others. Such a man will definitely treat his family in the same manner, he will demand his own benefit and ignore the needs of his wife. This attitude will cause him to bring his wife as a *sotah* to the priest, for where there is no peace between the couple, the wife might look elsewhere."

The Stitchiner Rebbe explained the relationship between loving (*ahavah*) and giving (*chesed*) in the following manner. Love is in the internal and emotional realm of man what giving is in the external dimension of behavior. Giving is spreading myself and what I possess outward, these acts reflect an inner reality. My soul seeks to spread toward the recipient.

370. Frequently, we give to those who we feel are an extension of ourselves, who are united with us. See further Rabbi Shimon Shkop's introduction to his work *Sha'arei Yosher*. Rabbi Shkop explains that the Torah's demand of love to our neighbors is really a requirement that man have an expansive view of self. A lowly person sees his body as the extent of his being. A higher understanding recognizes that my soul is part of who I am, and I must act in a manner that helps my soul. I cannot only further the desires of my body. An even higher level sees the "I" as encompassing all the members of my family. A spiritual person sees the "I" as totaling his entire nation. He does kindness to a fellow man for his friend is connected to him, just as all the branches are extensions of and connected to the same tree.

> We usually think it is love which causes giving, because we observe that a person showers gifts and favors on the one he loves. But there is another side to the argument. Giving may bring about love for the same reason that a person loves what he himself has created or nurtured: he recognizes in it part of himself. Whether it is a child he has brought into the world, an animal he has reared, a plant he has tended, or even a thing he has made or a house he has built—a person is bound in love to the work of his hands, for in it he finds himself (Rabbi E. Dessler, *Strive for Truth*, pgs. 126-127).

days of Sukkos. They are Abraham, Isaac, Jacob, Joseph, Moses, Aaron, and David. Each one of these leaders excelled at feeling the Heavenly form of one of the seven emotions, reaching God through a different focus of service.[371]

Abraham was the paradigm of *chesed*. In the Torah we learn of the extent of Abraham's willingness to pour himself out into others. Even after a surgery at the age of ninety-nine, Abraham went out of his tent and sat at the doorway waiting for guests, When he saw a trio of pagan earth-worshippers, he ran out of his tent and begged them to come to his home for refreshments. Furthermore, when God told him that He planned to destroy the wicked inhabitants of Sodom, Abraham prayed with utmost dedication and entreated God to save them. Abraham's giving was unconditional. Absolute love motivated him to perform favors even for sinners and pagans who opposed his life's mission of teaching ethical monotheism.[372]

---

371. The *sukkah* (ceremonial tabernacle) that Jews sit in during the seven days of the holiday is meant to recall the miraculous clouds of glory that surrounded Jewry while we traveled through the Sinai Desert after leaving Egypt. There were seven clouds of glory around Israel; on the right (south), left (north), front (east), behind (west), above and below, and a seventh that traveled before them to flatten hills and smooth the terrain. These seven clouds were manifestations of the seven lower *Sephiros*. They displayed these Heavenly Lights in the dimension of place. Perhaps the *sukkah* that commemorates those clouds recreates their holiness. The seven shepherds who visit the *sukkah* are revelations of these seven in the realm of soul (man), and the seven days of Sukkos reveal these forces in the realm of time. See further Lesson Two for a discussion of holy concepts that appear in three dimensions.

372. The *Da'as Tefillah* writes:

> The purest form of giving has no admixture of harshness or justice. A giver who gives endlessly, with a disregard of the worthiness of the recipient, is connected to Heavenly giving. Hence the lesson of Maharal, "The *chesed* of God spreads to all.... It has no measure or limit. For *chesed* comes from Him, from the fact that He seeks to do good." Pure kindness is done because the giver is innately good and seeks to spread himself out, not because of the recipient (*Da'as Tefillah* pg. 92).

That is why Abraham who was connected to Heavenly levels of generosity sought to benefit even those who did not deserve favors.

Our world is filled with attraction.[373] There are masculine trees and feminine trees, male animals and female animals, and the force of attraction between genders can be overwhelming. The reason why this force is so potent is that attraction is a form of *chesed*. The foundation of the world is *chesed*. Consider the verse, *olam chesed yibbaneh*, "The world will be built on Kindness" (Ps. 89:3). A deep analysis of the Divine creation reveals that God's purpose in creating us was to perform an act of love, to give pleasure to mortals.[374] Since love is God's purpose for this world, all forms of love, the righteous forms such as generosity to the poor or love for God, and the wicked forms like lust and selfish pleasure-seeking, are potent.

The Jewish nation bears the mission of humanity, revealing the holiness that is latent within the physical world. The physical world's first pillar was God's love. The first patriarch of the Jewish nation, who established the character of its children, was Abraham, a personality who embodied and practiced Godly Love.

THE OPPOSITE OF *CHESED*

The opposite of love is *gevurah*—strong restraint. This emotion has several names; it is also called *yirah*, "fear," and *din*, "justice." When I am afraid I

373. According to the Midrash, even the earth has desires. The ground was called *eretz* for she desired to fulfill the will of her Maker (*Bereishis Rabbah* 5:8, *Yalkut Shimoni, Parashas Bereishis*, lesson 8). The mystics teach that the ground desires to be used for observance of God's precepts. The cement in front of the *yeshivah* is whispering, "Please walk on me to go study God's Torah." And Jeremiah wrote that the "paths of Zion are in mourning," for her children no longer visit during the festivals (Rav Wolfson's lessons about prayer).

374. Rabbi Aryeh Kaplan writes:

God had absolutely no need to create the world. God Himself is absolute perfection, and He has no need for anything, even creation. Thus, to the best of our understanding, we can say that God created the universe for the purpose of bestowing good upon man. God Himself calls His creation an act of goodness. It is for this reason that, at the end of the first six days of creation, after making man, the Torah says, "And God saw all that He had made and behold it was very good" (Gen. 1:35). We are being told that the creation of the universe was an expression of His goodness (*Innerspace*, pg. 9).

recoil and withdraw. Justice also demands a withdrawal. The judge must stay within the bounds of the law and prevent his feelings of compassion from bursting out of his heart and tainting his legal decisions.[375] Love is focused on others; it is the desire to spread out. Fear is the opposite movement, focusing on oneself and pulling all inward. A being that is fearful or induces fear in others bears a trace of this *Sephirah*.[376]

The second day of creation revealed this force. God then created a barrier, the firmament in the Heavens, to divide the spiritual waters from earthly waters. He pulled the spiritual into its domain, and the physical recoiled into its dimensions. The personality who inculcated fear of God into the Jewish soul was our second father, Isaac. Isaac's relationship with the Almighty is called in the Torah, *Pachad Yitzchak*, "the fear of Isaac" (Gen. 31:42).

Abraham was creative, while Isaac excelled in staying within the bounds of the behavior his father had modeled. Isaac dug his father's wells that the Philistines had sealed. During famine he did as his father did—he traveled to Gerar and presented his wife as his sister. Isaac's finest moment was when his father brought him atop Mt. Moriah[377] to

---

375. Rabbi Kaplan writes further:

> *Gevurah*, "restraint," parallels *din*, "law." In interpersonal relationships of *chesed* and *gevurah*, if one person relates to another with *chesed*, he could pour out his most personal feelings. If he related to his friend with *din*, however, his relationship with him would become totally structured and restrained within very narrow limitations. A judge, for example, cannot say, "I like this man and I want to do him a favor. I want to be altruistic to him." A judge cannot be altruistic; he has to be very delineated. Hence, *gevurah*, "restraint," is *din*, "judgment" (*Innerspace* pg. 62).

376. *Gevurah* literally means strength. One might question why restraint is called strength. Why isn't it called *tzimtzum*, constriction? Couldn't love have also been called strength, for sometimes you must overcome inhibitions and obstacles to practice giving? The answer is that restraint conflicts with the core of creation. The essence of creation is something from nothing, namely it is a process of revealing Divine forces into an empty space. Restraint is a process of hiding one's self and personality, the opposite of the very nature of existence. To embody restraint one must go against the grain of existence, hence the term *gevurah*—it requires added strength (heard from the Stitchiner Rebbe).

377. The Temple Mount in Jerusalem.

be bound and offered as a sacrifice. Abraham had heard a command from God to offer his son. Isaac had not heard such a decree, and nevertheless Isaac held himself back. He displayed enormous strength and restraint when he did not stir with a single protest as his father tied him for slaughter.[378]

In religious practice, *chesed* and *gevurah* find expression in Judaism's twin pillars of service, love of God and fear of Heaven. Abraham is the first father of all Jewish souls. He filled himself with absolutely divine *chesed*, and all Jews have within their souls an innate desire to love God as a genetic endowment from him. As descendants of Isaac all our souls harbor an innate fear of Heaven. Jewish practice does not demand behaviors that are foreign to one's nature. All one must do is draw forth feelings that are latent within the Jewish personality.

Displays of *Chesed* and *Gevurah*

Water emerged from the *Sephirah* of *chesed*, Heavenly giving. Pour water onto your table, it will spread out. Warmth is also from *chesed*; heat the table and the water will bubble and evaporate spreading its tiny particles over a greater area. Cold weather emerged from *gevurah*, as it causes one to recoil and draw inwards. Remove the heat in the room by adding a blast of frigid air, and the water will not spread anymore—it will turn into a solid block of ice.

---

378. Rabbi Kaplan writes:

> Concerning the relationship of the Patriarchs with the *Sephiros*, we saw that Abraham is the paradigm of *chesed*, "love." He is the pure altruist. Isaac is the person who totally subjugates his ego. In fact, you see this to such a degree, that after being bound upon the altar, Isaac's life becomes a perfect parallel of Abraham's life. He digs the same wells that Abraham dug; he goes down to the Philistines and calls Rebecca his sister, just as Abraham had done with Sarah. The reason for this is that Isaac is a person who totally gives up his ego. Abraham is the initiator; *chesed* is essentially initiating a new idea. Whereas Abraham initiates the new movement, Isaac sees himself as a transmitter. He is a perfect disciple (*Innerspace*, pg. 63).

A lion is a creature that engenders fear in others. He causes others to retreat and withdraw. The Hebrew word for "lion" is *aryeh*. These letters also spell the word *yirah*, for this creature's essential nature is connected with fear since it emerged from the *Sephirah* of *yirah*, or *gevurah*.

According to the prophet Elijah, the right hand is the part of the human body that corresponds to *chesed*, while the left hand corresponds to *gevurah*. The right hand is usually more active, and since *chesed is* linked to spreading and doing, it is represented with the right. The left hand restrains, that is why it is associated with *gevurah*. For example, when I cut meat, my right hand will wield the knife while my left hand will hold the steak in place.

In Jewish law the right is preferred to the left. For instance, when performing the service in Jerusalem's temple the priest had to turn to the right side whenever he ascended the altar. Furthermore, when arising in the morning, we begin the process of washing our hands with our left hand serving the right through pouring water on it. When getting dressed we are to first put on the right shirtsleeve and right shoe. Since the right symbolizes *chesed*, preferring the right is a reminder to ourselves, and a prayer to God, that love should dominate fear.[379]

In the Torah, the direction south was the right side since the individual would stand facing the east.[380] Thus Abraham, who personified *chesed*, is frequently found traveling to the south for he was attracted to a place that had the spiritual force of giving.[381] Colloquially, the south is usually

---

379. Perhaps this was the symbolism of the binding of Isaac. Abraham, the paradigm of love, had to assert supremacy over the limitations of fear, so that more Divine Love would flow to this world than Divine Recoil. The reason why the first Mitzvah in the morning is washing the hands with water might also be an expression of the supremacy of love. Water emerged from the *Sephirah* of *chesed*; pouring water over the hands is a symbolic act that arouses love to become manifest and proceed before all other emotions (Rav Wolfson).

380. According to the Midrash, Adam was created with his face to the east. There are several Torah sources that prove the importance of the east. In Biblical Hebrew, *kedem*, the word for "beginning," also means, "east," and the direction *panim*, "faceward," is "east," while *achor*, "behind," is "west" (Heard from the Stitchiner Rebbe). See further Rashi on Exod. 19:2 s.v. *neged ha-har*.

381. Heard from the Stitchiner Rebbe. See further *Pri Tzaddik* of Rabbi Tzadok Ha-Cohen, *Parashas Pinchas*, Lesson 8.

a place of greater warmth, and *chesed* is associated with warmth.[382] The north represents *gevurah*, harsh withdrawal. Cold weather is found in the north. When the Torah delineated the borders of the Land of Israel it began with the south, for in the Jewish perspective, kindness is primary and paramount (see Num. 34:3).[383] When waving the four species during Sukkos, a Jew first waves to the south, the right, and then to the north, as a further manifestation of this norm.

Many secular cultures prefer the left to the right. Mystically, their natures prefer harsh limitations and laws to the generosity of kindness. That is why in some societies their shirts button left over right, to place the left as supreme above the right. Furthermore, they produce maps in which you face the west, north becomes affiliated with the right, the most active hand, showing that restraint, harshness, and self- absorption are the usual and preferred modes.[384]

TIFERES

The combination of *chesed* and *gevurah* together produces a third emotion, *tiferes*, "harmony," which is more than just the sum of the first two. When generosity sweetens restraint, harmony is the feeling of pleasure that emerges. Harmony emerges from the blend of opposites. Imagine a choir: the high-pitched voices that are difficult to produce might be viewed as *gevurah*. The deep low voices can be considered

---

382. Heard from the Stitchiner Rebbe.

383. Heard from the Stitchiner Rebbe. See further Rav Wolfson in *Tzion Ve-Arehah* pgs. 145-149. He provides an alternative explanation for the borders of Israel beginning with the south.

384. Even though these thoughts might not have been the conscious motivation for these actions they may well have been the reason why their souls guided them to arrange their maps and clothes in this manner. See further *Megillah* 3a, and Rashi there s.v. *mazaleihu*.

Since Judaism focuses on giving, the Torah only speaks of obligations. Secular society's focus on itself leads to a concentration on rights that all should receive. For more about the difference between the Jewish perspective and secular perspectives about giving and kindness see "The World of Obligation" by Rabbi Akiva Tatz in *Worldmask* pgs. 99-113 (ZR).

sounds of *chesed*. The merger of both together is *tiferes*. Sugar is sweet and desirable, it is from *chesed*. Lemons are tart, and tasting them causes one to withdraw from further ingestion, thus they have a trace of *gevurah*. When you mix the sugar and lemon juice in a perfect blend to produce the new taste of lemonade you have discovered *tiferes*. There is a certain transcendent sweetness that you feel when you encounter harmony or perfect blends and balances of opposites. Consider a master painting: the beauty lies in the merger of the different colors to produce a satisfying feeling in the heart of the beholder. That feeling is *tiferes*.

Our forefather Jacob is the paradigm of *tiferes*. He merged together within himself the kindness and originality of Abraham together with the discipline and restraint of Isaac. His personality was a balanced blend that was greater than the sum of the two.[385]

In the lesson of Elijah the right hand and arm displayed *chesed*. The left hand and arm manifested *gevurah*. The torso, in which the right and left are blended together, is the location of *tiferes*.

---

385. According to the *Zohar*, Jacob is *Tushbechasa she-ba-avos*, "the greatest of the three Patriarchs."

"Take pure white and pure black. Pure white would be *chesed*—love—and pure black would be *gevurah*—restraint. There is no harmony or beauty in each one by itself, but as soon as I take black and white and mix them together I can make all kinds of beautiful pictures, not by merging, which would just give grey, but by a blending of the two. Again with pure *chesed*, you can take a whole pail of paint and just pour it on the canvas. With pure *gevurah* you hold a brush in your hand and you are unable to touch the canvas. *Tiferes* means you are able to harmonize and blend these two extremes. In terms of the human body, *chesed* is the right arm while *gevurah* is the left arm. *Tiferes* is not both hands together, however, but rather the torso with all its complexity,

Whereas *chesed*—light—was created on the first day, and *gevurah*—firmament—was created on the second day, on the third day, God separated the seas and the dry land. In other words, the third day set boundaries: not all sea, not all dry land, but a balance between the two. In addition, plants were created on the third day. A plant grows, so that you have the element of *chesed*. Yet a plant is enclosed; it has a barrier between itself and the outer world, which is the element of *gevurah*. A plant is like a controlled, aesthetic growth (*Innerspace*, pg. 62-63).

The Tetragrammaton, Y-H-V-H, reflects the fact that God is the source of all love (*chesed*). The name *Elokim* represents the fact that He is a strict judge (*gevurah*). When the two names are written together as *Hashem Elokim*, it teaches that He is the source of the balance of both in harmony.

Males are associated primarily with the *Sephirah* of *chesed*.[386] The feminine bears a strong trace of *gevurah*.[387] That is why in the *halachic* ceremony for marriage the man must give the ring that the woman receives. If a woman gives a ring to a man, *halachic* marriage is not created, for it is a duty upon the male to manifest *chesed* and for the female to withdraw and display *gevurah*. Marriage is a merger of love (male) and restraint (female) and is a paradigm of the balance and harmony of *tiferes*. Hence, the verse states:

Ke-tiferes Adam lasheves bayis. The beauty [*tiferes*] of mankind [is] the established [harmonious] home (Isa. 44:13).

A harmonious home is not just a place where there is an absence of friction. The ideal home contains an atmosphere in which each individual is true to himself and herself. The blend of the differences creates a feeling of transcendent beauty and harmony.[388]

Initially the world was created with harshness, as a result, the name of God that is employed in the story of creation is *Elokim*, the name of restraint. However, in the tale of the first human marriage the name of God is expressed differently: *Va-yomer Hashem Elokim lo tov heyos ha-adam le-vaddo e'eseh lo eizer ke-negdo,* "And Hashem Elokim said it is not good for man to be alone I will make for him a helpmate opposite him" (Gen. 2:18). Marriage is a display of the harmony emerging from the blend of opposites, which is why it is introduced with a Divine appellation that recalls the attribute of *tiferes*.

386. In the biological process of creating life the male gives to the female.
387. To foster life, the female is empty and receives.
388. The word *shalom*, "peace," shares a connection with the word *shalem*, "complete," and "whole." Furthermore Rabbi S. R. Hirsch on Num. 25:11-13 explains that Pinchas's act of violence was in fact peaceful since it restored the harmony of forces. Rabbi Wolfson in *Emunas Etecha* on *Parashas Pinchas* has a different explanation for why Pinchas's violence merited a reward of Divine peace.

Why Emotions May Lead Man Astray

The seven lower emotions are also called *sheva kefulos*—the seven doubles—for these feelings can be intrinsically holy or sinful. For instance, one can employ the innate human drive of generosity to give money to the poor. Alternatively, a loving person might misdirect innate goodness and love a prohibited woman, such as a sibling or a woman married to someone else. If the emotion of fear engenders fear of performing a sin and harming our relationship with the Divine, it is being used correctly. However, if a judge allows fear to inhibit him from stating a controversial truth, then he is lowering fear into the realm of evil (*kelippah*). Art, music, and poetry are expressions of *tiferes*, which can be used to increase one's service of God,[389] or heaven forbid, to arouse an abdication of holiness.[390]

The Keys to Leadership:
Netzach, *Hod*, *Yesod*, and *Malchus*

Netzach, "dominance," and *hod*, "subservience," or "empathy," are represented by Elijah with the right and left foot respectively. The feet allow an individual to stand; these two behaviors represent two modes of survival, how to remain standing despite challenges. They are the two ways of dealing with adversity, fight or flight. For instance, if a man is walking to his destination and suddenly a devastating winter storm attacks. If he continues walking, unbent, fighting through the elements, overwhelming the enemy, he is embodying *netzach*—dominance or victory. If he stands off to the side, or if he crouches and waits for the storm to pass before he continues, he is acting with *hod*—survival through submission. When a storm wind blows and a stout tree stands

---

389. Poetry that is sung on Shabbos as a *zemirah* and religious poetry that is filled with love of God, such as the poems of Rabbi Yehudah Ha-Levi, inspire love of God and His service (Rav Wolfson).

390. There is a form of music that is empty of meaning, rock music. This music has no wisdom, it does not display great harmony; rather it is a cacophonous collection of noises that stimulate man towards lust, violence, and a general rejection of all limits and laws (Rav Wolfson).

upright, seeking to defeat the gales, it is a picture of *netzach*. The grass that bends with the wind waiting for the opportunity to rise again when the tempest passes is a paradigm of *hod*. The word *hod* shares a root with the term *modim*, meaning, "they admit." It represents a withdrawal of self and acceptance of the other person's viewpoint. *Hod* can be viewed as empathy, because empathy is an experience where I entirely accept the needs of the other.

There are two types of leaders. Some overpower their followers with charisma or message, others are seemingly overwhelmed by their people. Moses was a paradigm of forceful leadership; he was the personality of *netzach*. When he descended Sinai and found the nation cavorting before the Golden Calf, he immediately stopped the party, crushed the idol, and killed the ringleaders of the idolatrous group.

Aaron is a paradigm of *hod* leadership. He was an accommodationist, allowing whatever he could. When the people demanded a Golden Calf, Aaron did not fight them. He did not attempt to frighten them into submission. He took his cue from the nation as to what it wanted, and then he went along with their plans, seeking to derail them through obfuscation and delay.[391]

---

391. See further *Innerspace* pg. 42. To walk one must use both legs as it is impossible to walk with one leg. However, if one has only a right arm, such an individual can still use it to give charity, its primary purpose. *Netzach* and *hod* always work in tandem, while the other forces, such as *chesed*, can exist independently. Of the seven shepherds, all the other leaders occupied their own moments in history while Moses and Aaron were leaders during the same era. The Jewish nation always needs both modes of leadership, some individuals can thrive under a Moses; others resent his forcefulness, and for their sake there is a need for Aaron-like leadership.

The two legs are outside the core body, thus *netzach* and *hod* come into play when someone extends himself past his body. An individual who has a certain truth has *tiferes* (which is also called "truth"). When he educates a student he is extending this truth outside of his body, then *netzach* and *hod* are utilized. The *netzach* teacher overwhelms his student. If the student is doing something wrong he will tell him off or overwhelm him with criticism. The *hod* teacher, however, will smile at the disruptive student, so as to keep the student within the community to eventually bring him back to observance. *Hod* literally means, "glow." It is an external light, for the glow is the external aspect of the sun. A teacher who is *hod*-like might be churning internally when he sees his student's infractions, yet externally he presents a smile, acting as if the student is controlling the dynamic (heard from the Stitchiner Rebbe).

Yesod, "foundation," is a blend of all the feelings that preceded it. It is the channel of blessing. It is a most holy force, the ability to procreate, to produce another human who also has the ability to sire future generations. *Yesod* literally means "foundation." The ability to sire descendants blessed with fruitful capabilities of their own is the pillar of continuity.

This ability and force are concentrated in the organ of the body through which man creates a new life. *Tzaddik yesod olam*—the *tzaddik* is the foundation of the world—because he is an embodiment of the holiness of *yesod*. A *tzaddik* such as Joseph used *yesod* in the perfect manner.

Marital intimacy is a realm of enormous holiness, which is why the temptations in this regard are so difficult. The greater the potential for good, the more difficult it is to attain that good. Joseph was the embodiment of holiness in this realm, as evidenced in the fact that he ran away from the allurements of Potiphar's wife.[392]

Just as *tiferes* was born of the merger between *chesed* and *gevurah*, *yesod* blends *netzach* and *hod*. A *tzaddik* is a master leader who knows when to employ *netzach* and when to employ *hod*; he balances and blends both in a perfect balance.

Joseph was the paradigm of this attribute. He was a great manager who knew how to lead subjects in the correct manner. *Yesod* led him to step forward and assert his views and to step back and absorb the needs of others, each at the appropriate time.[393]

Yesod means perfectly balanced giving. I might earn five hundred dollars in one week. If I only had the force of generosity (*chesed*), I would give it all away to help the poor. If I only possessed restraint (*gevurah*) I would give none of it to the poor and keep it all for myself. Harmony (*tiferes*) would lead me to a balance; I would give something, but not everything. I would give ten percent, a personal optimum. If I give fifty dollars to an alcoholic who needs ten dollars for his rent, I am overwhelming him (*netzach*). The extra cash will probably cause a

---

392. In Gen. 39:6-20 the Torah relates the story of Joseph and Potiphar's wife. Joseph had been sold as a slave to an Egyptian nobleman. The nobleman's wife sought to seduce Joseph for a long time. Once, they were alone in her home, and she grabbed his shirt and asked him to sleep with her. He ran outside the house to escape her entreaties and left his garment with her.
393. Heard from the Stitchiner Rebbe.

deepening of his chemical dependency. If I were to give the fifty dollars to someone who needed five hundred thousand dollars, my giving would disappear, and be overwhelmed in the face of need (*hod*). *Yesod* would be where I give my fifty dollars to an individual who needs fifty dollars. Such a gift is a true blessing; it is balanced, both from the perspective of the giver as well as the perspective of the recipient.[394] Joseph was a master giver, history's best distributor of scarce resources in times of distress.

Balance is needed to truly create new life.[395] A master teacher creates new life as his students are his children. A master teacher ideally embodies *yesod*. His balanced presentations allow for the message to be conveyed. Joseph was a master teacher. He succeeded in teaching his children, Menashe and Ephraim, how to maintain the traditions of Jacob, despite living in an Egyptian society that was their theological antithesis.

---

394. Rabbi Kaplan writes:

> If I am dealing with another person, it is not just a question of giving or holding back, because essentially, the more I give (*chesed*), the more I am changing this person, the more I am overwhelming him (*netzach*). The more I restrain myself (*gevurah*), the more I give way to the needs of another, the more I allow him to assert his own individuality (*hod*). What is required is a harmonious balance between Dominance and Empathy, and it is this that leads to a perfect *yesod*-relationship.
>
> The word *netzach* comes from *menatze'ach* meaning to "conquer" or "overcome." One can see this implication in a male-female relationship. Some men in a relationship feel that they must totally overwhelm the woman, who is not left with much personality of her own. Some women also have a *netzach*-relationship with their husbands, where they have to dominate them in every way.
>
> Hod—empathy—is just the opposite. It is a relationship where I totally give in to the other person. In *hod*—empathy—I essentially annul myself and lose all account of myself. For instance, if a person allows himself to be seduced, this would be the ultimate *hod* relationship (*Innerspace*, pg. 65-66).
>
> The idea of *netzach* and *hod* is a question of asserting your identity on the one hand, or total compliance with the other person's identity, on the other. The perfect *yesod* relationship is of course the balance between the two. What is important to emphasize is that this rule holds true both in the relationship between man and God as well as between man and woman (ibid.).

395. *Innerspace* pg. 66.

An expert teacher pays special care to remain a source, one who influences, and he does not become a product, a subject who is influenced. Good teachers transform their disciples. If the students are pulling the teacher to the lower level, the teacher will not remain a great pedagogue. There are grade-school teachers who are wonderful; they relate to the children and have a great impact upon their young charges. Sometimes, these teachers invest so much of their own thought into the world of the child that they become immature themselves and talk with the cadences and vocabulary of elementary school students. These teachers did not maintain *yesod*. *Yesod* leads the master teacher to be totally tied to a heightened spiritual level that is truly appropriate for him. Since he is rooted in realms above, he can descend to domains below and maintain his integrity and stature. In Kabbalistic literature, this concept is expressed with the phrase *Achid bi-shmaya u-bi-ara'a*, "United with the Heavens and the earth." The personality of *yesod* has an iron bond with heights of service; as a result, he can engage the material world fully, for it will not have an impact upon him.[396]

Malchus is a difficult concept to define. It too is a composite of all the earlier feelings. It is an empty vessel that receives the gift from all the other six feelings. *Malchus* is associated with revelation; it receives the other feelings and reveals them.

For man, the concept of a vessel connotes the ultimate degree of humility, emptying oneself fully in order to receive. According to Elijah, the organ of *malchus* is the mouth. The mouth reveals the thoughts of man, and the observant Jew uses his mouth to recite *Shema Yisrael* and thus accept upon himself the yoke of Heaven's rule. The obligations upon the Jew are absolute. When I use my mouth to recite the *Shema*, I am totally humbling myself. Ideally, I should desire and commit to fulfilling whatever demands God may make of me.

---

396. The Stitchiner Rebbe explained that eating is an example of *netzach*, *hod*, and *yesod*. Eating is outside of the body. Some people conquer the desire of excess food ingestion through *netzach*. These individuals meditate on the fact that food is really no better than excrement, and that the only important part is the Godly spark within the food. Too much concentration along this line of thought will overwhelm a person, who won't be able to eat at all (*hod*). The personality of *yesod*, though, is totally rooted in the realm above. Since he is so secure in his spiritual connection, the *tzaddik* engages in the material world and eats without any fear that he might be corrupted.

Malchus literally means "kingship." The ideal Jewish king is an individual who personifies nullification of self. He feels that he is merely a vehicle for the revelation of God's kingship. He turns his authority over to Heaven, feeling, "Whatever I accomplish, it is God who is truly doing the act." The honor of God is his paramount concern. King David is the seventh shepherd of the Jewish people, and he embodied this concept, that is why he said of himself, *Ve-anochi tola'as ve-lo ish*, "I am a worm not a man" (Ps. 22:7).[397] King David's rule is compared to the moon,[398] for the moon merely reflects the light of the sun. King David felt that he was a mere reflection of Divine power with no innate right to honor or power.[399]

Monarchy implies having followers, subjects who obey the decrees of the king and do not follow the whims of their own hearts. Secular kings and Gentile rulers seem to be authorities, to have others nullified, and fully committed to them. In truth that is an external commitment. Their subjects fear punishment so they listen to the king's edicts. Internally, at the core of their character the citizens of most lands are not followers. They usually hate their king and curse him in their hearts. External leadership is appropriate for the manifestations of the *kelippah* forces, the evil copies of the saintly realm. *Malchus* of holiness entails total nullification, or truly absolute leadership. When someone I respect, such as a Torah scholar, or King David, merely reveals his will, I am so subservient that I follow him for my inner being is committed to

---

397. See also *Chullin* 89a. The Talmud teaches that God loves Israel for when he gives its leaders, such as Abraham, Moses, Aaron, and David, greatness they humble themselves more.

398. Rema on *Orach Chaim* 428:2.

399. The Stitchiner Rebbe explained that *malchus* is an externalization, a ray off of the sun. *Malchus* is associated with the mouth, for through the mouth and my speech I reveal myself. What I reveal, though, is a fraction of my essence—the depths of my being. Relative to who I really am what I say is meaningless. The physical world is a manifestation of *malchus* for it is a mere ray from the Divine, relative to His infinite Light, we would vanish. A true king is someone who has fully internalized the fact that he is a mere ray from the Almighty, he demands no honor for himself and is entirely subservient and nullified before the Almighty. The *kelippah* of *malchus* takes itself too seriously. Secular kings feel that that they deserve regard and respect for they are truly special individuals with enormous worth. The root of their error is that they look at rays while ignoring the source. See further *Da'as Tefillah* pgs. 321-384.

following him. The organ of *malchus* is the mouth, for an ideal Jewish leader does not need a stick to keep his people in line; he merely expresses his wishes with his mouth and the nation flows in that direction.[400]

The *Sephiros* and God's Name

The pattern of the universes and the letters of God's name is the same as the pattern of the *Sephiros*. *Keser*—innate will—is the expression of one's very identity. It emerged from the apex of the letter *yud*, the soul part *yechidah*, and the world of *Adam Kadmon*, "Primordial Man." In some Kabbalistic writings this level is called *Atik*, representing ancient grandfatherly wisdom. *Chochmah* is called *abba*—fatherly inspiration that corresponds to the soul part *chayah*, the letter *yud*, and the world of *atzilus*, where life begins adjacent to God. *Binah* is *imma*—mother—which corresponds to *beriah*, the soul part *neshamah*, and the first *heh*. *Chesed, gevurah, tiferes, netzach, hod,* and *yesod* are called *ben*, "son,"[401] and correspond to the *vav*[402] and the universe of *yetzirah*, emotions. The final *heh* produced the world of *asiyah* and the *Sephirah* of *malchus* as well as the soul part *nefesh*. This is called by the Kabbalists, *bas*, "daughter."[403]

There is no letter for *da'as*, nor is there a "family member" to represent *da'as*. Apparently, *da'as* is not to be considered as a discrete concept. *Da'as* is linked in an intrinsic manner with *keser*. Thus the apex of the *yud* and the concept of *Atik* include *da'as* as well. What is the nature of this link? Why is *da'as* part of *keser*?

Lesson Twenty-Two will further refine the definition of *da'as* and thus explain the link between internalization and will.

---

400. Heard from the Stitchiner Rebbe. See further the Vilna Gaon's *Kol Eliyahu* on *Parashas Vayeishev*, quoted in *Da'as Tefillah* pg. 321.
401. In some sources these six *Sephiros* are called *ze'ir*, "small face."
402. Rabbi Aryeh Kaplan points out that the *gematria* of the letter *vav* is six, and this letter is the Hebrew term for connection. The six *Sephiros* of *chesed* through *yesod* are hinted in this letter, for they enable perfectly balanced giving. Thus, perfect connection between people is accomplished through the interplay and weaving together of these six concepts. (See further *Innerspace* pgs.42-43.)
403. Heard from the Stitchiner Rebbe.

Lesson Twenty-Two

Will and Internalization[404]

DA'AS IS THE force that decides how much of a particular emotion will appear. What causes me to balance my love of candy with restraint? *Da'as*. *Da'as* begets responsibility, it directs my soul to acknowledge context and to reveal only a measure of love or a measure of fear. According to Jewish law children are exempt from religious duties since they do not have it. A child possesses *chochmah* and *binah*; he can think creatively and can comprehend difficult ideas. He also has all seven feelings: generosity, fear, harmony, dominance, submission, creative balance, and humility, but he is missing responsibility; he has no *da'as*. A child does not have full control over his feelings. He does not know when to stop crying and how to take matters in their true context, which is why he is not obligated in Mitzvos.

What determines context? Why do doctors' warnings about the dangers of smoking resonate with me while concerns over sugar consumption do not lead me to refrain responsibly from sweets? The depth to the nature of *da'as* is the key to responsibility. *Da'as* is more than focus and concentration; it is the part of the brain that decides whether an idea will be truly internalized.

Sometimes you hear a lecture and your life changes. You become a different person whose actions reflect what you learned. At other times you will hear speakers, and they will say things that you fully grasp and comprehend yet your life does not change. The force of *da'as* determines what you assimilate and make part of yourself and what you do not let in to your essence.

---

404. The entirety of this lesson is derived from Tape 7 of the Stitchiner Rebbe's lessons on the *Tanya*.

Lessons that a student feels are truly relevant become part of the individual and are heeded, while warnings that one feels are not truly relevant for his essence are ignored.

Why do some ideas become part of your very personality, fostering feelings and behaviors? Because those ideas resonated with your unique soul. Your soul has a particular character. It might be a very loving soul, because the most powerful part of you is *chesed*, or you might have a very poetic soul since *tiferes* is the primary force of your personality. Certain presentations correspond to your core. For the giving individual, Talmudic legends (*Aggadah*) will resonate. His essence is Love (*chesed*); the Talmudic stories contain moral ideas that stem from the same source, and they are compared to water, another manifestation of *chesed*. The poet might find that Jewish poetry, such as the heartfelt songs of Rabbi Yehudah Ha-Levi, enter him in an intrinsic manner.[405] *Da'as* is a manifestation of your very essence. *Da'as* is the awareness of what is truly relevant, for what is meaningful and relevant to my essence is what I will internalize.

Examples of *Da'as*

The *Code of Jewish Law*[406] details the ideal attributes for the one who leads the prayers on the High Holy Days. He should be married, well-liked, at least thirty years of age, a Torah scholar, and have children. In the town of Brisk they found an individual who had all these qualifications. However, he had a poor voice and did not pray in a manner that would arouse the emotions of the community. Rabbi Chaim of Brisk rejected this cantor. "The lessons of the *Code of Law*," he explained, "are advantages among prayer leaders, but this individual is not a prayer leader in the first place!" R. Chaim was displaying *da'as*. What is truly relevant is that a cantor himself pray with devotion and arouse his listeners. The other qualifications were not fully relevant when compared to something as essential as a melodious voice and heartfelt prayer manner.

---

405. The examples of the poet and the kind soul are my own (ZR).
406. *Orach Chaim* 581:1.

The focus of Chasidim is *da'as*, to be aware of what matters. Some criticize the Chasidim for seeming to flippantly ignore the laws of prayer times. It is an unfair critique. Chasidim are very stringent about the essentials. Prayer is the "Service of the Heart."[407] They are stringent in ensuring a devotional, full hearted service, so they insist on preparing for prayer.[408]

DA'AS AND KESER

In light of *da'as* as an extension of essence it can be understood why *da'as* is linked to *keser*. *Keser* represents will. Will is an extension of essence. I want that which corresponds to my very essence, the real me.

Why do some dedicate their lives to teaching Torah, and others spend their days serving God through ethical business practices? Each soul leads a person to a life mission that conforms to the nature of one's essence. The innermost will, or the *Sephirah* of *keser*, is an expression of one's essential core, and it corresponds to the soul part of *yechidah*. *Da'as* is externally what *keser* is internally; they both reveal the essence of a person.

One perspective sees *keser* as the name of this concept within the ten *Sephiros*. A different point of view feels that discussion of *keser* is too exalted for mere man. As a result, it sees the *da'as*-aspect of innate essence, and its *Sephiros* are *chochmah*, *binah*, *da'as* and the lower seven. Both approaches express the same truth, for *keser* and *da'as* are two sides of the same element. The root of *da'as* is *keser*, a display of the essential life of the individual.

TEN NOT ELEVEN

The realm of holiness is symbolized with the number ten, while the realm of impurity is either nine or eleven. In holiness there are ten forces

---

407. See *Mechilta de-Rabbi Shimon bar Yochai, Devarim* 22:25.
408. Chasidim are extremely stringent in their efforts to maintain purity in the realm between men and women, for they know that violating Abraham's covenant is the source of enormous spiritual impurity. *Da'as* leads them to acknowledge the lesson of the *Zohar* that this misdeed is the worst of all sins (the Stitchiner Rebbe).

that emerged from the ten *Sephiros*. In impurity there are corresponding forces; however, in evil they become eleven forces. The reason for this is that only in holiness are *keser* and *daas* united. When I internalize an idea of holiness, that is an expression of my essence. However, in the realm of evil, will and internalization are two separate elements. *Daas* of evil states that holiness is irrelevant, materialism is what matters. Such a perspective is not an extension of the true essence of man. The realm of evil has essential life that it has captured from the realm of the holy. That is why in evil, *daas* and *keser* are divided and there are eleven forces of evil.

Perhaps these are examples of the basic forces of evil. Wisdom of evil would be the study of basic philosophical principles that lead man away from love of God. Understanding of evil might be the investigation of the thought of a heretic. Internalization of evil is the cynic who claims that miracles are irrelevant, and therefore one should not change his life based on them. Love of evil would be lust. Fear in evil would be to recoil from the observance of a difficult Mitzvah. Harmony of evil would be arrogance, such as a slavish commitment to wearing the most beautiful clothing in order to feel haughty and proud. Rock music that engenders a renunciation of all authority other than one's own wishes would be another example of harmony in evil. Dominance in evil would be a totalitarian regime. Subservience would be following an evil man's advice. Foundation of evil would be misuse of human seed, instead of creating life, squandering its potential. While *malchus* of evil would claim that the ruler deserves his own honor, or misuse of language, such as haughty tale-bearing. *Keser* of evil would be an innate intrinsic opposition to the message of the Jewish nation.

The innate anti-Jewish hate might be linked with the *daas* of evil. *Daas* of evil divides the heart from the mind. It claims that one should not be inspired to change from miracles or Torah lessons. It says that they are not truly relevant, they should not be internalized. This divisiveness stems from an innate opposition to Jewry and God. But there is still an innate hidden advocate for good even in the realm of evil; this *keser* is not the same as the *daas* of evil. This spark of good has been captured by evil, and evil has masked it to make it appear evil, at its core though, it belongs to the realm of holiness. As a result there are really eleven forces in evil.

EXAMPLES OF EVIL ELEVENS

The number eleven is often found in the realm of evil. The Sinai desert was a distance that normally took eleven days to walk through (see Deut. 1:2). The desert was the place of the four *kelippos*.[409] Noah's ark was submerged eleven *ammos* (cubits) into the waters of the flood. Noah's ship was a refuge that saved holiness from the clutches of evil. It reached to the very depths of the realm of the unholy, to the eleventh *ammah* and preserved sparks of the Divine from that depth.[410] The *ketores* (incense) had eleven spices, and its secret was taught to Moses by the angel of death, the head of the force of evil.[411] The incense would stop plagues, for it had the ability to remove all the life force out of the realm of evil.[412] Since evil has eleven forces, there were eleven spices in the incense mix.[413] The tabernacle was covered with a roof of eleven goat skins. The Hebrew word for goat is *aiz*, whose *gematria* is 77, which is seven times eleven. This symbolizes a state where the physical seven are controlled by the eleven forces of evil. The roof of the tabernacles was also meant to break the entire realm of evil, all eleven of its powers. Goats are a symbol of *kelippah*, which is why on Yom Kippur the sacrifice that symbolized misdeeds was the goat that was sent to the wilderness.[414]

---

409. See further *Shem Mi-Shmuel* at the beginning of *Parashas Bemidbar*.

410. Heard from Rav Wolfson.

411. See further *Shabbos* 89a.

412. "The idea of transforming evil by elevating it back to its source in holiness is intimated in the incense" *(Innerspace*, pg. 86).

413. The desert was the place of evil, of *kelippah* forces. Hence the verse in the Song of Songs, *Mi zos olah min ha-midbar ke-simros ashan mekutteres mor u-lvonah mi-kol avkas rochel*, "Who is she that arises out of the desert, she is perfumed [with *ketores*] of sweet myrrh and galbanum, [sweeter] than all the spices of the cosmetician" (Song of Songs 3:8). The Jewish service in the desert was to break the forces of evil that inhered there. The incense symbolizes breaking evil through removing its life-force which is why the entire desert sojourn is symbolized in the above cited verse with the sweet smell of the *ketores* (heard from the Stitchiner Rebbe).

414. The word *shaatnez* (שעטנז)—a prohibited mixture of wool and linen—can be rearranged to spell *satan aiz* (שטן עז). This teaches that the goat (*aiz*) is the symbol of Satan.

DA'AS AND AMALEK

Da'as of *kelippah* is epitomized with the ancient nation Amalek. Amalek attacked the Jews, and the Bible called their attack a "cooling down" (Deut. 25:18). After the miraculous exit from Egypt, the entire world was scared of God; in awe of His people, Amalek challenged that lesson. Amalek claimed that the miracles were happenstance, that there was no need to internalize the ten plagues. Amalek stated that morality was irrelevant and there was no need for the mind's ideas to filter down to the heart and behavior.[415] Spiritually, the war with Amalek represents a struggle to attain internalization, to fully assimilate what is true and to reject unholiness.

Before any receipt of the Torah it is necessary to defeat Amalek. The Torah is not given to those who are cooled down. People who need a committee meeting to decide whether or not God's word is relevant will not receive the Torah. The Torah demands passion. Torah is given to a nation that has an open heart. People who will internalize Torah's directives and change their behavior accordingly—without any hesitation—are the ones who can merit God's Torah. Those who view Torah as the voice of their inner soul can hear its directives. Defeat of Amalek taught Israel to avoid vacillation and to allow for internalization of Torah.

After passing through the Red Sea, the Jews had to defeat Amalek before they could arrive at Mt. Sinai. Similarly, in the aftermath of the first exile, Haman—a descendent of Amalek—had to be defeated before the Jews could reclaim the Torah, which was done through the holiday

---

415. According to classical commentators, the spiritual damage Amalek performs is that they divide the letters of God's name. The Tetragrammaton has four letters, Y-H-V-H. These letters correspond to the *Sephiros*, The first two letters, the *yud* (with its apex) and the *heh*, are the sources of the three intellects, *keser*, *chochmah*, and *binah*. The last two letters are the sources for the lower seven *Sephiros*. The *Sephiros* of *chesed*, *gevurah*, *tiferes*, *netzach*, *hod*, and *yesod* are from the *vav*, and *malchus* is from the last *heh*. Amalek divides the first two letters from the last two letters—they divide the intellect from the heart. Amalek is said to divide parents from children. Within each man, his intellects are the parents that sire emotions as their children. Amalek sets up a wall between the mind and the heart by claiming that the lessons of miracles should not be internalized (the Stitchiner Rebbe). See also Rashi on Exod. 17:16 s.v. *ki yad*.

of Purim.[416] Purim celebrates the defeat of Amalek. If Amalek is the antithesis of correct *da'as*, Purim must be a manifestation of holy *da'as*.

At the beginning of this lesson, we learned that a child does not have *da'as* because he lacks responsibility. A child is not aware of context. A child lacks control. He does not realize what really matters and what is irrelevant. On Purim we all seem to act childlike. According to the Talmud's directive, we are to drink to the point of no control.[417] Purim seems to be the antithesis of *da'as*, so how can it be a celebration of *da'as*?

In light of our analysis, true *da'as* is an expression of innermost will, *keser*. *Keser* is sheer vitality, a vividness and passion that transcends reasonable limits. The rules of nature reflect a world of God's *chochmah*; the miracles that play with the rules of nature are expressions of God's *Ratzon Ha-Elyon*, His Highest Will, His *keser*. The term for will is *ratzon*, which connotes a connection with the word *ratz*, "run." When God jumps ahead of the cloak of nature and clearly reveals how He controls all, it is a sighting of *keser*. Within my personality, when I feel my innermost will, I rush to fulfill it, with absolute disregard of how to accomplish my goal.

Da'as of evil, Amalek-type thinking, entails dividing the mind from feeling and behavior. Evil *da'as* means excessive hesitation and trepidation before permitting a moral concept to change behavior or feeling. The defeat of Amalek merits a grand display of holy *da'as*. Purim is a celebration of the roots of *da'as* of holiness. That is why it leads to passionate celebration and it demands intoxication. When one loses self-control through drinking wine, the essence of man emerges. The excitement of the observant Jew on Purim reveals essential life-force. This is especially true about *tzaddikim*. Once a *tzaddik* is drunk on Purim, his innermost core emerges. The way Torah insights pour out of the mouth of the inebriated *tzaddik* on Purim is a display of the root of holy *da'as*—the innermost, essential will that wishes to fulfill every religious precept.[418] Purim attunes the mind and heart to the innate holy

---

416. According to the Talmud in Tractate *Shabbos*, the Jews at Sinai accepted the Torah against their will, and after defeating Haman they accepted the entire Torah willingly.

417. *Megillah* 7b.

418. In earlier lessons, this will was called the *yechidah* part of the soul.

desires, and it reveals the nature of holy *da'as*—unbridled, passionate, devotion for God and His law.

Knowledge of the *sephiratic* view of the personality can inspire. Knowledge of the depths of internalization and its connection to innermost will and essence can arouse the soul of a Jew to serve God with greater spirit. Celebrate Purim by letting your soul express its soaring self. When you do, you will have merged internalization with will; you will have defeated Amalek who divided them. Within your personality, you will have killed the eleven of evil, who are represented by Haman and his ten sons who were hung together, and in turn, you will cause a reaffirmation of the ten commandments of holiness.

Lesson Twenty-Three

From Ten Plagues
to Ten Commandments

The Ten Tests of Abraham

THE CONCEPT OF *Sephiros* is the meaning of all the tens in the Jewish tradition.[419] Creation occurred through ten statements.[420] These ten commands were the ten *Sephiros* in a physical, almost tangible, form as the roots of the material universe.[421] There were ten generations from Adam to Noah,[422] at which time the entire physical world was decimated with a deluge of water. The reason for this time span was that mankind's mission was to fully refine the ten Godly forces within themselves and to reveal how the ten key elements that underlie the world are from God.[423] However, they failed. Instead of disclosure, humanity covered the ten expressions of Divinity with thick veils. They cloaked their personalities with sensuous character traits, and as a result, civilization was destroyed in a flood.

After the flood, the descendants of Noah were given another chance to accomplish their task. Again, the human race received ten generations.[424] Once more they did not succeed. In the ten generations from Noah until Abraham, humans covered the ten Heavenly roots with yet another shell. The process of hiding the true nature of the Divine's relationship with the created world culminated in the generation of dispersion.[425]

---

419. *Pri Tzaddik* to *Parashas Noach*, Lesson 1.
420. *Ethics of the Fathers* 5:1.
421. *Sfas Emes* to *Parashas Yisro* (5632).
422. *Ethics of the Fathers* 5:2.
423. *Pri Tzaddik* to *Parashas Noach*.
424. *Ethics of the Fathers* 5:3.
425. Genesis 11.

The *dor haflagah*, "generation of dispersion," sought to wage war against God. They attempted to build a giant monument in testament to the supposedly infinite power of man. They were arrogant and assumed that they were disconnected from a Creator. They embodied many of the traits that lead to evil behaviors.[426] In punishment for that generation's misdeeds the human race was eternally divided into factions and nations.

Abraham was tested with ten trials.[427] He passed all of them, maintaining his belief despite the ten challenges. The ten challenges forced Abraham to acknowledge God in each of the ten statements of creation. Thus, he was the purpose of the universe, for he began the process which was man's original task for life: finding God in each of the ten basic elements. His discovering God, despite the barriers earlier generations had constructed, caused him to receive all the reward that those earlier generations could have accrued.

THE TEN PLAGUES

The Jewish nation was tested in Egypt, its first exile. Despite enormous difficulty, we maintained the commitment to our heritage and refused to change our Hebrew names, our mode of dress, and our unique language. In reward for maintaining this residual faith in the Almighty, we were redeemed from Egypt. How did God redeem the Jews? With ten plagues. Why ten? Because the ten plagues revealed that God was the source of the ten statements of creation and the Authority who controlled the entire physical dimension.

According to the Ari, the ten plagues correspond to the ten *Sephiros* in inverse order. The last plague, death of all Egyptian firstborn, was a revelation of the first *Sephirah*, *Keser*. *Keser* is the initial point within the human mind, will. In the ten statements of creation it is represented with the word *Bereishis*, "In the beginning," a level before language. When God killed the Egyptian firstborn He proved that He is the Authority who controls all beginnings, all firsts.

When talking of this plague the Torah spells the word for firstborn without the vav, *b-ch-r-s*. These same letters rearranged can spell *b-k-s-r*,

---

426. See Lessons Fifteen and Sixteen for a description of the realm of evil.
427. *Ethics of the Fathers* 5:4.

literally, "with *keser*." Perhaps the Torah chose to spell the word without the *vav* to hint that this plague rectified misconceptions in the realm of *keser*.

The second statement of creation was, "Let there be light," which corresponds to the *Sephirah* of *chochmah*[428]—intuition or wisdom. The ninth plague was darkness. This punishment blackened the light for all Egyptians while allowing light for the Jews. It demonstrated that God is sovereign over illumination and darkness.

The third statement of creation was, "Let there be a firmament." This Godly barrier divided heavens from the earth. The eighth plague was locusts. Their swarms covered the sky and hid the earth from the Heavens, thus demonstrating that God is the Authority who decides if, when, and how, heaven is linked with earth.

The Heavenly firmament separated physical water from its spiritual root and thus corresponds to *binah*, the ability to discern details within a principle. The key phrase for *binah* is, *meivin davar mitoch davar*, "Comprehending one matter from another." Once one begins to acknowledge details latent within a rule, many thoughts come to mind. One detail leads to another, which leads to yet another. The locusts were many creatures, and they increased in a most prodigal manner, just as understanding begets many thoughts.[429]

How to calibrate the other plagues with the seven lower *Sephiros* is a matter of dispute.

Some say that the first seven plagues corresponded to the first seven *Sephiros* in the regular order. This view argues that the first plague, blood, in which water was affected, demonstrated God's authority over the world of *chesed*, since water emerged from the *Sephirah* of *chesed*. According to this view, the seventh plague, *barad*—hail stones that contained fire—corresponded to *malchus*—kingship.

In the context of the plague of hail stones, the Torah makes reference to the Egyptians who feared God. According to Rashi[430] the plague of

---

428. According to some commentators, the light referred to in the verse is really the Torah, the ultimate and most perfect wisdom (Rav Wolfson). Furthermore, even in English light is connected with the concept of wisdom as evidenced by the word, "enlightenment."
429. Heard from the Stitchiner Rebbe.
430. Rashi on Exod. 9:10 s.v. *ba-adam*.

pestilence also demonstrated that some Egyptians feared God, yet the Torah makes no explicit mention of them. Perhaps the reason for this discrepancy between hail and pestilence is the correlation between hail and *malchus*. Since the plague of hail corresponded to *malchus* during the downpour of physical stones, there was also a spiritual flow from on High of *yiras shamayim*—fear of Heaven. Due to the special appearance of a Divine spirit that caused all to accept His rule, the Torah writes that even Egyptians had true fear of Heaven. Numerology confirms this thesis. The *gematria* of the word *ha-barad*, "the hail," is 211, which equals the value of the word *yarei*, "one who fears," which is the first word in the phrase, *ha-yarei devar Hashem*, "One who fears the word of God" (Exod. 9:20).

The Midrash Tanchuma[431] teaches that at the time of the great war of Gog and Magog, which will precipitate the Messianic era, the rest of the hail stones from Egypt will fall. *Tzaddikim* have revealed that the war of Gog and Magog is primarily a spiritual battle to maintain faith and commitment to God despite cultural beliefs that reject God and His authority. Since the hail brought with it a flow of *malchus*, obedience to God, it will also fall in the times of Gog and Magog, when man will need God's help to maintain faith and observance.[432]

Others argue that blood relates to *malchus*[433] while hail corresponds to *chesed*.[434] The first night of Passover and the *Seder* meal recall the ten

---

431. Exod. 9:32.

432. *Emunas Etech*a, *Parashas Vaera*, pgs. 193-196.

433. Perhaps they link the first plague to kingship because blood's red color is related to *tzimtzum*, strict withdrawal (*gevurah*). *Malchus* is a force that has within it much *gevurah*, much harshness.

434. See further *Bnei Yissachar* about Passover, and *Zohar* 2:36a. The Stitch-iner Rebbe explained this view in the following manner: Blood corresponded to *malchus* because the plague of blood punished the Nile River. The Nile was the real king of Egypt. It provided the water that allowed for life in Egypt. In fact, the Nile was a supreme authority to many Egyptians, and they viewed it as a god. When *malchus* of holiness appeared, the kingship of evil was stricken.

The plague of frogs corresponded to *yesod* because it entailed excess procreation. *Yesod* of holiness means that one displays an unbridled passion for Mitzvos. The practitioner of a holy *yesod* has an ever increasing, vigorous commitment to God. *Yesod* is called a river of blessings, for a river symbolizes constantly replenishing waters, and blessings symbolize a state of eternal

plagues in Egypt. The ten plagues revealed the ten *Sephiros*. The *Seder* plate also represents these forces. The three *matzos* correspond to the first three *Sephiros*. Atop the plate we arrange six food items that parallel generosity, restraint, harmony, dominance, submissiveness, and procreation (foundation). The plate itself is a vessel, thus a parallel to *malchus*.

To further impress upon the Jews that God is the Sovereign of the world's roots, the ten plagues of Egypt were repeated at the Red Sea.[435] After these displays, the Jews fully accepted the power of the Divine in all the forces that emerged from the ten *Sephiros*. In reward for this dedication of the heart the Jews merited to receive the Ten Commandments.

---

growth and receipt of new gifts. In holiness *yesod* entails constantly increasing the amount of good deeds an individual is performing; in the realm of the unholy it was expressed as an ever increasing scourge.

The plague of lice corresponded to *hod*. *Hod* is the root of the word *hodaah*, "admitting." During the plague of lice the Egyptian sorcerers admitted that the plagues were the handiwork of God and not the product of black magic and sorcery.

The plague of wild animals causing damage to humans corresponded to *netzach*. *Netzach* is the fourth *Sephirah* of the lower seven Godly lights. The Mishnah, the record of conversations that serve as the foundation for the Oral Law, is divided into six orders. Rabbi Isaac Luriah taught that the orders correspond to the *Sephiros*. The first order, *Zeraim*, which contains agricultural laws, corresponds to *chesed*, and *Mo'ed*, the order of holiday law, corresponds to *gevurah*. The fourth order is *Nezikin*, tort law. This order details how observant Jews are obligated to safeguard the property of others and ensure that no damage occurs to others from one's ox or flames. *Nezikin* corresponds to *netzach*. Since in holiness, *netzach* is expressed as ensuring that one's animals not damage others, when the force of *netzach* was revealed in the world, it caused animals to damage the property and persons of the realm of evil.

The plague of pestilence was a plague of death and it corresponded to *tiferes*. *Tiferes* entails balance and harmony, and it is also called *rachamim*, "compassion," and *emes*, "truth." Truth requires a balance. A man of truth will sometimes display *chesed*, and at other times he must display *gevurah*. Truth is eternal and everlasting. The hallmark of falsehood is its transient nature. Our forefather Jacob, the paradigm of *tiferes*, was a man of truth. According to our sages, our forefather Jacob never died. Since pestilence corresponded to *tiferes* it caused death in the realm of evil.

The plague of boils corresponded to *gevurah*. Fire is a display of *gevurah*. The plague of boils caused the Egyptians to feel heat on their skin. The hail stones that affected water corresponded to *chesed*.

435. *Ethics of the Fathers* 5.

THE TEN COMMANDMENTS

The Ten Commandments (Hebrew, *Aseres Ha-Dibros*) revealed the *Sephiros* in the realm of Torah thought and service to God.

The first Commandment, "I am God your Lord," corresponds to the first *Sephirah—keser* (innate will)—and the last plague, death of the firstborn. *Keser* is the foundation of personality, and the first Commandment, faith in God, is the foundation of Judaism. This Commandment is not stated as an obligation that Jews must fulfill. God did not say, "Believe in Me." Instead, the first Commandment is phrased as a statement of fact, "I am God your Lord."[436] The first statement of creation, *Bereishis*, "In the beginning," is missing the introductory phrase, "And God said...." It is presented as a self-evident truth and not a decree. A Jew has no choice whether or not to believe in God. Faith is innate, and it is harbored with the soul-part *yechidah* from birth.[437]

A Jew can ignore this inner voice of belief. He has choice as to whether to listen to the voice of *yechidah*, but he has no choice as to the possession of the innate advocate of faith. Just as *yechidah* is a reality, the first Commandment, which represents *keser*, is phrased as a statement of the way things are.[438]

The plague of darkness corresponds to the second Commandment, "Do not have any other gods before me." The plague of locusts corresponds to "Do not bear God's name in vain." The fourth commandment, "Keep the Sabbath," corresponds to the plague of hail.

Sabbath is the seventh day of the week, and it is the day when *malchus*, the seventh *middah*, is revealed. On the Sabbath we demonstrate that God is King. We show complete subservience through cessation of creative work. On Sabbath, we are to empty our minds of the inflated ego that stems from material accomplishment. On Sabbath, the liturgy proclaims, *Yismichu be-malchuscha shomrei Shabbos*, "Those who observe the Sabbath will rejoice in your kingship [*malchus*]." Among the plagues, the seventh one, hail stones, corresponds to the *Sephirah* of *malchus*.[439]

---

436. See *Sfas Emes, Parashas Yisro* (5635) s.v. *u-ma'amar anochi*.
437. See Lesson Fourteen.
438. See Rav Wolfson's book, *Wellsprings of Faith*.
439. As with the plagues, there are other ways of linking the commandments with the *Sephiros*.

FROM STATEMENTS TO COMMANDMENTS

The ten statements were very close to the physical realm and were quickly hidden by shells that men constructed. The Ten Commandments displayed Godliness in a transcendent manner.[440] It took 2448 years to progress from the ten statements of creation and arrive at the Ten Commandments, the ultimate purpose of life.[441] In the human realm, this lesson is a source of comfort.

Do not feel bad if you are still a person who is physically inclined and spiritually distant. The entire world began on an exclusively material plane. Only after millennia of fitful progress did spiritual heights, the Ten Commandments, appear. Within each personal history as well, man is initially born as a physical creature with an inclination primarily for evil.[442] It takes a great deal of time to reach a spiritual elevation.

Never be frustrated and upset by spiritual setbacks and failures. How many times did the universe fail before it reached the radiance of Sinai? Each of the twenty generations from Adam until Abraham[443] failed to reach any spiritual light. So do not despair that man, a spiritually weak being, might endure several decades of setbacks. Just as eventually the great universe merited the Ten Commandments, if one perseveres, one will see his personal small universe,[444] the human body and soul, reach the realm where every part of body and soul reflect the holiness of the ethereal Ten Commandments.

---

440. According to Jewish tradition, when God would relay a commandment, the souls of the listeners would leap out of their bodies. Thus, the revelation at Sinai was an experience in which souls left the physical world and then were miraculously restored to their bodies.

441. See further Rashi on Gen. 1:31, who says that had Israel not accepted the Ten Commandments at Sinai God would have reversed the creation and destroyed the world. *Da'as Tefillah* suggests that the ten statements of Creation are a *chochmah*-like element. They are the raw building blocks. The Ten Commandments are the *binah*, the understanding, the inner meaning and purpose of the ten statements.

442. The *yetzer tov*, the desire for holiness, only fully enters at age thirteen.

443. Twenty generation from Adam until Abraham. After Abraham, it still took six generation until Moses, and then the Jewish nation experienced Sinai.

444. See Lesson Nine for an analysis of the parallel between the universe and the human soul.

LESSON TWENTY-FOUR

MORE LESSONS FROM THE *SEPHIROS*

THERE ARE TEN basic colors. Each color corresponds to one of the ten *Sephiros*.[445]

THE COLOR WHITE

White is the color of *chesed*. That is why milk is white and not green or red. Most of our food comes at some cost. Consider the efforts one must expend to earn a livelihood and thus purchase food. Human pain, discomfort, and frustrating failures are usually part of the process. This lesson can be found in the etymology of the Hebrew word for "bread," *lechem*. *Lechem* shares the same three-letter root with the words, *lechimah*, "battle," and *milchamah*, "war." The reason for this association is that acquiring bread demands perseverance through a struggle. Bread is the universal food staple and thus symbolizes all food.

Why is it so hard to provide food? Man's first sin was eating from the tree of knowledge. As a result of this sin, Divine *gevurah*, harsh restraint, was aroused. God then cursed man:

Because you listened to the voice of your wife and ate of the tree about which I commanded you saying, "You shall not eat of it," accursed is the ground because of you; through suffering shall you eat of it all the days of your life. Thorns and thistles shall it sprout for you, and you shall eat the herb of the field. By the sweat of your brow shall you eat bread until you return to the ground, from which you were taken (Gen. 3:17-18).

---

445. *Tikkunei Zohar*, foreword pg. 1a.

Due to this curse most efforts to attain food entail contending with *gevurah*, Divine harshness.

Most food items have a trace of this harshness within them. Milk is different. Milk is the gift of a mother to her child. The love from a mother to her newborn is absolute and overwhelming. The nourishment the baby receives is pure kindness. A baby is never asked to earn his food in any manner. This is why a mother's milk is lily-white. It is pure *chesed*.[446]

The manna in the desert required little effort to attain. It was the bread of kindness, imbued with the light of *chesed*. This is why Moses states that manna's starkest characteristic was its white color (see Exod. 16:31).

During Shavuos, which celebrates the receipt of the Torah, we have the custom of eating dairy products. Maybe the reason for this custom is that dairy products are all products of milk and as a result these white foods are expressions of Divine *chesed*. The gift of Torah was a display of unmitigated love, hence the custom of eating food that displays Divine giving.[447]

The first stage in the creation of the physical world was a display of Divine *chesed*. King David expressed this fact with his phrase *olam chesed yibbaneh*, "The world is built on kindness" (Ps. 89:3). The first place that God created was the Temple mount in Jerusalem. The Temple mount contains a stone, called *even shesiyah*—the foundation stone—for it was the foundation of the world. Since the world began with kindness, the Temple mount is a place where there are continual downpours of Godly generosity. That is why Moses called it *Levanon* (Lebanon), from the root *lavan*, "white." White is the color of giving and the Temple, and its moun-

---

446. *Emunas Etecha, Parashas Devarim*, pg. 211, s.v. *u-vein tofel ve-lavan*.
447. There are many things humans do as a result of subconscious motivations. Some of those motivations are directives from the soul. Perhaps the reason why doctors wear white is that the healing profession is a vocation of *chesed*. Since white is the color of kindness and love, these practitioners wear its color. In recent years it has become quite widespread for many doctors to wear scrubs that are blue and green. Perhaps the reason for this is that they are no longer motivated by pure kindness to engage in healing the ill, which is why their souls no longer seek to be clothed in white (Rav Wolfson).

tain are the places where Divine gifts, accompanied with tender feelings that resemble a mother's concerns for her newborn, continually appear.[448]

During the beginning of the Hebrew month *Av* the Jewish nation suffered many tragedies.[449] As a result, there is a custom to refrain from eating meat during the first nine and a half days of the month.[450] Perhaps this custom is meant to encourage the ingestion of dairy products. Food from milk is usually white and has within it traces of *chesed*, Divine giving. At a time of year when the Jews suffered Divine limitations, traditional custom mandates eating white foods to arouse Divine mercy, compassion, and generosity.[451]

---

448. In the realm of time the world began on Rosh Hashanah, the first day of the month *Tishrei* (*Tikkunei Zohar* pg. 81b). The numerical value of *Rosh Hashanah* (861) equals the value of the words for Jerusalem's Temple, *Beis Ha-Mikdash* (*Emunas Etecha, Parashas Ki Savo* pg. 2, s.v. *u-matzasi*, quoting the *Imrei Noam*). Rav Yitzchak Hutner in his work *Pachad Yitzchak* (*Rosh Hashanah, Kuntres Ha-Chesed*) posits that the very nature of Rosh Hashanah demands that observant Jews perform acts of kindness. Since Rosh Hashanah is the beginning of the world, and the beginning was an appearance of Godly kindness, man must emulate his maker and at the time of beginning give gifts to all.

One might ask on this lesson of Rav Hutner and on what was written in the text the following question: As first beginnings one would think that Rosh Hashanah and the Temple should be manifestations of *keser*? The text described their essence as *chesed*? In a private conversation, the Stitchiner Rebbe told me that, in truth, both *keser* and *chesed* are displays of kindness. *Keser* is the love and kindness that transcends reason while *chesed* is acts of kindness that emerge from intuition, understanding, and internalization. If I feel that it makes sense to help someone and then I help him, it is *chesed*, while instinctual, trans-logical giving is *keser*. Thus, Rosh Hashanah as the day of *keser* demands a display of kindness that is above logic and justification and the Temple Mount as the place of *keser* is the place where there are constant flows of spiritual gifts, emerging from a Love that transcends logic, understanding, or explanation.

449. The Mishnah states: "On the ninth of *Av* it was decreed that our forefathers [the generation that had left Egypt] would not enter Israel, the first and second Temples in Jerusalem were destroyed, the city Beitar was captured, and the city was plowed over" (*Ta'anis* 26b). As a result of its sad history the beginning of the month of *Av* is a time of mourning (see *Code of Jewish Law, Orach Chaim* 550-559).

450. *Orach Chaim* 551:10.

451. *Emunas Etecha, Parashas Devarim* pg. 211.

FLAMES OF FAITH

THE COLOR OF *GEVURAH*

Red and black are the colors of *gevurah*—restraint. Even the secular soul senses this directive, which is why a red light is the universal stop sign. It tells the driver or pedestrian, "Restrain yourself." According to the Talmud, black is really spoiled red,[452] so black is also a color of restraint.[453]

THE GREEN MEAN

Green is the color of *tiferes*—harmony. Harmony is the key to Judaism. According to Maimonides,[454] balance and moderation, the blending together of extremes, is the approach one should use in all attributes. For instance, Jewish law states, "Do not be penurious, but do not throw away all your money either." According to the Maharal, the reason our holidays are in spring and autumn is to demonstrate that the ideal is a time that has some cold and some warmth, not a time of extreme swelter or ice.[455] The land of Israel is in the middle of the world[456] as it should be a place of the blending together of extremes and the discovery of the golden mean. Most of the natural world is green to demonstrate that harmony is the ideal and key to life.[457]

TEN TUNES

There are ten terms of song in the book of Psalms. There were ten authors of the Psalms. Each author excelled in one of these ten forms of poetry. Why ten and not seven or eight? The ten types of melody correspond to the ten *Sephiros*.[458] Each type of song can help purify an aspect of the

452. See *Sukkah* 33b.
453. Perhaps the white keys on the piano are displays of *chesed*, which is why they produce beautiful notes. The black keys are displays of *gevurah*, which is why their sounds are only appealing when they are combined together with the sounds of *chesed* (Rav Wolfson).
454. *Laws of Dei'os.*
455. During the extreme of heat, we have the fast of the ninth of *Av*, commemorating the loss of the Temple. And during the extreme of winter we have the month of *Teives*, during which evil forces have great potency.
456. The nations call this area, "the Middle East" (heard from the Stitchiner Rebbe).
457. Heard from the Stitchiner Rebbe.
458. See further the *Sfas Emes* to the Psalms.

human personality that corresponds to one of the ten *Sephiros*.[459]

---

459. Chasidim teach that the misdeed of a man spilling seed is a source of enormous spiritual damage. Maintaining purity in this realm is called *shemiras ha-bris*, "preserving the covenant." Rabbi Nachman of Breslov revealed a means of rectifying misdeeds in this realm. He called this healing prayer the *Tikkun Ha-Kelali*. It is a collection of ten chapters of Psalms, each of which begins with a different type of song. Through recital of the songs that parallel the ten *Sephiros* every aspect of the human personality and the world can be healed.

The following selections from Rabbi Aryeh Kaplan's commentary to Rabbi Nachman's stories clarify the lesson of the types of melody: "**Ten types of melody** Rabbi Nachman himself taught that the Ten Psalms were a 'General rectification' [*tikkun kelali*] for all sins, particularly sexual sins, and especially those involving emitting seed in vain [*Likkutei Moharan* 205; *Likkutei Moharan Tinyana* 92]. These involved the ten types of melody found in the Psalms. The Ten Psalms are numbers 16, 32, 41, 42, 59, 77, 90, 105, 137, 150."

"The Psalms as a whole also contain all ten different types of song [*Tikkunei Zohar* 13; *Likkutei Moharan Tinyana* 92]. King David ended the book with Psalm 150, which contains the expression *halelu-hu* ("Praise Him") ten times. The last of these is, "Praise Him with cymbals of *teruah*" (Ps. 150:5), because the *teruah* [staccato] also includes all ten types of song" (*Likkutei Halachos, Even Ha-Ezer, Peru U-Rvu* 3:10).

"Sin and spiritual damage are associated with sadness and depression. The healing is therefore through song, which brings joy" (Cf. *Likkutei Moharan* 24).

"The ten songs were also alluded to in the ten sounds of the shofar. On Rosh Hashanah the shofar is sounded in the following manner: *tekiah shevarim teruah tekiah; tekiah shevarim tekiah; tekiah teruah tekiah*. Thus, there are a total of ten sounds. These allude to the ten types of song. Furthermore, on Rosh Hashanah, in the *Musaf* service, ten verses of *malchiyos* [kingship], ten verses of *zichronos* [remembrances], and ten verses of *shofros* [trumpet blasts] are recited. Each set of ten also parallels the ten types of song. Rosh Hashanah is the beginning of the ten days of repentance; therefore it has these ten types of song. Song is the basis of repentance, since song leads to joy and joy brings one to the side of merit (*Likkutei Moharan* 282). It is only through the ten types of song that those who are far from God can be brought back (*Likkutei Halachos, Peru U-Rvu* 3:10).

"The ten days of repentance also parallel the ten types of song. We begin these ten days with Rosh Hashanah, where all ten types of song are brought into play through the ten sounds of the shofar. Shofar is the rectification of these ten types of song, as it is written, "Make song good with the *teruah* sound" (Ps. 33:3). The Psalm says, "God will rise in *teruah*; God will rise in the sound of the shofar. Sing to God sing" (Ps. 47:6) (*Likkutei Halachos, Peru U -Rvu* 3:10).

"The ten days of repentance end with Yom Kippur. This completes the ten types of song" (*Likkutei Halachos, Peru U-Rvu* 3:11, *Rabbi Nachman's Stories* pgs. 418-420).

SHABBOS AND THE *TZADDIK*

A *tzaddik* is also clothed with the ten lights, the ten forces of holiness that emerged from the ten *Sephiros*. His first thoughts are holy (*chochmah*). His comprehending intellect is dedicated to understanding the Divine and increasing love for Him (*binah*).

His internalization is a reflection of his essence (*daas* as an expression of *keser*). He channels *chesed* to absolute generosity. He knows when to withdraw (*gevurah*), and he balances giving with withholding (*tiferes*). He knows when to dominate (*netzach*) and when to submit (*hod*). He uses his creative organ in a holy manner (*yesod*). And lastly, he views himself as a humble vessel of his Maker (*malchus*).

In Lesson Two we learned that the *tzaddik* is a person through whom all members of mankind are blessed. The ten *Sephiros* are the reason for this central role of the *tzaddik*.

The ten *Sephiros* are the keys to the Universe. God sends life to all creatures through His ten *Sephiros*. The *tzaddik* is clothed with a glow from all ten, which is why the *tzaddik* is the channel through which the life-force of the entire universe flows.

We also learned in Lesson Two that the *tzaddik* is a manifestation of Shabbos in the realm of person. Shabbos is a time when all ten forces of creation are partially revealed. In Psalm 29, which is recited as an acceptance of Shabbos, these forces are mentioned. The psalm begins as a song to David. Then it states,

Havu la-Hashem bnei eilim, havu la-Hashem kavod va-oz, havu la-Hashem kevod shemo.

Bring forth to God mighty sons. Bring forth to God honor and strength. Bring forth to God the honor due His name.

The psalm mentions the word *havu*, "bring forth," three times. These three gifts are the first three *Sephiros*—the first three statements of creation. The chapter proceeds to describe seven sounds of God. These seven sounds are the seven notes of music, and they parallel the seven lower *Sephiros*. This psalm is recited to usher in the holiness of Shabbos. It mentions all ten *Sephiros*, since on Shabbos all ten holy forces of creation, and the ten holy personality parts of man, are revealed in some measure and are spiritually renewed.

LESSON TWENTY-FIVE

LESSONS FROM
THE *SEPHIROS* PATTERN

EARLIER LESSONS TAUGHT that within the statements of creation there is a difference between the first three and the latter seven. The primordial trio speaks of other-worldly concepts, while the lower seven speak of the dimensions of Godliness that appear in the physical realm. Within the human these two classes are represented as the intellects and the emotions and behaviors.

The ten plagues are also divided in a similar fashion. The first seven plagues are discussed in the Torah portion of *Vaera*. The last three plagues (locusts, darkness, and the death of the firstborn) parallel the first three *Sephiros* and are discussed in the Torah portion of *Bo*.

Prior to celebrating the receipt of the Torah, on the holiday of Shavuos, Jews first count the days of seven weeks. This ritual is called *sefiras ha-omer*—the *omer* count. The *omer*'s seven weeks are dedicated to the perfection of emotions and behaviors, the seven lower forces within man. After perfecting all seven emotions, we commemorate Torah's revelation at Sinai. The Torah perfects the three intellects: intuition, understanding, and internalization.

Ideally, each Jew should focus each week during the counting period on refining one of his emotional tendencies. To help in this endeavor there are special parts of Torah that are learned during the *Shabboses* of these weeks. On the first Shabbos (which is during the holiday of Passover) we publicly read the Song of Songs. This text teaches what Heavenly love is supposed to be. Love is an aspect of the *Sephirah* of *chesed*. Learning the Song of Songs is meant to inspire the reader to increase his love of God and correct his use of *chesed*.

On every subsequent Shabbos of the *omer* count, we study a different chapter from *Avos* (*Ethics of the Fathers*). The first chapter details the order of *mesorah*—the exact and precise transmission of Jewish oral law. To transmit precise instructions, much harsh *gevurah* is needed. Those passages teach that we must perfect our attribute of *gevurah*—restraint and precision. On the third Shabbos, the chapter begins with the lesson of R. Judah the Prince:

Aizo hi derech yesharah she-yavor lo ha-adam, "What is the straight path man should choose?" *Kol she-hi tiferes le-oseha ve-siferes lo min ha-adam,* "Any path that is *tiferes,* [a harmonious blend that produces glory], for those who perform it and for those who see the act."

This chapter seeks to inculcate sensitivity to perfection of *tiferes.* Each subsequent chapter corresponds to the specific emotion that should be perfected during that week. After perfecting the emotions we celebrate Shavuos. Shavuos recalls the receipt of the Torah. Torah insight and knowledge help perfect man's three intellectual components.

INTELLECTS SIRING BEHAVIOR

The order of the statements of creation was first the three Higher statements and then the seven earthly statements. This organization conveys a lesson. The ideal arrangement is when the first three forces, the intellects, proceed before the seven emotions. Throughout history, if an experience occurs and God first reveals His three Heavenly *Sephiros* and only later the lower seven abilities, then it is an ideal experience.[460] Within man, this pattern teaches that the intellects should always come first. A holy individual has his mind control his feelings and emotions. He does not react in an instinctual and emotional manner.

---

460. Consider the Ten Commandments. God first presented the commandment, "I am God Your Lord." This commandment paralleled *keser*—innate will—the highest of the three intellects. The revelation at Sinai was an ideal experience. At Sinai there was a partial recreation of the Garden of Eden experience (see *Shabbos* 146a). As a result, the manifestations of the primordial three proceeded before the expressions of the lower seven.

Rabbi David Yungreis, of blessed memory, a teacher in Yeshivas Ohel Moshe in Jerusalem, used to relate the following story:

Jerusalem was once a town that survived on handouts. In those days, residents of the holy city needed the support of the Jews from their homelands to make ends meet. The help would arrive during the holiday season. For example, Jerusalemites who were descendants of Lithuanian Jews would receive holiday stipends from a fund called the Vilna Kollel. This Kollel was financed by the donations of the observant Jews of Lithuania.

Rav Yeshaya Bardaky, a well known righteous man, was the financial secretary of such a Kollel. A bitter individual once entered R. Yeshaya's office and asked for some financial help. "I know that now is not the time of *chalukah*," when resources were usually distributed, he said, "but I need the help desperately, so I am asking for an emergency loan."

R. Yeshaya checked his safe and found that it was empty. "I am sorry," he said, "I cannot give you anything for I have no funds left to disburse."

The fellow was incensed. He lifted his hand and slapped R. Yeshaya across the cheek.

R. Yeshaya did not slap him back. Instead he immediately apologized.

"I am so sorry," he told the insolent individual. "I had no idea that your financial situation was so dire. Please wait here for a moment."

R. Yeshaya then ran upstairs to his residence and borrowed money from his wife and several neighbors. Once he had a respectable sum in hand he ran downstairs, gave the money to the man, and again apologized for not having appreciated how difficult the situation was. Had he realized, he would have immediately found a way to help out.[461]

Rabbi Yeshaya was a holy individual. His intellects controlled his feelings and behaviors. Faced with a sudden attack he did not let his emotional impulses, his lower seven forces, rule him. He asserted the supremacy of the three intellects. He immediately realized the pain the poor man was in and he overcame his natural urge of anger to perform an act of kindness.

---

461. *Leket Amarim*, Volume 1, pg. 66. The Talmud in *Chullin* 89a states, "Rabbi Illai taught: The world exists in the merit of the individual who restrains himself and does not respond during disputes."

The *tzaddik* acts like R. Yeshaya. When faced with a conflict between reason and feeling, his logic wins out. Furthermore, he uses his mind to trigger his emotions. His feelings are born from his intellectual analysis and decisions.

This is the meaning of the passage[462] which teaches that after Moses died, the Jews forgot three hundred laws and were in doubt about seven hundred others. The three hundred forgotten laws are a loss in the realm of the three intellects. The seven hundred doubts correspond to the seven emotions, the source for all actions. Loss of intellectual capabilities caused seven hundred practical ambiguities, for the mind had been siring the feelings and behaviors.

The Chasidim of Lubavitch advocate this ideal. They feel that the best type of love of God is one that is the product of *chochmah*, *binah*, and *da'as*. Love of God that emerges from a soulful song might not be real. Song is an emotional arousal. Emotions are by definition ephemeral. Lubavitch thought advocates use of the mind as a means to love of God. Love that emerges from the intellects is long lasting and thus real. Even when the full measure of its passion passes, residual benefit remains eternally.

The following meditation is one that has the mind arouse and direct the heart:

Consider the grandeur of the universe. Think about how large it is. Picture all of the stars, microscopic creatures, animals, plants, and other forms of life that fill the spheres of existence. They are yours. God has given man the entire world as a gift to enjoy. If you delve into the details of this gift, and focus with great concentration on how much God has done to benefit man, love for Holiness will burst forth from the heart.

Since they emphasized the use of the mind, the Rebbes of Lubavitch delivered lengthy, intricate, discourses that delved into the details of hidden universes, such as *atzilus*. They felt that such mind stretching exercises perfect logical thought and lead the mind to spark the heart. As a mark of their commitment to intellectualism, Lubavitch Chasidim call their movement *Chabad*, an acronym for *chochmah*, *binah*, and *da'as*, the three intellects.

---

462. *Temurah* 16a, s.v. *amar Rav Yehudah amar Rav be-sha'ah she-niftar Mosheh Rabbeinu.*

EMOTIONS FIRST

The ten statements of creation were a display of an ideal pattern of the *Sephirah* array. The ten plagues also revealed the ten *Sephiros*. During the ten plagues, however, it was the lower seven first, and then the three Heavenly Intellects appeared. In the weeks prior to Shavuos, as well, Jews first focus on emotional rectification, and only after complete character refinement do we focus on our intellect as we reaccept the Torah. The reason for the dissonance between the statements of Creation and the pattern of plagues is that during the exodus from Egypt we confronted the non-ideal world.

Egypt tainted the Jewish nation. After 210 years of slavery, the Jews were not ready for the high levels of spiritual energy contained in flashes of holy intuition (*chochmah*), understanding (*binah*), and internalization (*da'as*). In the corrupted world of Egypt there first had to be a revelation of the lower seven forces; only then could the higher forms, the first three *Sephiros*, appear. When our forefathers left Egypt they were still on a low spiritual level. They could not appreciate the Divine lights of intuition, understanding, and internalization. They first had to perfect their seven emotions. After the seven weeks of character refinement they were able to appreciate the three intellects when they appeared at Sinai. Since we relive their experience on a yearly basis, we too first refine the seven emotions during the *omer* count that follows Passover, and then we receive the three intellects on Shavuos.

Many Chasidic groups, other than Chabad, feel that we should focus on emotions first, even those that do not emerge from the intellects. They believe that the average human mind was not created with the ability to truly comprehend the details of the Heavenly worlds that the mystics reveal. These groups emphasize *Chagat Nehim* (the seven emotions and behaviors). They might emphasize the glory and beauty of Judaism (*tiferes*), or love for all Jews (*chesed*), or the importance of precise observance of Mitzvos (*gevurah*).

Both approaches, Chabad and *Chagat Nehim*, are necessary. Different Jews are drawn to varied approaches of serving God. Each Jewish soul is rooted in a unique point in Heaven. The path of service a Jew will find most appealing is the one that corresponds to his root in Heaven. Some souls are rooted in *mochin*. These individuals are great intellectuals who can comprehend abstract concepts and Chabad is the approach they should follow. Other souls are rooted in the emotional areas of Heaven and they will find that the approaches of Chasidic groups that emphasize *Chagat Nehim* are best for them.[463]

OUR GENERATION

We are presently on a low spiritual level. Since we are on a lower spiritual plane every act of holiness is treasured by our Father in Heaven. Perhaps, due to the weak nature of our generation, even an imperfect love of God, one that stems from the heart and not the mind, is of great value.

Rabbi Isaac Luriah revealed that our lowly world affects the value of deeds:

Rabbi Chaim Vital once asked his teacher the Ari, "How could you tell us that you have an exalted soul? Even the simple Jews in the generations of the Tannaim and Amoraim [the Sages of the Mishnah and the Talmud] accomplished more than you in their prayers and devotions!" The Ari answered, "They did not live in my era. In my era, when observance is difficult, when sin and lust fill the air, to continue to observe anything displays greatness."

If the Ari, who lived in the holy atmosphere of Safed in the Sixteenth Century, felt that any level of observance was a mark of distinction, how much more so is that true today. We live in a secular society that is filled with temptations. Our era is filled with denial of God and disbelief in His providence. We are a mere two generations from the horrors of World War II and Holocaust, which ravaged our nation. If today, one is

---

463. In truth, each Jewish soul is rooted in a letter in the Torah. There are 600,000 letters to the Torah and 600,000 primary Jewish souls. The Jews rooted in the intellectual parts of the Torah are primarily intellectual while the Jews rooted in the emotional parts are primarily reached through the heart.

willing to call himself a Jew, that is already a mark of awesome greatness. As a result of all the difficulty entailed in observance, the Almighty loves our deeds a great deal. Perhaps they are worth more than the accomplishments of earlier generations.[464] [465]

---

464. Heard from Rav Wolfson.

465. The lowly nature of our generation affects the attribute of *yesod* as well. We have learned that the seven days of the week correspond to the seven lower *Sephiros*. In light of such a parallel, Sunday is the day of *chesed*, and Friday would be the day of *yesod*. According to Jewish law the day begins with the night before, thus, the sixth day starts with Thursday night. *Yesod* is concentrated in the organ of procreation. Chasidim used to have the custom that on Thursday night they would stay awake all night studying Torah as a rectification of any possible misdeed in the realm of *yesod*. On Friday Chasidim used to, and still do, go to the *mikveh* (ritual bath) to further purify whatever misdeeds they might have in the realm of *yesod*. Our generation is a weak one. If we would stay awake all of Thursday night, we might not feel the pleasure on Shabbos.

We should therefore find other ways to fix *yesod*. Perhaps one should dedicate a small part of Thursday night studies to review of one's Torah learning for the week and to write down all the novel Torah ideas, the intellectual children, which were spawned that week. Due to our meager level such activities are very meaningful in the eyes of God (Rav Wolfson).

LESSON TWENTY-SIX

THE SECRET OF MUSIC

THE VITALITY AND depth of music trigger many questions. Music seems to capture almost any mood. To express sadness and pain there are mournful dirges. To arouse the war-making ability of soldiers there are military marches. To inspire dancing at weddings and joyous occasions there are celebratory ditties. Why can the same institution express so many different facets of emotional experience? Music also has great spiritual importance.

The Levites in the Temple would serve God by accompanying the sacrifices with song. Clearly, song reaches great spiritual heights, for the Levites were disrupting their Torah study and prayer to sing. Why do melodies reach such lofty levels?

There is a tradition that Heaven contains a palace of song. According to the *Zohar*,[466] the doors of this palace only open to melodies. King David was world Jewry's greatest singer, and he is the master of this palace. When simple Jews sing the Psalms, King David's songs, they too gain entry into that palace.

People say that the palace of *teshuvah*—returning to God—is near the palace of song. "They are wrong," revealed the Rebbe of Modzhitz. "The palace of song is the palace of return. The way to return to God is song."[467] Why is song the means of reattachment to God?

The concept of the *Sephiros* as the root of reality is the reason for the uniqueness of harmonious melodies. Our world emerged from the seven lower *Sephiros*. Music contains a manifestation of all seven *Sephiros*. An

---

466. *Tikkunei Zohar* 11.
467. *Imrei Shaul, Inyanei zimrah ve-simchah*, Note 15, quoting Rabbi Yisrael of Modzhitz (1849-1921).

emotional experience is a display of one of the seven *Sephiros*. Since music contains all seven *Sephiros*, it expresses all emotions.[468] In a small way, singing displays our spiritual roots; hence the enormous spiritual significance and potency to melody. Evidence of the connection between music and the seven *Sephiros* is the connection Jewish sources draw between music and the number seven.

THE SEVEN NOTES

In the Jewish tradition, the number seven is associated with music. According to the *Pirkei de-Rabbi Eliezer*, there are seven major bodies of water, and the seventh is the *Kinneres* (Sea of Galilee), which lies east of Tiberias, Israel. The word *Kinneres* comes from the word *kinor*, "harp," for it is a lake shaped like a harp that leads all the other lakes in song to God.[469] The Midrash states further that there are seven major land-masses: the six continents and the Land of Israel. The Land of Israel is the land of song. When Jacob told his sons to take some of the produce of the land, he said, *Kechu mi-zimras ha-aretz*, which can be translated, "Take some of the song of the land" (Gen. 43:11).[470]

The seventh day is Shabbos, and in Psalms we read, *Mizmor shir le-yom ha-Shabbos*, "A joyous song for the Shabbos day" (Psalm 92). The wording of the verse suggests that the Shabbos day sings. Our liturgy confirms this reading when it states, *Ve-yom ha-shevi'i mishabbe'ach ve-omer: Mizmor shir le-yom ha-Shabbos*, "And the seventh day praises God

---

468. *Divrei Yisrael, Parashas Miketz* pg. 66a.

469. "All the bodies of water sing to God. This is the meaning of the phrase in our prayers: *illu finu malei shirah ka-yam u-lishoneinu rinnah ka-hamon gallav*, 'Were our mouths filled with song like the ocean, and our tongues with praise like the multitudes of waves.' Apparently, the ocean and its waves are viewed by Jewish thought as a great song to God, and we are saying that we too should sing like them. The Kinneres Lake is the cantor leading all the waves and oceans in their musical chant" (*Tzion Ve-Arehah* pg. 90).

470. When Messiah will arrive, we will hear the songs that the stones and pebbles of Israel are singing. Then we will merit the fulfillment of the verse, *Mi-kenaf ha-aretz zemiros shamanu*, "From the edges of the land we heard songs" (*Tzion Ve-Arehah* pg. 50, quoting Isa. 24:16).

and chants: 'A song for the Shabbos day.'" Song is central to the Shabbos experience. It has been said that "Shabbos is a cloak woven out of the songs the Jew sings."[471]

The Jewish nation has been blessed with seven great leaders. The seventh was King David. King David was the sweet singer of Israel who composed the songs that fill the Psalms and our prayer-book.[472]

Why is the seventh the organ of tunes? Because there are only seven lower *Sephiros*, and they appear in the seven notes of music.

The Western musical system organizes all sounds into seven full notes: C, D, E, F, G, A, and B. Sing a C, raise your voice and sing a higher note, it is a D; these are two distinct tones. However, if you continue to raise your pitch your eighth sound will once again be a C, this time in a higher octave. If you continue to sing higher notes you are just repeating the D, E, F, and other notes, at the elevated pitch.

All the sounds on earth can be classified in this musical system. A peal of thunder might be a C note. A door creaking might be a D. We usually do not realize what note household sounds are because the octave they are in is either too high or low. A gifted musical soul, blessed with perfect pitch hearing, will be able to discern the musical note for every sound of life. Why can all sounds be classified within seven notes? The answer is that there are only seven *Sephiros* that appear in our realm. Music has only seven notes, just as the week has only seven days, for our realm of reality has only seven *Sephiros* in a fully manifested way.

The *Sephiros* can appear in many different forms. For instance, water, from *chesed*, can appear as a liquid, solid, or gas. Similarly the note C, which is the note of *chesed* can appear in different forms: hence the appearance of C in the different octaves.

Now we can better understand the answer to the question of music's unique abilities to arouse the heart. The seven emotions of the heart (giving, harsh restriction, harmony, dominance, empathy, continuity/foundation, and kingship/humility) are displays of the seven *Sephiros*. Since the seven notes of music represent the same pattern and embody the Heavenly *Sephirah* forces they have the ability to arouse these feelings.

---

471. *Tzion Ve-Arehah* pg. 89.
472. Even in the animal realm one will find the seventh associated with song. *Parashas Re'eh* lists seven kosher animals. The name of the seventh *zamer*, literally, "song" (Deut. 14:5. See *Tzion Ve-Arehah* pg. 50).

THE SOUL OF SHABBOS

A musician needs all seven notes to produce music. Without a single note of the seven, say he possesses a guitar that cannot produce the note A, he cannot compose a tune. That is why the seventh day is associated with song.

On Sunday the note C is recreated, on Monday the note D. On Sunday one only has a single note, on Monday only two notes. However, on Shabbos one finally has all seven notes at his disposal. That is why on Shabbos one can sing, and the sensitive soul feels, "I must sing." Shabbos is the day when all the seven lower *Sephiros* appear in the world. On Shabbos, a Jewish heart realizes that it should sing, for every note within it is being plucked by the Divine musician. In fact, the Rebbe of Lechovitz taught, "I would sooner believe that all seven oceans dried up before I would believe that a Jew who knows how to sing does not sing on Shabbos."[473]

The Lands of *chesed* have only one note. The Land of Israel is the seventh in the series of land bodies, which is why it has all seven notes. Israel was blessed with seven types of fruits: wheat, barley, grapes, figs, pomegranates, olives, and dates. These seven fruits correspond to the seven lower *Sephiros*. Israel is the place where the seven lower *Sephiros* are displayed in some measure. Since the seven notes of music are also a display of these forces, the land itself arouses song. Prior to its liberation, the land was called Canaan; this name contains a hidden reference to song. Canaan (כנען) is the acronym for the phrase *kinor* (כ) *naim* (נ) *im* (ע) *navel* (ן)—the sweet harp together with the navel instrument.[474]

The different oceans throughout the world display only one of the *Sephiros*. The *Kinneres* as the seventh body of water displays all seven *Sephiros* and notes of music. The seventh water body was shaped like a harp, because it is a place of song. King David as the seventh leader possessed all seven notes of the *Sephiros*, which is why he was the sweet singer of Israel.

---

473. *Tzion Ve-Arehah* pg. 90.
474. *Tzion Ve-Arehah* pg. 49.

Shabbos, Oaths, and *Tzaddikim*

Lesson One taught that an oath is related to the number seven and the arousal of all the forces of a person. From the nature of music we can better understand that lesson. In music one can sing the same note in many different octaves. So it is with the *Sephiros*.

The *Sephiros* are the bounded lights of Divinity. These lights appeared in the "octave" of statements of creation. Since our earthly world was created with the last seven statements, in the "octave" of physical creations we primarily experience revelations of the seven lower *Sephiros*. Every week, these seven heavenly forces appear in the "octave" of seven days. In each person the *Sephiros* appear in the "octave" of the seven emotions and behaviors (*Chagat Nehim*). An oath causes all seven forces to appear within the "octave" of a commitment. Since an oath is a display of the *Sephiros*, it arouses all seven emotional forces within the heart. Shabbos is the day when the seven *Sephiros* appear in the "octave" of a single day, which is why Shabbos is like an oath, in that it inspires every emotional facet of the person.

Since Shabbos is the time when all seven Sephiros appear and our world is a display of the seven *Sephiros*, Shabbos is the channel through which new life flows to the physical universe. Shabbos and the world are like two parallel harps that only differ in size. When the *Sephiros* appear in the dimension of time (Shabbos) and person (the Shabbos-observing heart) they cause a corresponding revelation in the realm of world. Once the *Sephiros* reappear, new life arrives as well.

Earlier lessons taught about the *tzaddik*. The *Sephiros* and their corresponding parts of the soul[475] are the personality maps that teach man how to become a *tzaddik*. It is hard to become a *tzaddik*; there are many barriers that must be broken. Yet if one asserts the mind over the heart, or if one engages in holy emotional activities, or if one

---

475. See Lesson Twenty-One. It was mentioned there that the *Sephiros* are like the parts of the soul in that they emerged from the letters of God's name. Thus, *keser* corresponds to *yechidah* and the *kutzo shel yud*. *Chochmah* corresponds to *chayah* and the *yud*. *Binah* corresponds to *neshamah* and the first *heh*. *Chesed, gevurah, tiferes, netzach, hod*, and *yesod* correspond to *ruach* and the *vav*. Finally, *malchus* corresponds to *nefesh* and the final *heh*.

employs internalization that corresponds to innate will, one can defeat the *kelippos* and become a *tzaddik*. A *tzaddik* uses his personality in holiness thus embodying the holiness of the *Sephiros*. That is why he, like Shabbos, is the channel through which life for the world flows.[476]

SONG AND RETURN

In holiness, due to the chain-like nature of creation, every level is linked with the stage above it. Thus, the seventh note of music has within it traces of the realm of eight. Lessons Seventeen and Eighteen revealed that the number eight is associated with the fiftieth year, the force of *Yovel* that returns all to their roots. After the seven lower *Sephiros*, there is the intellect of *binah*. *Teshuvah*—returning to God—stems from the universe of *binah*. The light of *Yovel* is a display of the *Sephirah* of *binah*. Hence, the lesson of the Rebbe of Modzhitz: the palace of return, the level of eight, is the palace of song, the level of seven. For when one reaches a complete experience of the seven lower forces one finds oneself already in the realm of the level of eight, the world of Return.

King David wrote that in the future, when the Messiah will have come, we will sing to God a "new song" (Ps. 98:1). Perhaps the Talmud's lesson about David's harp is the deeper meaning of that new song. The Talmud teaches that in the Temple in Jerusalem, King David used to play a seven-stringed harp. When the Messiah will come, David's harp will have eight strings. In the World-to-Come it will have ten.[477]

The *Sephiros* are the significance of these strings. In our dimension of reality only seven *Sephiros* are fully revealed, hence a seven-stringed instrument. The Messiah will return all to their root. He will personify Bethlehem, the place of *Yovel*. During his reign, a great light of *Yovel* will glow—the *Sephirah* of *binah* will express itself. As a result, music will change. A new note will appear, all tunes will be enriched, and David's

---

476. In Lesson Twenty-Four we learned that Shabbos and the *tzaddik* display all ten *Sephiros*. That does not contradict the text. The first three *Sephiros* do not appear fully in our world. A mere echo of their sound resonates in our world. The seven lower *Sephiros* are more fully expressed. Thus, Shabbos and the *tzaddik* fully display the seven lower *Sephiros* and posses only a meager revelation of the top three.

477. *Eirchin* 13b.

harp will possess eight strings. In the ultimate future David will have a ten-stringed harp. Then the fullest revelation of all ten *Sephiros* will be with us.[478] A new world will exist then; in that Messianic world, there will be ten different notes in the musical scale. The *Sephiros* will then be fully revealed in the world and internalized within man.

It is my prayer that the lessons in this book help us merit to see those days, soon.

---

478. The Land of Israel was controlled by ten nations before the Jews conquered it. These peoples were the shells covering the lights of the ten *Sephiros*. When Joshua entered Israel, the Jews only conquered seven of these nations. The territories controlled by the Keni, Kenazi, and Kadmoni were not conquered. We only received the land of the seven nations, for only the seven lower Sephiros have emerged fully in our world. Once the Messiah arrives, we will inherit the land of Keni, Kenazi, and Kadmoni, for in that era all ten *Sephiros*-like lights will appear (see further *Tzion Ve-Arehah*, pgs. 49-51, 149- 157).

There are three *Shabboses* in the summer months when the readings from the Prophets are predictions of destruction. After the ninth of *Av*, for the next seven *Shabboses* we read sections of consolation. The first three readings correspond to the Three Intellects. Since our world has not merited a true and full display of those Heavenly lights, those readings are of destruction, and the time of year is a time of mourning for the destruction of Jerusalem and Jewry's subsequent exile. Since our world has a revelation of the seven lower *Sephiros*, we read seven readings of consolation. Each reading helps restore one of the *Sephirah* lights which dimmed with Jerusalem's fall. When Messiah will come there will be ten readings of joy, for then there will be a display of all ten *Sephiros* (adapted from *Mishbetzos Zahav, Parashas Nitzavim-Vayelech*. 5753, pg. 283).

GLOSSARY

Abba, lit., "father": According to the Kabbalists, a display of Heavenly forces that resembled the *Sephirah* (the Godly light) of *chochmah*.

Adam Kadmon, "supernal man": An extremely exalted spiritual universe. It is a display of Godliness that is the Heavenly root and source for the parts of man.

Adar: The last month of the Jewish calendar. During Adar Jewry celebrates the hidden hand of Divine Providence and the holiday of Purim.

A-do-n-ai: The name of God that denotes His mastery and rule.

Afar, lit., "dirt": The element of earth or solids.

Aggada: The Talmudic passages that contain legends, philosophy, and Biblical homilies.

Ahavah, lit., "love": An amplification of *chesed* (kindness, giving), the desire to extend oneself into someone else.

Aish, lit., "fire": The element of fire or energy.

Aish Mislakkachas: An ever igniting fire (Ezek. 1:4), which is one of *kelippos* Ezekiel penetrated to see the Divine and His chariot.

Aiz: A goat. Often perceived as a satanic image.

Aleph (א): The first letter in the Hebrew alphabet.

Alma de-isgalya, lit., "the revealed world": The realm of the seven lower statements of creation. It is the dimension of reality where the seven lower *Sephiros* (Godly lights) are somewhat apparent.

Alma de-iskasya, lit., "the hidden world": The realm of the first three statements of creation that correspond to the first three *Sephiros*.

Alma de-prodah, lit., "the world of separation": The domain of evil, for evil emerges from disconnectedness.

Alufo shel olam: A phrase for God denoting the fact that he is the first of the world.

Amalek: An ancient nation that sought to destroy the Jews (see Exod. 16:8-16). They attacked the weakest members of Israel, the elderly and infirm, before the Jewish nation arrived at Sinai to receive the Torah. Haman was a member of this nation (see Esth. 3:1), and he tried to annihilate world Jewry during the reign of Achashveirosh.

Anan kaved, lit., "heavy cloud": One of the *kelippos* that Ezekiel had to penetrate before he could see the Divine and His chariot (See Ezekiel 1).

Arich, lit., "long": Long face; a name the Kabbalists use to denote the *Sephirah* of *keser*, "essential will."

Aseres Ha-Dibros: The Ten Commandments.

Asha"n: An acronym of the Hebrew words for the three dimensions: space (*olam*), time (*sha'ah*) and person (*nefesh*).

Asiyah, lit., "physical action": The lowest of the four supernal universes, which is attached to the physical realm.

Asur, lit., "tied, tied up": Forbidden.

Atik, lit., "ancient": The ancient one. The Kabbalists used this name to refer to the grandfather-like love that God displays through his attribute of *keser*, "essential will."

Atzilus: The highest of the four supernal universes that is "next to"(*eitzel*) unlimited Divinity.

Aveirah, pl. *aveiros*: A sin.

Avodah, lit., "work": Service to God, such as sacrifices and prayers. Also a section of prayers and supplications traditionally recited on Yom Kippur that recalls the sacrificial service to God that the High Priest would perform in Jerusalem's temple.

Avraham: The Hebrew name for the Biblical Abraham, the father of the Jewish people.

Ayin: Nothingness. The *Sephirah* of *keser*, "essential will," is sometimes called *ayin*.

Baal Shem Tov (also known by the acronym *Besht*): Rabbi Israel of Mezhibuzh (born in Okup, Ukraine in approximately 1698). The title means "Master of the Good Name." He started the Chasidic movement in order to inoculate Jewry against the ravages of secularism.

Baal Tzefon: An Egyptian idol that symbolized a hidden and intransigent opposition to Israel and Judaism (see Exod. 14:2).

Barchi Nafshi: A phrase which King David wrote five times in his psalms, meaning, "My soul shall bless" (God).

Bas, lit., "daughter": The Kabbalists call the revelation of the *Sephirah* of *malchus*, "humble kingship," the daughter of wisdom, intuition, and understanding.

Bechinah: An aspect of, a comparative or relative value.

Be'er Sheva: The city of Beersheba, Israel. Literally, "the well of seven."

Beinoni (pl. *beinonim*): An intermediate person, an individual who can achieve spiritual perfection in deed, speech, and thought but who will always have a virulent urge for sin.

Beis Ha-Mikdash: The Temple in Jerusalem. It was first built by King Solomon, son of King David, approx 950 B.C.E. Destroyed by Nebuchadnezzar, king of Babylonia, 586 B.C.E. The second Temple was built approx. 538-515 B.C.E., and destroyed by Titus and the Romans in 70 C.E. The Temple was the nexus between Heaven and earth. The rules of space were suspended within its walls. All spiritual blessings for the world would flow through it, and it revealed the seven lower bounded lights of God (the seven lower *Sephiros*).

Beis Lechem: The Biblical city of Bethlehem, Israel.

Ben, lit., "son": According to the Kabbalists, feelings that are derived (the son of) wisdom and understanding. These derived emotions are the six lower *Sephiros*: *chesed* (giving), *gevurah* (restraint), *tiferes* (harmony), *netzach* (dominance), *hod* (empathy), and *yesod* (perfect balance), often known collectively by the acronym *Chagat Nehi*.

Bereishis: "In the beginning," the first word in the Torah. It also refers to the first statement of creation, which was a level of Godliness that transcended articulation.

Beriah, lit., "creation": The second highest of the four supernal universes, where human thoughts are formed.

Besht: See *Baal Shem Tov*.

Betzalel: The architect who constructed the Tabernacle in the desert (Exod. 31:1-6).

Binah: Understanding, the ability to understand one matter from another, the mental capacity to comprehend details.

Be-sheim kol Yisrael, lit., "In the name of all of Israel": The last line of the unification prayer, traditionally recited prior to the fulfillment of a religious precept. It attaches the individual to the heavenly world of *Adam Kadmon* where all Jewish souls are bound together in unity.

Chabad: An acronym for *chochmah* (intuition), *binah* (understanding), and *da'as* (internalization), the three highest *Sephiros*. Within man these Godly lights became the three components to intellectual thought and comprehension, which is greatly stressed in the *Tanya* and by the Lubavitch Chasidim.

Chagat Nehim: An acronym for *chesed* (giving), *gevurah* (restraint), *tiferes* (harmony), *netzach* (dominance), *hod* (empathy), *yesod* (perfect balance), and *malchus* (kingship), which are the seven lower *Sephiros*, and within man represent the seven primary emotions.

Chai: Animal life, the third highest class of existence after *domeim* (rocks) and *tzome'ach* (plant life).

Chametz: Leavened dough, its ingestion and possession are prohibited during the Passover holiday.

Chananyah, Mishael, and Azaryah: Three prophets who were exiled by Nebuchadnezzar prior to the fall of Jerusalem's first Temple (See Daniel 3). When the Babylonian regent erected an idol and demanded that all bow to it, these brave Jews refused and were thrown into a lit furnace. A miracle occurred, and they emerged out of the flames unharmed.

Chanukah candles: Candles lit during the eight-day festival of Chanukah to commemorate the miracle of the Temple's candelabrum burning for eight days on one day's jar of oil.

Chasidus: The Jewish movement and school of religious thought that was started by Rabbi Yisrael Baal Shem Tov.

Chayah: The part of the human soul that parallels the world of *atzilus*. This part of the soul is total attachment to God. It is beyond a person, and it is sensed in the feeling of absolute union with holiness, when vessel and light become one.

Chazir: A pig.

Chesed: The Heavenly attribute of generosity and giving.

Chetzyo la-Hashem, lit., "half of it for God": This Talmudic phrase teaches that half of the festival holiday should be dedicated to God.

Chetzyo lachem, lit., "half of it for you": A Talmudic phrase that declares that half of the festival holiday is for human enjoyment.

Chevron: The Biblical city of Hebron, Israel.

Chomer: Matter, a vessel that is influenced by its *tzurah*, "form."

Chomrius: Materialism.

Davar Kelali: An all-encompassing entity. It is a microcosm that contains minute amounts of the essences of many items, moments, or people. Shabbos, Jerusalem, and righteous individuals are examples of this concept.

Derash: The analytical meaning of the Torah text.

Deveikus: Attachment to God; a connection with Heaven that is so strong that through it one leaves the physical dimension and becomes attached to infinity.

Dibbur: Speech.

Dibros: Commandments. The *Aseres Ha-Dibros* are the Ten Commandments.

Din, lit., "justice": The Heavenly *Sephirah* of *gevurah*, "strong restraint."

Domeim: The lowest class of existence, which includes water, stones, and earth.

Eden: The Garden of Eden.

Eliyahu Ha-Navi: The Biblical prophet Elijah. He directed Israel to a life of faith and ascended to Heaven in chariots of fire while still alive. He periodically reappears on earth to save the Jewish nation from dangers, and he will be the harbinger of the final redemption. Also called *Eliyahu Ha-Tishbi*.

Elul: The sixth month of the Hebrew calendar and commonly a time of repentance and introspection, immediately preceding *Tishrei*.

Emunah: Faith in God.

Eser kisrin de-misaavusa: The ten crowns of impurity; ten powerful forces of sin, evil, and spiritual filth which counteract the ten forces of holiness that emerged from the ten *Sephiros*.

Esrog: The citron fruit, which Jews ritually shake during the holiday of Sukkos along with the *lulav* (palm frond), *hadasim* (myrtle) and *aravos* (willow), based on Lev. 23:40.

Eved Ivri: A Jewish slave, whose term usually did not exceed six years. However, if at the end of six years he would insist on remaining in his master's home, then he would remain a slave until the year of Jubilee (*Yovel*).

Gehinnom: Hell, the opposite of the Garden of Eden.

Gematria: The homiletic device of numerology. Two words that seem disconnected might have the same numerological value, indicating a hidden connection.

Gilgul: Reincarnation.

Gog and Magog: The nations that in the future will battle Israel in the final war before the coming of the Messiah (see, e.g., Ezekiel 38-39).

Gumra de-isha: A burning ember. The consonants of this phrase are similar to the word *Gemara*, the part of the Talmud written after c. 200 C.E.

Hispashtus: Spreading, the movement of spreading out.

Halachah: Traditional Jewish law.

Ibbur neshamah: Soul impregnation, when the spirit of a soul enters a living individual to inspire him to greater levels of Torah knowledge and Mitzvah fulfillment.

Ikvasa di-meshicha: The heels of Messiah; the generation that will precede the ultimate redemption, which will hear his footsteps, and in comparison to other eras, is as unfeeling and coarse as a human heel.

Imma, lit., "mother": The name the Kabbalists use to describe revelations of the Heavenly force of *binah* (the understanding of details).

Kalem: Embarrassment and cessation of existence.

Kapparah, taharah: The two elements of Yom Kippur, the day of atonement; atonement from the punishment due to misdeeds (*kapparah*) and purification of the spiritual filth of sins (*taharah*).

Kaved: The liver.

Keli (pl. *keilim*), lit., "vessel": Filters that partially obscure the spiritual lights so that they might be appreciated by mortal man.

Kelippah (pl. *kelippos*) lit., "shell, peel, husk": In mystical terminology, symbols for evil, such as tragedy, illness, misfortune, evil desires, and sins.

Kelippas Nogah, lit., "the shell of light": A veil of light surrounding the holy sparks, which contains items that can, under the proper circumstances, become holy.

Keser, lit., "crown": The Godly light of the first *Sephirah*; the Heavenly will to create a world and teach Torah to Israel. The love, pleasure, and desires of this will are beyond rational comprehension, hence it is symbolized by a crown, which sits atop the head, above the place of logical thought.

Ketores, lit., "incense": A combination of eleven spices burned in the Temple to produce a special smell, and offered to the Almighty on the inner altar.

Ketz, lit., "end": The date of redemption.

Kiddush, lit., "sanctification": One of several prayers recited over wine on the eve of Shabbos or holidays to acknowledge its holiness, and again during the daytime.

Kinneres: The Sea of Galilee, a lake in Northern Israel that abuts the city of Tiberias. It is shaped like a harp, and mystically it leads all the oceans in song.

Kinor: A harp.

Koach ha-galgalim: The force of the spheres, which according to the ancient astronomers was believed to be a hidden physical force that caused the planets to rotate.

Koach ha-moshech, lit., "the force that attracts": Gravity, the force that attracts physical items to each other.

Koach mah: (1) The force of something. (2) The force of nothing. (The multiple meanings are based on the two meanings of *mah*: "what," and "nothing.")

Korbanos: Animal sacrifices that were offered to God.

Lag Ba-Omer: The thirty-third day of the *omer* count. It is the birthday and day of passing of Rabbi Shimon bar Yochai.

Lechah Dodi: A prayer composed by the sixteenth-century Kabbalist Rabbi Shlomo Alkabetz, traditionally recited Friday nights to accept the holiness of Shabbos.

Lechem: Bread.

Lechimah: Battle, struggle.

Le-Sheim Yichud: The Prayer of Unification, traditionally recited prior to fulfilling any religious precept. A declaration of intent by the one reciting it that he is about to perform a Mitzvah for the sake of unification, to combine God with the Jewish people and other-worldly holiness with the Divine essence that is hidden within physical creation. Its final words are *be-sheim kol Yisrael*, "for the sake of all Israel."

Lev: The heart.

Ma'aseh mitzvah: An act of Mitzvah.

Machpelah, lit., "cave": The Tomb of the Patriarchs in Hebron where Adam and Eve, Abraham and Sarah, Isaac and Rebecca, and Jacob and Leah are buried.

Machshavah: Pure thought.

Makkifin: Worlds and levels of soul that are so Heavenly and exalted that most men cannot fully internalize them, which hover above man and envelop him with ethereal light and inspiration.

Malach, lit., "messenger": An angel.

Malchus, lit., "kingship": The *Sephirah* of humble kingship.

Malkos: Lashes. According to Jewish law if a Jew flagrantly violates a Biblical commandment in the presence of two witnesses who warned him not to perform the sin, the court may punish the guilty by lashing him thirty-nine times.

Mashgiach: A spiritual guidance counselor to boys in a *yeshivah*.

Mashiach: The messiah.

Mayim, lit., "water": Liquids; one of the four elements believed to compose everything in the world, along with *eretz* (earth, solid), *ruach* (wind, gas), and *aish* (fire, energy, electricity).

Medabber, lit., "speaking": Human beings who have the ability to speak. The highest rank of existence above *domeim* (rocks), *tzome'ach* (plants), and *chayah* (animals).

Melech: King.

Merkavah la-Shechinah: A chariot of the Divine Presence, a righteous individual whose behavior reflects Godly holiness on which the Almighty's Glory resides.

Mesiras nefesh: Self-sacrifice.

Mesorah: The glorious chain of transmitted Torah wisdom.

Middos, lit., "measurements": The seven measured emotions of man. See *Chagat Nehim*.

Midrash: A collection of homiletical interpretations of Biblical verses.

Migdal Eder: A place in Israel, mentioned in Gen. 35:21. It seems from Scripture that it is the vicinity of Bethlehem. Our forefather Jacob camped in the environs of Migdal Eder after he lost his wife Rachel, who was buried in Bethlehem. According to the translation of the second-century sage Yonasan ben Uziel, Migdal Eder is the place of the Messiah, as well as his name.

Mikveh: A ritual immersion pool. In Jewish law, some changes of status, such as conversion, repentance, and ritual purification require ritual immersion in a pool of 40 *seah*, approximately 200 gallons, of pure water.

Milah: Ritual circumcision.

Milchamah: War.

Mishkan: The Tabernacle, the mobile sanctuary Temple that God commanded be built for the Jewish sojourn through the Sinai Desert after the departure from Egypt (see Exodus 25-40).

Mishnah: The basic text of the Oral Law, written in the second century by Rabbi Judah the Prince.

Mitzvos: The commandments of God to the Jewish nation, whose fulfillment attaches man to God and refines man's body and soul.

Mitzvos aseh: Positive commandments, Godly commands of behaviors a Jew must perform.

Mitzvos lo ta'aseh: Negative commandments, Godly prohibitions that a Jew may not commit.

Moach (pl. *mochin*): The mind. See *mochin*.

Mo'adim: Jewish holidays.

Mochin, lit., "minds": The three intellects, which have been categorized as *chochmah* (intuition), *binah* (understanding) and *da'as* (internalization); or *keser* (will), *chochmah* (intuition), and *binah* (understanding).

Musar: A category of Jewish thought focused on ethical refinement and character development.

Muttar, lit., "released": permitted, especially in reference to an object or an act permissible according to Jewish law.

Nafash: He rested.

Nefesh: The lowest level of soul, attached to the body and expressed through sacred acts.

Nefesh Elokis: The Godly soul, a piece of God that He has placed within man to animate and inspire.

Nefesh ha-bahamis: The animal soul, the source for the biological life of man, the root of his natural urges and proclivities.

Ner ma'aravi: The Western candle of the menorah, the Temple's Candelabrum, which would always remain lit, and towards which all other flames would miraculously turn.

Neshamah: The highest level of soul most men might internalize, concentrated in the mind and experienced through pure, abstract thought.

Neshamah kelalit: An all-encompassing soul, an individual to whom all other souls are connected, to receive Heavenly blessings when Divine gifts.

Neshimah: Breath.

Neta Revai: The fourth-year fruit of a tree in Israel, which must be eaten in Jerusalem, or else exchanged for money which must be spent on food to be eaten there.

Nisan: The first month in the Jewish calendar, which heralds the onset of spring, and is a time of Divine blessings. It is also the month when the Jewish nation departed Egypt.

Nitzotz (pl. *nitzotzos*), lit., "spark": A particle of Divine light and Godly life.

Nogah: A glow or sheath of light; the fourth of the four major *kelippos*. See *Kelippas Nogah*.

Ohel Mo'ed: The Tent of Meeting, where God would communicate with Moses.

Olam: World, universe. (Related to *he'elam*, "hidden," and *ne'elam*, "unknown.")

Olam ha-kissei: The universe of God's Throne; the universe of Creation (*beriah*).

Olam katan: A miniature universe; mankind, whose spiritual makeup is a of the universe's soul parts.

Or, lit., "light": Often used to refer to soul-like entities. See also *Or Ain Sof, Or penimi, or makkif*.

Or Ain Sof: The Infinite Light.

Or penimi, or makkif: An inner light; an enveloping light. "*Or makkif* is a light that does not appear gradually. It does not appear in a form that corresponds to the capabilities of the recipient. Since it is so high the recipient cannot internalize this light, and it hovers above his understanding. *Or penimi* is a light that appears gradually; it is limited to correspond with the capabilities of the receiver. For example, consider a teacher who would like to impart to his student a very deep thought. If the teacher limits his presentation of the concept, if he translates the abstract principle into parables and real life anecdotes and thus teaches his student, it is an *or penimi*. If the teacher simply relates to the student the depths of the abstract principle as he, the teacher, comprehends it, the student will not grasp the idea, and it will be an *or makkif. Or makkif* is a light that surrounds an individual, yet it is too bright for internalization and comprehension."[479]

Orlah: (1) The first three years' growth of a tree in Israel. Fruit of an Israeli tree from the first three years of its existence. It may not be eaten and must be destroyed. (2) The skin that is removed during ritual circumcision.

Osiyos mischalfos: Interchangeable letters.

Oveid Hashem: One who is working for Heaven.

Pachad Yitzchak, lit., "the fear of Isaac": According to the Torah, the Being that Isaac feared (Gen. 31:42).

---

479. *Razei Ha-Bosem* pg. 33, s.v. *or makkif*.

Parashah: Section, especially a weekly Torah reading.

Pardes: An acronym for the four methods of Biblical interpretation: *peshat* (the simple meaning), *derash* (the homiletical meaning), *remez* (the hinted meaning), and *sod* (the hidden meaning).

Pasach Eliyahu, lit., "Elijah began": A key lesson of Kabbalah that Elijah the prophet taught Rabbi Shimon bar Yochai and his disciples.

Periah: The part of ritual circumcision in which the *mohel* lifts a piece of skin to reveal the circumcision.

Peshat: The literal and most simple interpretation of the Torah text.

Pesukei de-Zimra, lit., "verses of praise": The section of morning prayers before the blessings of *Shema*, containing Psalms praising God, which enables prayers to rise heavenward.

Pintele Yid: The little piece of a Jew that remains in the heart of even the most estranged descendant of Abraham.

Pirkei Avos: The Mishnaic tractate *Ethics of the Fathers*, which deals primarily with ethical teachings and homilies.

Purim: A Jewish holiday celebrating the downfall of the wicked Haman who sought to annihilate the Jews.

Rasha (pl. *resha'im*): A sinner, a sinful individual.

Rasha gamur: A thoroughly wicked individual.

Rasha she-eino gamur (also *rasha ve-tov lo*): A wicked individual who possesses an advocate for holiness.

Remez: The hinted meanings of the Torah text.

Reshus ha-rabbim, lit., "the public domain": A symbol for the realm of evil, caused by disconnection and detachment, places containing many disconnected individuals.

Reshus ha-yachid, lit., "the private domain": The realm individual privacy of holiness. Just as in a private home there is one owner, in holiness there is unity of purpose and mind. The realization that relative to God there is no power and that God owns the entire created world is the foundation of ethical behavior.

Rosh Chodesh, lit., "the head of the month": The beginning of each month on the Jewish calendar, and considered to be a minor festival.

Roshei teivos: The first letters of words, used as homiletical tool for uncovering hidden meanings in Biblical passages, similar to *gematria*.

Ruach, lit., "wind": (1) The element of air, one of the four elements believed to compose everything in the world, along with *eretz* (earth, solid), *mayim* (liquid), and *aish* (fire, energy, electricity). (2) The soul that is the source of emotions and speech, above *nefesh* and below *neshamah*.

Ruach se'arah, lit., "stormy wind": One of the *kelippos* that Ezekiel had to penetrate before he could see the Divine and His chariot (See Ezekiel 1).

Saraph: A fiery angel.

Seder hishtalshlus: The order of evolutionary descent; the process of drawing from the spiritual to the physical, in which pure spiritual light devolves to a progressively lower levels of light until the physical emerges out of a much limited spiritual entity.

Sephirah (pl. *Sephiros*): Any of the ten limited lights of Divinity which God used to create the world, and are the sources for all of creation. Since man was created in the image of God, man contains within his personality abilities that parallel the ten *Sephiros*. Other creatures only have similarities to one or two of the *Sephiros*.

Shabbos: The Sabbath.

Shad-dai: The name of God indicating that He sets limits to His world.

Shalosh kelippos ha-teme'os: The three impure shells; the three categories of items that contain sparks of holiness that are irredeemable by man: a stormy wind, a heavy cloud, and ever igniting fire (see Ezek. 1:4).

Shalsheles: A chain.

Shavuos: The Jewish holiday that celebrates the receipt of the Torah at Sinai.

Shechinah: (1) The Divine Presence. (2) The *Sephirah* of *malchus*, "humble kingship." (3) The yoke of Heaven.

Shefa, Shefa Eloki: An overwhelming and ever increasing flow of Divine energy.

Shefa Chaim: A heavenly flow of life.

Shema: The Jewish prayer beginning with, "Hear, O Israel, God the Lord is our God, the Lord is One" (Deut. 6:4), which Jews recite to declare their faith and accept upon themselves the sovereignty of Heaven.

Shemiras ha-bris, lit., "preserving the covenant": Safeguarding the connection between man and God and man and his spouse by ensuring that there is no misuse of seed.

Shemoneh Esreh, lit., "eighteen": The silent devotional prayer, which originally contained eighteen blessings.

Sheva kefulos, lit., "the seven doubles": The seven emotions of man that can appear in a holy or unholy form. See *Chagat Nehim*.

Shevua: An oath.

Shiras Ha-Yam: The Song of the Sea (Exod. 15:1-19), which the Jews sang after God miraculously split the Red Sea to enable Jews to cross on dry land.

Shiur Komah, lit., "the measure of height": A phrase referring to a complete complement of forces and abilities.

Shlit"a: An acronym for *she-yichyeh le-yamim tovim arukkim*, "May he live many more years of a long and good life."

Simchas Torah: A Jewish holiday on the last day of Sukkos, celebrating the completion of reading the Torah.

Sitra achra, lit., "the other side": The realm of materialism, selfishness, and evil, so called because it is the backside of holiness.

Sod: The secret meanings of the Torah text.

Sukkah: A temporary booth that Jews reside in for the seven days of the Sukkos holiday.

Sukkos: A seven-day holiday beginning on 15 *Tishrei*, which celebrates the harvest, the Divine Providence that protected Israel in its Desert sojourn after it left Egypt, and is a time to pray for rain and water. Its special rituals include waving the four species, *lulav* (palm frond), *hadasim* (myrtle), *aravos* (willow) and *esrog* (citron); dwelling in the *sukkah* for seven days; and in the times of Jerusalem's Temple, pouring water libations on the altar.

Tefillah: Prayer

Tefillin: Phylacteries, leather boxes which adult Jewish men don daily to remind themselves of the Exodus from Egypt and their commitments to God.

Teshuvah: Return; repentance; the process of return to God and one's innermost self.

Tikkun: Rectification of soul, fulfillment of life's mission.

Tikkun ha-kelali, lit., "the general rectification": The ten chapters of Psalms (16, 32, 41, 42, 59, 77, 90, 105, 137, and 150) whose recital can cause a general and all encompassing rectification.

Tishrei: The seventh Jewish month, which contains the holidays of Rosh Hashanah, Yom Kippur, and Sukkos.

Tzaddik: A holy, righteous individual.

Tzaddik gamur (also, *tzaddik ve-tov lo*): A completely righteous person. According to the *Tanya*, an individual who does not possess an evil urge and is only attracted to holiness.

Tzaddik she-eino gamur (also, *tzaddik ve-ra lo*): An individual who is mostly, but not completely, righteous.

Tzafon: North.

Tzafun: Hidden.

Tzefuni, lit., "hidden": The hidden evil urge.

Tzelem Elokim: The image of God, used in Gen. 1:27.

Tzimtzum: Constriction or self-limitation.

Tzome'ach: Plant life; the second lowest class of existence, above *domeim* (rocks) and below *chai* (animal life).

Tzurah: Form, soul, inner character.

Yaakov: The name of the Biblical Jacob.

Yechidah: The highest level of soul, the unique essence of man, above *nefesh, ruach, neshamah,* and *chayah.* The part of the soul that is inextricably attached to God; the source of an inner advocate for sacred behavior. This advocate can never be fully silenced.

Yesh me-ayin: Creation *ex nihilo*, something created from nothing.

Yesh mi-yesh: Creation *ex materia*, something formed out of a preexisting matter.

Yetzer hara: The desire for evil deeds, feelings, and thoughts.

Yetzer tov: The desire for good deeds, feelings, and thoughts.

Yetzirah: The spiritual universe of formation, below *beriah* and above *asiyah*. It is the place where emotions are real.

Yirah: Fear.

Yiras Shamayim: Fear of Heaven.

Yitzchak: The name for the Biblical Isaac.

Yom Kippur: The Day of Atonement.

Yom she-kullo Shabbos: A day that is all Shabbos, specifically the Messianic era.

Yom Tov: A religious festival.

Yovel: Jubilee, the fiftieth year, when servants would return home and ancestral lands would return to their original possessors.

Ze'ir, lit., "small": Small face, another name for the Kabbalistic concept of *ben*.

Zemirah: (1) Pruning. (2) Song (pl., *zemiros*).

www.ingramcontent.com/pod-product-compliance
Lightning Source LLC
Chambersburg PA
CBHW021048090426
42738CB00006B/234